Rightly Dividing the Word of Truth

Drawing of Metropolitan Kallistos by Noel White.

Rightly Dividing the Word of Truth

Studies in Honour of
Metropolitan Kallistos of Diokleia

Andreas Andreopoulos and
Graham Speake (eds)

PETER LANG

Oxford · Bern · Berlin · Bruxelles · Frankfurt am Main · New York · Wien

Bibliographic information published by Die Deutsche Nationalbibliothek.
Die Deutsche Nationalbibliothek lists this publication in the Deutsche National-
bibliografie; detailed bibliographic data is available on the Internet at
http://dnb.d-nb.de.

A catalogue record for this book is available from the British Library.

Library of Congress Cataloging-in-Publication Data

Names: Kallistos, Bishop of Diokleia, 1934- honouree. | Andreopoulos,
　Andreas, 1966- editor. | Speake, Graham, 1946- editor.
Title: Rightly dividing the word of truth : studies in honour of Metropolitan
　Kallistos of Diokleia / Andreas Andreopoulos & Graham Speake.
Description: 1 [edition]. | New York : Peter Lang, 2016. | Includes
　bibliographical references and index.
Identifiers: LCCN 2016007930 | ISBN 9783034319973 (alk. paper)
Subjects: LCSH: Orthodox Eastern Church--History. | Orthodox Eastern
　Church--Doctrines. | Kallistos, Bishop of Diokleia, 1934-
Classification: LCC BX250 .R544 2016 | DDC 281.9--dc23 LC record available at
　https://lccn.loc.gov/2016007930

Cover image: Metropolitan Kallistos serving the Divine Liturgy at Simonopetra
monastery on Mount Athos in May 2014. Photo © Hadrian Liem.

ISBN 978-3-0343-1997-3 (print)　•　ISBN 978-1-78707-152-0 (ePDF)
ISBN 978-1-78707-153-7 (ePub)　•　ISBN 978-1-78707-154-4 (mobi)

© Peter Lang AG, International Academic Publishers, Bern 2016
Hochfeldstrasse 32, CH-3012 Bern, Switzerland
info@peterlang.com, www.peterlang.com, www.peterlang.net

All rights reserved.
All parts of this publication are protected by copyright.
Any utilisation outside the strict limits of the copyright law, without
the permission of the publisher, is forbidden and liable to prosecution.
This applies in particular to reproductions, translations, microfilming,
and storage and processing in electronic retrieval systems.

This publication has been peer reviewed.

Printed in Germany

Contents

Acknowledgements ix

Message from His All-Holiness Ecumenical
Patriarch Bartholomew xi

Address by His Eminence Archbishop Gregorios
of Thyateira and Great Britain xiii

ANDREAS ANDREOPOULOS AND GRAHAM SPEAKE
Introduction 1

PART I Tributes to Metropolitan Kallistos

FRANCES JENNINGS
1 The Spiritual Father 7

NIKOLAI SAKHAROV
2 The Monk 13

STEPHEN PLATT
3 The Pastor and Bishop 19

MARCUS PLESTED
4 The Teacher 23

† EPHREM LASH
5 The Translator and Writer — 27

ANDREW LOUTH
6 The Theologian — 33

ANDREAS ANDREOPOULOS
7 An English Orthodox Bishop? — 41

PART 2   Papers in Honour of Metropolitan Kallistos

SEBASTIAN BROCK
8 An Early Syriac *Exposition of the Holy Mysteries* — 49

MAXIMOS CONSTAS
9 'Nothing is Greater than Divine Love':
Evagrios of Pontos, St Maximos the Confessor,
and the *Philokalia* — 57

HILARION ALFEYEV
10 St Symeon the New Theologian and the
Studite Monastic Tradition — 75

ELIZABETH JEFFREYS
11 On the Annunciation: Manganeios Prodromos, no. 120 — 105

JOHN CHRYSSAVGIS
12 *Philokalia*: A Vocabulary for Our Time — 113

NIKOLAOS HATZINIKOLAOU
13 The Desert, *Hesychia*, and Ascesis: Then and Now — 131

JOHN BEHR
14 Patristic Texts as Icons   151

ROWAN WILLIAMS
15 Deification, Hypostatization, and Kenosis   171

ELIZABETH THEOKRITOFF
16 Priest of Creation or Cosmic Liturgy?   189

DIMITRI CONOMOS
17 C. S. Lewis and Church Music   213

Epilogue

KALLISTOS WARE
18 Fifty-Four Years as an Athonite Pilgrim   237

Notes on Contributors   253

Index   259

Acknowledgements

Most of the papers included in this volume were first delivered at a symposium which was held by the Friends of Mount Athos in honour of Metropolitan Kallistos's eightieth birthday at Madingley Hall, Cambridge, in February 2015. A few more papers were specially commissioned after the event. All the contributions are written by former students, colleagues, or friends of the Metropolitan and we are grateful to them all for agreeing to participate in both the conference and the subsequent volume.

The society would like to acknowledge with grateful thanks the generous sponsorship that it received from the Gerald Palmer Eling Trust, the A. G. Leventis Foundation, and the Prince of Wales Foundation in support of the conference. The editors in their turn would like to thank the Friends of Mount Athos for generously contributing towards the cost of publishing the proceedings. They are also grateful to Hadrian Liem for kindly supplying the photograph that was used to illustrate the front cover of the book and to Noel White for giving permission for his drawing of Metropolitan Kallistos to be used as a frontispiece.

It goes without saying that neither the symposium, nor the volume, nor much of what today constitutes Orthodoxy in the West would have been possible without the inspiring presence of His Eminence, our beloved bishop. We are delighted to include his own contribution to the symposium as an epilogue to the book; and we are proud to offer the entire volume to him as a token of our affection and admiration for all that he has achieved in his first eight decades. In the time-honoured phrase, we wish him many years.

A.A.
G.S.
Feast of the Transfiguration 2016

Message from His All-Holiness
Ecumenical Patriarch Bartholomew
to the Friends of Mount Athos Conference
in Honour of His Excellency Metropolitan Kallistos,
Madingley Hall, 6–8 February 2015

Beloved colleagues, students, and friends of Metropolitan Kallistos,
Esteemed conference speakers and participants,
Dear Friends of Mount Athos,

It is our sincere pleasure and privilege to respond to the gracious invitation of your Chairman, Dr Graham Speake, that we address a brief paternal message to the participants of the residential conference organized in honour of His Excellency Metropolitan Kallistos. We are delighted to do this through our Exarch in Great Britain, His Eminence Archbishop Gregorios of Thyateira.

There is no greater honour for a Church than to pay tribute to one of the most eminent hierarchs and prominent scholars of the Ecumenical Throne, who for many years has served as spiritual father, academic teacher, metropolitan bishop, monk, theologian, and author-translator. We understand that speakers will address the manifold virtues of Metropolitan Kallistos's life and the diverse aspects of his work: the 'one face' and 'many facets' of the productivity and legacy of this respected leader of our Church.

Our beloved brother Metropolitan taught numerous students at the University of Oxford for thirty-five years and ministered as a clergyman for over forty-five years. He recently celebrated his eightieth birthday and has variously supported and presided over the Friends of Mount Athos, which is currently celebrating its twenty-fifth year of growth.

One could endlessly describe the contributions of Metropolitan Kallistos to the Orthodox Church in general and the Ecumenical

Patriarchate in particular. However, we shall confine ourselves to highlighting the fact that one could never calculate the number of people who have embraced or admired the history and teaching of the Orthodox Church through his classic works, *The Orthodox Church* and *The Orthodox Way*. Moreover, one could never imagine the number of people whose lives have been informed and transformed by the translation of the writings on prayer and spirituality, known to us through the *Philokalia*.

We would like to assure you that, while our numerous commitments regrettably prevent us from attending in person, as we certainly would have liked to, we shall nevertheless be with you in thought and in prayer as you consider and celebrate the acclaimed career and vocation of the recipient of your tribute and homage.

Therefore, υπέρ τούτων και απάντων [for this and for all things], we give thanks to the Lord for the gifts shared with us by His Excellency Metropolitan Kallistos, to whom we pray that God may grant many years 'rightly to divide the word of His truth'.

Prayerfully yours,

† BARTHOLOMEW
Archbishop of Constantinople-New Rome
and Ecumenical Patriarch

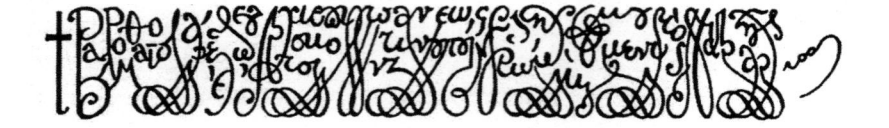

Address by His Eminence Archbishop Gregorios of Thyateira and Great Britain

It is a great privilege to be present at this conference celebrating the eightieth birthday of my brother bishop, Metropolitan Kallistos of Diokleia, and to have had the honour to read the august message that His All-Holiness the Ecumenical Patriarch Bartholomew I has addressed to the gathering.

I think I am right in saying that the first time that I saw Metropolitan Kallistos (or Timothy Ware, as he was then) was with a group of people who had come to visit the church of All Saints in Camden Town where I was then serving as a priest. I got to know him better and appreciate his abilities and talents some time later when I was driving the car in which he and my predecessor of blessed memory, Archbishop Athenagoras, were travelling; and I vividly remember how they were discussing the question of his ordination and how he agreed to become a clergyman of the Orthodox Church and of this Eparchy of the Ecumenical Throne. Indeed, it was I who, as a priest, gave him the Canonical Letter of Witness (*Symmartyria*) prior to his ordination as a deacon in the Greek Orthodox Cathedral of the Divine Wisdom (Agia Sophia) in London, which took place almost exactly fifty years ago (on 10 March 1965).

When he was ordained to the priesthood the following year (after having been tonsured as a monk of the monastery of St John the Theologian in Patmos), I remember him assuring me that the community in Oxford was now guaranteed a priest for the next fifty years. For me, this showed not only his humility but also his humour. In that university city he taught both academically and spiritually, putting the Greek Orthodox community on firm foundations and being one of those responsible for the building of the church of the Annunciation of the Mother of God (today shared with our Mother Church's parish within the Archdiocese of Orthodox Parishes of Russian Tradition in Western Europe).

Although his name is inextricably linked to Oxford, it has become well known throughout the world. It is already engraved in letters of gold on the pages of theological writings and studies, and the internet reveals the titles of his books and the numerous papers, articles, and translations that bear his name. He has glorified the name of the Patriarchate that has honoured him with the episcopate, and he is also a compliment to the nation that gave him birth. As an assistant bishop of the Archdiocese of Thyateira and Great Britain, we always had excellent relations with him and his co-operation has always been beyond reproach.

He has passed the Royal Years and has already lived for ten years those that the Psalmist claims are – even at the best of times – years of toil and trouble, 'because meekness came upon us, and we shall become disciplined'.[1] And yet – even if a little less physically strong than of previous years – he has proved the Psalmist wrong as he continues to teach and instruct, 'rightly dividing the word of [God's] truth', maintaining evangelical humility, and being an example and inspiration to thousands of Orthodox Christians and those who are not, who have delved the depths of the 'Orthodox Way' by way of his teaching and academic ability.

In brief, it is right and proper that we should be celebrating this eightieth anniversary of Metropolitan Kallistos's birth, and at the same time the fiftieth anniversary of his entry into the ranks of the clergy of the Orthodox Christian Church. May Almighty God grant him length of days, good health, and sharpness of mind for many years to come.

---

[1] Psalm 89 (90): 10; NETS translation.

ANDREAS ANDREOPOULOS AND GRAHAM SPEAKE

Introduction

Most of the papers collected in this volume were delivered at a conference organized by the Friends of Mount Athos to mark the eightieth birthday of their President, Metropolitan Kallistos of Diokleia, that took place in Madingley Hall, Cambridge, from 6 to 8 February 2015. It was always the intention of the organizers that the proceedings should be published in the form of a Festschrift.

Another volume was published in the honour of Metropolitan Kallistos in 2003 by St Vladimir's Seminary Press under the title *Abba: The Tradition of Orthodoxy in the West*. While both books may be thought of as Festschriften in the sense of a scholarly volume that the students and colleagues of the honorand have taken the initiative to compile, there are two differences that encouraged us to contemplate a second book in this tradition, without wishing in any way to discredit the first, especially since several of those who contributed to the first collection have also contributed to the second.

The first difference is that the present volume is a more focused offering, being set firmly within the context of the Friends of Mount Athos. Metropolitan Kallistos is the President of the society, but this means much more than the holding of an administrative office: in many ways he is the human embodiment of the society; when people speak of the Friends, he is the first person who comes to mind; he has been the keynote speaker at every Madingley conference that the society has held (including this one, which was the seventh!); and for many years he has led its annual pilgrimage, to places such as Cappadocia, Russia, Romania, Serbia, and Georgia, opening with his presence many doors that would normally remain closed to the average pilgrim.

The other reason for proceeding with a second Festschrift is that the activity and the impact of Metropolitan Kallistos on the spiritual life of the UK and of the Orthodox world as a whole are ongoing: one could say that he has become even more important, even more influential, in the last few years, as he has become ever more deeply involved in official and unofficial ecumenical dialogue. We therefore felt that it was more appropriate to think of these celebrations of his continuing guidance and inspiration not so much as full stops, but rather as a series of semicolons: the first shortly after his retirement; the present one after his eightieth birthday; there may yet be a third ...

Following the format of the Madingley conference, this volume consists of two parts. In the second part we are proud to include scholarly contributions by colleagues, students, and friends of Metropolitan Kallistos who are distinguished in their various fields. Dr Sebastian Brock opens the order with a discussion and translation of an early fifth-century Syriac commentary on the Divine Liturgy, a concise work of scholarship that touches on several of the themes that pervade the thought of Metropolitan Kallistos. Archimandrite Maximos Constas follows this with a presentation of the spiritual strand that connects Evagrios of Pontos with St Maximos the Confessor and its influence on the *Philokalia* – something that helps us appreciate the very foundations of the ascetic tradition. Metropolitan Hilarion Alfeyev's chapter focuses on the relationship of St Symeon the New Theologian with his spiritual father, Symeon the Studite, or Symeon the Pious, thereby honouring Metropolitan Kallistos as his doctoral supervisor. Professor Elizabeth Jeffreys offers, 'as a small token of esteem', a short discussion of a twelfth-century epigram on the Annunciation to the Theotokos. In the following piece Deacon John Chryssavgis reflects on the value of the *Philokalia* and its relevance for today, emphasizing some of its most fundamental concepts in simple and straightforward language. Metropolitan Nikolaos Hatzinikolaou casts new light on the long-running debate about the distance between the 'then' and the 'now' of the monastic life, speaking both as a monk and as a scholar in order to examine both traditional and modern practice. Fr John Behr starts from the concerns of the 'neo-Patristic synthesis', that we usually associate with theologians such as Sergei Bulgakov and Georges Florovsky, and develops an inclusive view of biblical exegesis and the Patristic tradition, offering us a sophisticated and beautiful image of that tradition as a symphony of voices. Dr Rowan

Williams draws on his deep understanding of Orthodox Christianity as he explores the traditionally Eastern Orthodox area of deification, hypostasis, and self-emptying, with reference to the thought of theologians such as Vladimir Lossky and also a fondly remembered and much-loved figure of modern British Orthodox spirituality, Fr Sophrony Sakharov. Dr Elizabeth Theokritoff discusses the cosmological dimension of the royal priesthood of Christianity and the liturgy of all Creation as it finds fulfilment in its Creator. Finally Dr Dimitri Conomos examines C. S. Lewis's response to sacred music, thereby paying tribute to the wider cultural and spiritual context of the sacred arts.

These contributions highlight different strands of current scholarship. The authors were invited to write about something that reflected their interests, offering one of the finest gems in their collection that would be appropriate in honouring Metropolitan Kallistos. In this regard the second part does not differ very greatly in style and content from other similar collections of writings.

The first part, however, is different. Instead of scholarly contributions, we solicited presentations from a number of individuals who have had a personal relationship with Metropolitan Kallistos, and whose friendship or collaboration with him enabled them to bring here something distinct, a unique appreciation of his work. Here we have the presentation of several different aspects of the presence and the influence of Metropolitan Kallistos on his generation: as a spiritual father, as a monk, as a pastor, as a teacher, as a writer and translator, as a theologian, and as an Orthodox bishop in the West. The list, of course, could go on, but even these seven brief presentations make the point.

We felt that this personal approach, this attempt to put together different aspects of a rich and multi-layered life, was appropriate for a volume that expresses the respect and the love of the generations that Metropolitan Kallistos has touched. To pretend that such an approach covers all of the layers of the personality and of the impact of a single human being is, of course, an impossible task. We can never know which sphere of influence on our generation, or which set of ideas that we now hold in high esteem, will be the one that will be appreciated in the future more than the others. Even those areas in which we may feel we have failed may yet prove to be our greatest legacy – as was the case of Sts Cyril and Methodios, who died under the impression that their mission and their work had been a complete failure. Nevertheless, in bringing together a few personal testimonies of appreciation, we hope that the first part of this volume will at least demonstrate that the work and contribution of Metropolitan Kallistos, whether we speak about the spiritual father, the monk, the pastor, the teacher, the writer and translator, the theologian, the Orthodox bishop in the West, or any of the other aspects that could not be included here, is far too complex and too multi-dimensional to be described by a single label.

For all of us who are connected with this book we can safely say that it has been an enormous privilege to know Metropolitan Kallistos in whatever capacity we have known him. For all of us he has been, and indeed is, someone who has touched our lives in ways that defy description. It is our humble hope that the contributions to this volume will demonstrate to our readers who may not have had that privilege that this is a man who has made the world a better place.

PART I

Tributes to Metropolitan Kallistos

FRANCES JENNINGS

1 The Spiritual Father

I first met Bishop Kallistos nearly eight years ago with my husband Simon, who at that stage was exploring whether he should become Orthodox. To be frank, Simon was half-Orthodox already and had been for some time, but wanted to talk to the Bishop about the possibility of being received. I went along for the ride. Having tried and failed to persuade Simon to join me in the Church of England, I went along very defensively, with my hackles up. I was not happy about Simon's getting involved with this ethnic bunch of people in a rather strange and, to me, very foreign religion and I listened very, very hard and I asked a lot of questions. I asked stupid questions because I was very ignorant. I asked what the Jesus Prayer was and I was not patronized. I received a straightforward answer, and a helpful little booklet, which made me realize that it was almost exactly the same prayer as my Methodist grandmother had taught me in my childhood. Listening to him, I felt I could discern links between the Orthodox and my position as a life-long High-Church Anglican.

I had no intention of becoming Orthodox myself. I had been Anglican all my life, a child of the vicarage, and never dreamt I would ever leave. It was Fr Andrew Louth who first raised the question of my becoming Orthodox, which I dismissed immediately, but the seed had been sown. Furthermore, it had always been fundamentally important that Simon and I worshipped together: it is not an area where we could 'agree to disagree', although I should stress that I was never under any pressure whatsoever from Simon. I had to face the fact that I was seeking to build a life with somebody who was clearly going to be Orthodox from a sense of real conviction and of homecoming, and we needed to be in the same church worshipping together. At first, after Simon's reception and our wedding, I skulked rebelliously in the back of Orthodox churches, but after a couple of months I cracked. I wrote to the Bishop to say, while I did not really want to do it, would he please receive me as a 'work in progress'. He immediately wrote back to me to say he would. He told me that, when I had been there while he was instructing Simon, 'I felt your eyes upon me and I knew you were listening'. The phrase is indicative of his patience and kindly humour.

That humour not only makes him a great communicator, but because he meets you where you are, it also actually opens doors that otherwise would be firmly shut. He had already decided, as I had sat there listening to him talk to Simon, and before I realized that this was my path, that when I was ready to ask, he would receive me as a 'work in progress', which I very much still am. There was no further formal instruction: I would learn on the job with Simon's very considerable and continuing help. He has never said so, but I think the Bishop realized that this would be good for both of us. It has certainly been an enormous help to me in my journey.

I have to say, I struggled. I really did struggle with the enormously complicated services in impenetrable languages with strange music you have to stand through, new services starting just as you think you have finished and can go home, and it all goes on for ever ... I remember saying how despondent I was about this to the Bishop and, with a light touch, he said: 'Yes, I remember my mother, when she became Orthodox, saying she now understood why the Orthodox pray so earnestly for those who have fallen asleep.' His humour is kindly but hits home, and with that help you can keep going, which is in essence what we have to do. I persevered and, eventually, the power and beauty of the services struck me and touched me deeply, even in languages I do not understand and probably never will. He recognizes where you are as his spiritual child, pokes gentle fun to make you see yourself as you are, and helps you to keep going. Most of us are on a long spiritual journey and what we have to do is just that, to keep going.

I remember the first hurdle I had was what we were going to do about my name. What is wrong with my name? My name is Frances. I have had it for over fifty years now, and it is part of my identity. I was not keen on a change. But the Bishop, with great sensitivity, said: 'What are you going to think, Frances, if you go up to a chalice in one of those strange Orthodox countries and say your name is Frances and they won't have you?' I know I would have been pretty cross, very hurt, and it would not have been helpful, so we had to decide what we were going to do. I wanted

The Spiritual Father

a married/non-monastic saint, but there are very few. We decided early on that probably Mary of Egypt was inappropriate on many levels. We worked out that I am domestic, very much a 'bossy boots'. In my defence, if you have seven children, two houses, and Simon to run, and, in your spare time, have to be a partner in a firm of chartered accountants, you need to have a good handle on your task list. The Marthas of this world are good at that: they get the dinner on, get things done and people fed; they may fuss and be abrasive, but they do move things along. However, they need to be reminded that there is more than this, and the name does remind me that there is a greater point to it all and the task list is not the end in itself, although I confess I sometimes lose sight of that. I thought at the time that it was my idea to choose Martha because I always felt that she was the effective sister and had an unfairly bad press. I now realize that it was probably the Bishop's idea all along and I, absorbed in my task list, did not notice he was making that decision for me. It is another example of his humour, but also his great perception.

So what is he actually like as a spiritual father? I would say the main thing is that he is careful, really careful. A spiritual father has immense power over his spiritual children, and can do immense harm. The Bishop is acutely aware of this, and he is very, very careful. He listens and observes very carefully and considers things. He must have a huge range of spiritual children, all at different stages of their journey. I am still at base camp, but he must be dealing with people who are a lot further on than me. He is very careful. His only question comes right at the start of confession, after the prayer, when he asks: 'Tell me, what is on your heart?' He does not drag confessions out of you, or suggest sins, even when he must have a pretty good idea of what is going on. He creates (in a dreadful phrase, but I am going to use it anyway as it is how it feels) a 'safe space' for you to talk, to accept where you are and why, to recognize and offer up your sins, and explore how you can do better. I think he must get awfully bored because I quite often end up repeating the same sins. Most of us are creatures of habit: we end up in similar situations, react in the same way because of the same weaknesses. So far he has never fallen asleep in one of my confessions and generally manages not to look bored. He makes it possible to talk with deep honesty and contrition. It is very difficult to make a confession, particularly when you make your first confession at fifty! You are exposing yourself in a way that you do not in any other forum; it is very important that that is carefully handled, and I feel that it is with him.

With me, because I really am a Martha, a lot of it is to do with priorities. I used to think that I was going to fit this Orthodox thing into my busy life, build it into my task list, and carry on as before, but it does not work like that. You have to put your Orthodoxy in the centre of your life and fit everything else around it. My priorities have had to change totally, but I still have to get it all done! When I was approaching Great Lent with dread at the thought of fitting in the extra services, he would say: 'Of course in Lent it is so much simpler.' I used to rail inside and think, 'What planet are you on? Have you any idea of the diary management it takes to get the two of us to a Presanctified Liturgy on a weekday in Lent, and at the busiest time of year for accountants?' But if you really listen, it is true: it is simpler, once the priorities are right. I come away from him with a reinforcement of faith and an ability to persevere, which is what I need to do. He tells me that I have to accept what cannot be changed – and we Marthas always think we can change everything – accept what cannot be changed, pray about it, and accept it. He gives very wise, thoughtful, sensible advice. I feel that he takes the burden of my sins and I come away lighter as a result. One of his other spiritual children once said to me, 'I come away feeling 10 kilos lighter'. That is quite something, but it means all that anxiety and sin is going somewhere and basically he is carrying it. That is an enormous thing to do.

I know that many theologians are cross with him because he has not finished the last volume of the *Philokalia*, but one of the reasons for that is because he has generously made himself available to people like me and has helped us along our road. He does not turn us away. I know there are many people like me whom he has helped in that way, and, of course, if he helps us along, then we can help other people. That is a very powerful thing. He has an ability to reach people from all walks of life. While I may be in the minority among the contributors to this book, out there, in the big wide world, I am in the majority in not being a theologian. He can reach me where I am, and as I am, and I think, because he has that ability, it affects the way that he writes. He is one of the few theologians whose books I read and actually understand, and which therefore have an impact on my life. The fact that he makes himself available as a pastor, with his skill and experience as a spiritual father, is a foundation stone of his lectures and writings. Another is, of course, his scholarship, but his great contribution as a spiritual father and its impact on his scholarship should not, in my view, as a non-theologian, be underestimated.

NIKOLAI SAKHAROV

2 The Monk

When I was invited to give this presentation, I found myself in a quandary: 'How much do we actually know about the monastic side of the Bishop's life?' We know him as a supreme theologian, an iconic lecturer, an outstanding hierarch of the Orthodox Church, a remarkable pastor of the people of God. All these qualities seem to eclipse in our minds his identity as a monk. When I asked the people who are close to him to share their views on Bishop Kallistos's monasticism, I was met with bewilderment on their faces. It all appears to be hidden from the public eye. Eventually I decided to confront the Bishop himself, to interview him on the subject. And he shared with me valuable insights into his monastic career.

His interest in the monastic life first arose when he was still an Anglican. At about sixteen years of age, he came into contact with the Anglican religious order, the Society of St Francis. Through one of their monks who visited his school he was attracted to the idea of becoming a Franciscan. But by the middle of his time as a university student, when he was about twenty-one, he began to realize that his calling was to become Orthodox. This did not change his desire to dedicate his life to Christ in the monastic way, attracted as he was by the idea of community life in mutual love as well as the services, the daily office. In the early 1960s he received a letter from Metropolitan Vitaly in Canada, encouraging him to visit his newly established monastery. His first Orthodox monastic experience lasted for six months, but soon it became clear to him and to Metropolitan Vitaly that this was not the right place for him to be. It was not the most encouraging start to a monastic career.

Back in England, it was Archbishop Athenagoras who encouraged the Bishop first to become a deacon, and then to live in the monastery on Patmos. In 1965 he spent ten months there, having meanwhile been ordained to the priesthood by Athenagoras.

He then received an invitation to come to Oxford to lecture and to take up the position of Spalding Lecturer. This fitted his second main interest, which was academic life and teaching. But before he left Patmos, there was an interesting convergence. One day he went down to see the *geronda* of the island, Fr Amphilochios Makris, well known as a spiritual father. The latter blessed him to take monastic vows. He said, 'Even if you are not going to live in the monastery permanently, you should still be a member of a monastic family.' So, on the one hand, there was clear direction from Fr Amphilochios. On the other hand, when he returned to the monastery, they said, 'There's letter for you from England.' The porter gave it to him: the letter was signed by Archbishop Athenagoras, and it said quite independently but simultaneously, 'It would be a good idea if you were to ask the abbot to profess you as a monk before you return to England.' So there these two important voices coincided in a most remarkable way, quite independently! When he went to tell the abbot what had happened, the abbot replied: 'Yes, this is a good wish on your part, but we don't usually have outside brothers who are not living in the monastery. But I will ask the monastic council.' And then, after a day or two, he said, 'I put it to the brotherhood, and they *all* said that they favoured your being professed a monk of the monastery, even though you are going to be working in Oxford. You have lived here for ten months, so we know you a little, and of course we know Archbishop Athenagoras, your bishop; and because he supports this idea, that too influences us favourably. We will make you straightaway a monk of the Little Habit.'

Back in England, he now took up his double duties as teacher and parish priest, but as we know the Bishop has maintained close links with Patmos ever since. His is not simply a formal connection with the monastery. He goes home every year, and spends a considerable time at his monastery.

This is his monastic story, as the Bishop himself shared it with me. He humbly ascribes to himself a vocation – one that in nineteenth-century Russia was called 'learned monasticism' – that combines monastic life with teaching, a vocation to be a monk in the world. However, there is far more to his vocation than appears at first sight. I would like to share with you my personal impression of the monk in the Bishop. What is it that betrays him as a monk?

I remember how, on one of those glorious afternoons of the Trinity term in Oxford, Metropolitan Hilarion and I invited Bishop Kallistos to join us punting on the river. Burdened by the weight of responsibility for such an enterprise and out of safety concerns, I asked the Bishop: 'Just in case, Your Eminence, can you swim?' 'Yes, if necessary', he replied.

We had a truly splendid time with the Bishop, as you would imagine, and Metropolitan Hilarion said to me afterwards: 'Amazing! Whatever the Bishop does, he gives himself fully to it. He knows how to work, he knows how to rest.' Indeed, in the case of Bishop Kallistos, I have noticed this remarkable trait to do things properly. (And this reminds me of a line in a book by Bill Bryson, called *Notes from a Small Island*, where he writes: 'If the British were to do Communism, they would do it properly.') The Bishop was a proper student, he is a proper lecturer, a proper theologian, a proper bishop, who serves the Divine Liturgy properly, a proper friend, a proper spiritual guide and father for many of us. He has also taught us by his example how to enjoy the gifts of life properly. Above all he is a proper Christian. And I might add that, for me, for us, he is a proper monk.

His monastic way is a remarkable example: it shows that if you really blend in with the Divine Providence, God will grant you your unique place, a unique ministry, and a unique name, which will express your personality in the most articulate way. And as far as I can see, monasticism is an integral and imprescriptible part of His Eminence's identity.

Orthodox monasticism does not have 'orders', such as are found in the Western tradition. Thanks be to God, it is rather 'disorderly' in the sense that God allows each person to find his unique way, his unique ministry to God and to the world.

It is common amongst the Holy Fathers of the Church to see in monasticism a form of martyrdom. In the Greek language the word *martyria* [martyrdom] has a double meaning: making a sacrifice for the sake of God, and also bearing a witness to God. In the case of the Bishop these two aspects of monastic martyrdom – sacrifice and witness – have become a harmonious *one*.

I have asked the Bishop how it felt, for an Englishman, to be a monk in his native environment, where monasticism scarcely plays a prominent part in mainstream spirituality. We have all seen how Bishop Kallistos would circulate in Oxford, lecturing in his cassock, ever faithful to the bidding of his *geronda*, Amphilochios, 'always to wear his cassock'. However, sometimes we may overlook what it cost him. The Bishop said to me, 'I realize that most of my colleagues considered me, if not eccentric, rather peculiar ... and in that way, I was somewhat set apart. I had, indeed, many friends in the theology faculty, but I think they considered me a little strange and not very typical.' As a monk myself, I do know the reality that lies behind his words, and how it feels once you put on your monastic habit in the midst of the world. 'I think they accepted me for what I was, yes, Orthodox, a priest-monk, that I went everywhere in my cassock, that I had a beard; though it did separate me off a little from the rest of the faculty ... I think I would have found my position isolated if it were not for the fact that I had the Orthodox parish here.'

I believe that through this sacrificial witness (martyrdom) of the Bishop, Orthodoxy in general and Orthodox monasticism in particular came to be accepted and respected at the highest level of British society. As a monk who studied at the same university where the Bishop lectured, I felt that it was due to his witness that I was not written off as some sort of looney, but I was accepted as an integral member of student life in Oxford. And the whole army of bearded clergy and monks who have studied under Bishop Kallistos have flourished socially in the shining rays of his brilliant personality – a personality that has become something of a legend in its own time, a legend that indeed continues to grow massively with time.

Also his inspiring example of spiritual stability as a monk has helped me and many other monks, his students there, to face the challenge over our monastic vocation, while we were living away from our monasteries.

His monastic *martyria* also overshadowed his academic career. I remember how his theological message in his lectures would bear an unmistakable stamp of authenticity: he taught Patristics at Oxford (most of the Holy Fathers were monks and bishops), and so his monastic presence would naturally blend with his theology. He taught us that authentic theology is the sort that affects and expresses itself in real life: when *theoria* becomes *praxis*. How remarkably his monasticism breathes life into his theology! And the opposite is true as well: his theology is a natural expression of his monastic way of life. We, his students, are therefore most grateful to the Bishop for this theological legacy that shuns any tendency to abstraction. Abstract theologizing, like an intellectual exercise in logical algebra over a cosy cup of coffee, is not for us Orthodox theologians. We see it in the Bishop. He always lived what he taught and what he professed. It is no surprise that Bishop Kallistos has had such a large number of students under his supervision.

Now when I look back at my Oxford years, when Bishop Kallistos was and will for ever remain my Oxford *geronda*, his guidance by word and by his overwhelming example embraces my life in its totality: my spiritual life, my theology, my monasticism, my church ministry. His example was and is 'the way to be', and not least 'the way to be a monk'. Neither words nor any length of time will ever suffice to express our eternal gratitude to him.

So, Your Eminence, Τὰ σὰ ἐκ τῶν σῶν, 'Thine own of the thine own', we offer unto you our everlasting thanks.

STEPHEN PLATT

3 The Pastor and Bishop

It is perhaps not coincidental that several of the contributors to this volume have included material about Bishop Kallistos's mother, and I must add to this.

I first met Metropolitan Kallistos when I was a schoolboy. I was fifteen and my English teacher was spending time in Oxford as a visiting scholar under the schoolteacher fellowship programme. She found herself working at Pembroke College and getting to know Dr Ware, as the Bishop was known in the academic community. I was terribly excited at this news because this was a name known to me through my reading. I asked my teacher whether it might be possible for me to visit her in Oxford, so that we might go together to visit Bishop Kallistos. She arranged this, so from Pembroke College we made the long walk up the Banbury Road to Staverton Road where we were met and shown into the study. The Bishop sat us down and asked if we would like tea or coffee and we indicated that we would both like coffee. At this point a rather older lady came into the room. He looked up at her and said, in a somewhat imperious tone, 'Two coffees, please.' She replied, 'Very good', and went off, and we continued our conversation. After a while the same lady came in with a tray, the lady that we had assumed to be the housekeeper, and put the coffee down on the table. The Bishop looked up at her and said, 'Thank you very much, that will be all!' She regarded him with a rather knowing look and said once again, 'Very good.' It was some years later, when I came to be one of his students, that I realized that this same lady was in fact his mother. On one rare occasion, when I was early and the Bishop was late, she showed me into the house and asked with exasperation, 'Well! You're here, but where is the Bishop? I don't know where he gets to these days. The only one of my children to remain a Christian, and he's turned Orthodox, you know!'

Some years later, I visited Bishop Kallistos on the eve of my ordination as a priest to ask for his advice, his 'good word'. He gave me two pieces of advice. First, as a priest, never go out looking for things to do. God will send you exactly what you need to do. Simply be prepared to respond to God's will for you. This has, indeed, proved to be very true. The second counsel he gave has proved instrumental in my own service: never pretend to be anything other than the Englishman you are. Strangely enough, when Bishop Kallistos told me the advice he had been given by the ordaining hierarch on the eve of his episcopal consecration, it was rather more down to earth: always fold up your own vestments at the end of the service.

Bishop Kallistos has now for many generations proved to be a true model of what it is to be an Orthodox pastor. We priests have all learned much from him, and to a great extent, many of us imitate him, even perhaps without realizing it at the time. This is obvious when observing the manner in which some clergy deliver talks and sermons. Some impersonations are more accurate and effective than others; some are, indeed, not terribly effective. Perhaps the worst impersonation of Bishop Kallistos I ever heard was that made by the late Militza Zernov, who attempted to impersonate his Queen's English using her own strong Russian accent. However, this rendition was only matched in its ineffectiveness when I once heard Bishop Kallistos trying to impersonate Militza.

The great Russian priest and theologian of the emigration Archpriest Sergei Bulgakov, in a prayer written for the Fellowship of St Alban and St Sergius, which has been used for many decades by the Bishop, asks God to grant certain gifts, in the context of a hope for restored unity between the divided Christians of east and west. He asks for a spirit of wisdom and of faith, of daring and of patience, of humility and of firmness, of love and of repentance. It occurs to me that our dear teacher and pastor has, through his many years of service, lived true to the hopes expressed in Fr Bulgakov's prayer. Bishop Kallistos is, in many ways, a spiritual father, a teacher, and a priest of contrasts, of unity in diversity. He may be considered a living example of *sobornost*, a true reflection of what he aspires to in his own deep faith in the Holy Trinity.

Just as the prayer asks, he has been granted wisdom and faith: able to hold together academic scholarship and the intellectual mind with the heart of faith; still able to stand, Sunday by Sunday, liturgy by liturgy, in front of the altar, with all sincerity and faith, looking towards the imminent yet transcendent God. He has been given daring and patience: rare indeed it is to find a pastor who is prepared never to give up on his spiritual children, and yet to be outspoken enough to suggest things which would put him in the line of criticism and of censure. I remember Bishop Kallistos telling me that he had once seen on the front page of the conservative Greek church newspaper *Orthodoxos Typos* the headline, 'Bishop accused of heresy', only to discover that it was him they were talking about.

The Bishop has been an example of humility and of firmness. As a pastor and teacher of priests, there is in him, above everything else, a deep kindness, a humanity, an approachability. Yet, at the same time, he is not afraid to point out when something needs correction. Many have been the occasions when people have caused problems in church life, have said things that should not be said, have behaved in ways which were unworthy. At such difficult moments, he with humility and firmness has spoken the truth in love, and put people in their place without any hint of personal animosity or of hatred. A rare gift for a pastor, one that many priests might learn from. Of love and of repentance: perhaps no more need be said about these qualities, other than that in all our individual relationships with him, a spirit of love and of calling us to repentance has characterized them.

This week the Church has been commemorating amongst the other saints a great bishop of the early Western Church, St Ansgar, the Archbishop of Hamburg, who was one of the first great missionaries to Denmark and Sweden. Only a few of St Ansgar's sayings are recorded, but one of them speaks pertinently in the context of this evening's gathering. St Ansgar writes, 'If I were worthy of such a favour from my God, I would ask that He grant me this one miracle: that by His grace He would make of me a good man.' Whether as a teacher, a pastor, or a spiritual father, leaving aside the whole question of his academic work, I think that those of us who have been influenced by Metropolitan Kallistos, or have learnt from him, will see there an answer to St Ansgar's prayer: God has made him a truly good man, and for that we are thankful.

MARCUS PLESTED

4 The Teacher

It is a great delight to be asked to offer a tribute to Metropolitan Kallistos as teacher. I am aware of being in an especially fortunate position for this task given that I was catechized by him, attended the various lecture courses he gave at Oxford as both undergraduate and post-graduate student, and wrote my doctoral thesis under his supervision. After that, in my time at the Institute for Orthodox Christian Studies in Cambridge (2000–13) I had the joy of sitting at his feet for almost innumerable courses and lectures – not to mention many and various other contexts.

One of Metropolitan Kallistos's favourite quotations from Plato comes from the *Theaetetus*: 'The beginning of philosophy is a sense of wonder'; and a sense of wonder is inescapable in anyone who has attended his lectures, talks, or sermons. This sense of wonder certainly has something to do with humour. While never flippant, Metropolitan Kallistos invariably peppers his presentations with a range of hilarious anecdotes. These have great pedagogical value, creating a sense of uplift, refocusing attention, and contributing to the overwhelmingly positive and affirmative character of his discourse. Humour, for the Bishop, has something fundamental to do with human nature (as does, in his estimation, a love of the railways). Having attended very many of the Bishop's presentations, I often find myself laughing at a joke or anecdote long before the punch line. Perhaps this will also apply to many of those reading this brief tribute and for whom the following prompts may raise a smile: Calvados; the Spanish aristocrat; Thomas Carlyle and his mother; the Revd W. A. Spooner and Aristotle; Fr Georges Florovsky's old and beautiful face. Like Tolkien's roads, the list goes ever on.

Perhaps the outstanding feature of the Bishop's teaching is its sheer clarity. His lectures are beautifully crafted and exquisitely lucid. This clarity is something the Bishop himself attributes to his classical education – a vanishing commodity in our own time. Metropolitan Kallistos's teaching deals with the profoundest of concepts in a manner that is always accessible. This is a rare quality in an age in which, at least in the theological arena, technical jargon and wilful obfuscation are all too prevalent. Then there is the style. I take Metropolitan Kallistos as a paradigmatic lecturer in terms of content, structure, and clarity. His delivery is quite remarkable: a sonorous but somehow also youthful voice coupled with a peerless command of the English language. Metropolitan Kallistos always speaks with a remarkable freshness and vision. One always leaves his lectures (and sermons) refreshed, reoriented, and inspired – a great 'yes!' ringing in one's ears.

As a doctoral student, I found Bishop Kallistos a very careful supervisor. We met perhaps once a term, when I had something to show him. I always received very precise and extensive comments and corrections on the work I produced. He was also very patient in deciphering my handwriting, which he once likened to the scratchings on the note left by the mice in Beatrix Potter's *The Tailor of Gloucester*. Every time we met I felt a return of a sense of direction and purpose that kept me going through the arduous years of graduate study. And I continue to be inspired by the example Metropolitan Kallistos gives of a scholar in whom head and heart are not separated, in whom the most meticulous academic standards are united with a faith commitment of unusual power and intensity. He is also – and this is not insignificant – someone who manages to be impeccably English while also uncompromisingly Orthodox. A very western Eastern Orthodox Christian.

I might also mention what might be called his quality of nuance. There is little room in his world-view for simple dichotomies, for instance between Greek East and Latin West or Orthodoxy and scholasticism. I can recall a tutorial in which he emphasized the sheer variety of the late Byzantine theological scene encompassing, for example, Palamite supporters of reunion with Rome, Palamite anti-unionists, anti-unionist Thomists, non-Palamite Palamites, Palamite Thomists, and various other permutations. Having been brought up, theologically speaking, to take the dichotomy of Orthodox East (represented by St Gregory Palamas) and Roman Catholic West (represented by Thomas Aquinas) very much as a given, this quality of nuance much surprised me and indeed planted a seed that emerged, eventually, as my most recent book. Nuance is not, however, tantamount to relativism. If lines need to be drawn, if distinctions need to be made, one can rely on him to do so with thundering clarity.

Lastly, I should like to acknowledge the element of sacrifice. Metropolitan Kallistos has devoted himself tirelessly and selflessly to his teaching. As Spalding Lecturer in Orthodox Christian Studies at Oxford from 1966 to 2001 he bore a very heavy load of undergraduate and postgraduate teaching. Both in that time and since his retirement he has consistently been remarkably generous in his acceptance of invitations to speak on both sides of the Atlantic and indeed across the globe. All this has come at a cost, especially when considered alongside his pastoral responsibilities. Had he taught less, had he restricted his pastoral commitments, he would surely have produced a great deal more published work – particularly in monograph form. But perhaps such a reflection rather misses the point. Metropolitan Kallistos's teaching has impacted millions – in print, by virtual means, and, especially, through the lived experience of the spoken word. He has also taught, and will continue to teach, through his many students from generation to generation. Look, for example, at his doctoral students scattered throughout the world in many and various teaching and pastoral roles. We can, in this respect, begin to talk of a Kallistian legacy. And let us not forget his undergraduate students at Pembroke College – of whom my wife was one. When I asked him to marry us he remarked that he quite approved of his students marrying one another. This is just one example of the wider and ultimately unquantifiable ramifications of his teaching – an extended community or family indelibly shaped by his remarkable vision and example.

There are many *Kallistoi*. My own studies in the Byzantine period have introduced me to Kallistos Angelikoudes, Kallistos Xanthopoulos, Kallistos Kataphygiotes, and others. But for me, as I suspect for many reading this, there is only one Kallistos. Our Kallistos has become a *hapax phenomenon* – a singular, unique, unrepeatable, and inimitable event. And if I may be indulged with yet another piece of Greek – *onoma kai pragma* [something by name, something by nature] – this is a man whose teaching is indeed most good and most beautiful.

Bibliography

Louth, Andrew, 'Biographical Sketch', in John Behr, Andrew Louth, and Dimitri Conomos (eds), *Abba: The Tradition of Orthodoxy in the West. Festschrift for Bishop Kallistos (Ware) of Diokleia* (Crestwood, NY: St Vladimir's Seminary Press, 2003), 13–27.

——, *Modern Orthodox Thinkers: From the 'Philokalia' to the Present* (London: SPCK, 2015), 332–48.

Plested, Marcus, *Orthodox Readings of Aquinas* (Oxford: Clarendon Press, 2012), 215–16.

† EPHREM LASH

5 The Translator and Writer

I want just to make one observation before I start: that I object to the translation in the title of this book. *Orthotomounta* does not mean 'dividing'. That crept into English with Tyndale, who I think got it from Luther, who uses the word *Teile*. It is a word in fact that occurs nowhere in Greek until the translation of the Hebrew Book of Proverbs. That is the first time it occurs anywhere in Greek: it is not a normal Greek word, but this is a different discussion.

Now I was sitting one afternoon in the porter's lodge in Dochiariou and two middle-aged Englishmen turned up. They were two doctors from Bristol, one a consultant and the other a GP. They sat in the corner while I was preparing what the Greeks always call *to kerasma mas*. They expect, as of right, to have their coffee and a particularly lethal shot of alcohol that we distilled ourselves: it was very dangerous. I saw them looking at me and, being English, they would not ask a direct question. So one said, 'Father, were you born in Bath?', to which I was able to reply, 'I am not Bishop Kallistos!' I knew that he was born in Bath – because his mother happened to be in Bath at the time – a most suitable place for him to be born, the city of Aquae Sulis, of Jane Austen and the Pump Room, particularly suitable for someone whose school chapel was to be Westminster Abbey!

I knew, of course, that he had written *The Orthodox Church*.[1] That is a remarkable book, still in print after half a century and more. It is quite the clearest and best introduction to the Orthodox Church that we have in English, and it is not full of that certain type of Anglo-Saxon Orthodoxy

---

[1] Timothy Ware, *The Orthodox Church: An Introduction to Eastern Christianity*, 3rd edn (London: Penguin 2015).

which gets a bit screechy about things. This is a very balanced and serious account.

While I am on *The Orthodox Church*, I would just like to remember his mother. His mother was a great character, and so was his father. In fact, his father and my father both sat at the feet of Colonel (as he then was) Bernard Law Montgomery at Staff College and my father said: 'You could follow Montgomery's campaigns from your lecture notes.' But his mother was a remarkable lady. Once I arrived at the house by the back door straight from Mount Athos, wearing the standard Orthodox Athonite *skouphia*. She always used my family name and she said: 'Ah Christopher, come in.' Then she looked, and she said: 'Timothy, why don't you get a fetching little felt number like Fr Ephrem?' He at the time had a rather splendid sort of purple Russian biretta, but it had seen its best days. I had never thought of an Athonite *skouphia* as a 'fetching little felt number'!

Metropolitan Kallistos's father lived and died a faithful and devout Anglican. After his death, his mother decided to become Orthodox and she said, 'It's nothing to do with you; it's my decision entirely and nobody has influenced me.' And then she said: 'Of course now I have a problem. I have to make my confession beforehand and when you are my age there is quite a lot. I see far too much of you lot in Oxford, so I have decided to wait until I go to Iona and be received by Fr John in Edinburgh', which is what she did.

Now next to *The Orthodox Church*, I think one of the best things Metropolitan Kallistos has ever done is *The Orthodox Way*, which was a sort of adult catechism.[2] It sets out the basis of the Orthodox faith in very clear, precise, and simple language and each chapter ends with an anthology, a sort of commonplace book of quotations from spiritual writers, mostly Orthodox, but all sorts of other people find their place. There is an ecumenical broadness, and if you want a commonplace book of quotations that can inspire your prayer, before you start making your own, then read *The Orthodox Way* and collect the quotations at the end. He is a scholar

---

2   Bishop Kallistos Ware, *The Orthodox Way*, 2nd edn (Crestwood, NY: St Vladimir's Seminary Press, 1995).

and all of them are listed at the back with the full references to where you can find the original text.

Apart from those two books, there are of course the translations and, first of all, the translations of *The Festal Menaion* and *The Lenten Triodion*.[3] But I would like to read you a passage from one of my favourite writers, John King, who in the late eighteenth century was chaplain to the English in St Petersburg. He wrote a marvellous book called *The Rites and Ceremonies of the Greek Church in Russia*. This is what he says of the liturgical texts:

> If I was to pass my judgement on the compositions themselves, I should venture to say, that, for the most part, they are a sort of rhapsody and bombast, difficult to be imitated, and scarcely possible to be reduced into common sense; this is generally allowed, even by those who esteem some of the ancient sublime and beautiful, to be the character of the most modern ones; for they are undoubtedly of different dates. The metaphors in these hymns are frequently so bold, they will not bear to be exhibited in our northern tongue: the reader therefore must expect to find the translations in the following pages greatly inferior to the original.[4]

Now I think that any of us who know the originals and the translations in *The Festal Menaion* and *The Lenten Triodion* will not always find that the translations are inferior to the originals. They are not easy to translate, I know, but Metropolitan Kallistos has a gift for putting the original Greek into straightforward but rhythmical and beautiful English. He did not translate the *Pentecostarion* but I do not think that he would ever have translated the four simple Greek words in Ode 3 of the Easter Canon, *deute poma piomen kainon* – 'come let us drink a new drink' – as one English translation manages to render it as 'come let us quaff a beverage new'. That is not how Metropolitan Kallistos translates. He translates the text, even if the text is simple. Many Americans are doing extraordinary things with our texts because they think that, if a troparion starts with *soson*, then you must start it as in the Greek. So they translate the troparion of the Cross

---

3 *The Festal Menaion*, trans. Mother Mary and Archimandrite Kallistos Ware (London: Faber & Faber, 1969); *The Lenten Triodion*, trans. Mother Mary and Archimandrite Kallistos Ware (London: Faber & Faber, 1978).
4 John King, *The Rites and Ceremonies of the Greek Church in Russia* (London, 1772), 18.

as 'Save, Lord, your people', as opposed to what would sound more natural in English, 'Lord, save your people', which is what Metropolitan Kallistos did. Can you imagine singing 'God save the Queen' in an American translation: 'Save God our gracious Queen'? It does not work, but I must not divert for too long on these things.

Now, of course, I occasionally have quibbles. I object to the introduction of 'and's into the Trisagion: 'Holy God, Holy Strong, Holy Immortal'. This is because in the Orthodox liturgical tradition it is Trinitarian, not addressed to one person. There are no 'and's in the Greek. This has crept in and I must say I have to take issue with that. We also do not agree entirely about the 'Our Father'. I was very struck the other morning by the ex-Canon Chancellor of St Paul's, Giles Fraser, who was on 'Thought for the Day' on Radio Four. He actually devoted it to the correct translation of the 'Our Father', which says, 'forgive us our debts, as we forgive our debtors'. I was discussing this once with Costa Carras, and he said: 'Ah yes, Father, but you see it's the difference between the English and the Greeks: we are interested in business and money and you are interested in property rights.' I did point out that in 'international' English language the only phrase in the Lord's prayer that our Lord gives his own explanation of is that one, which is in the parable of the unforgiving servant. So he actually provides his comment, but this could be developed further elsewhere.

Also those two volumes of translation give more than the translation. They give magnificent introductions to the services, to how they work, to the plan of them. It is an initiation into the Orthodox services of the Great Fast, and you will understand more if you read it, and about what Lent means, and what fasting means. They are not simply translations of the text: they are an explanation, they are something that you can feed on for your understanding of what is happening in the great services.

And then there is the *Philokalia*.[5] You will notice, by the way, that Metropolitan Kallistos's translations are all co-operative efforts. He does not live on his own in his private quarters; he has helpers and assistants and they all contribute. All his fellow contributors to the *Philokalia* are,

---

5   *The Philokalia: The Complete Text*, trans. G. E. H. Palmer, P. Sherrard and K. Ware, 4 vols (London: Faber & Faber, 1979–95); vol. 5 is shortly to appear.

I think, dead. We once presented to the Lord High Admiral, Prince Philip, Duke of Edinburgh, the first four volumes of the *Philokalia* in the English translation. I wonder what he made of it and where it is now in Buck House.

Well I just wanted to say a word about the *Philokalia*, and here is John King again on the monastic life in a passage worthy of Gibbon:

> The notion of making the height of virtue, and the perfection of human nature to consist in solitude and contemplation, is the most extravagant of all the unreasonable doctrines fanaticism and ignorance have ever conceived. A doctrine ... absurd in speculation, and productive of the greatest evils in practice ... subversive of every relative duty, destructive to human society, and contradictory to the first great law of God.[6]

I once found a bibliography of the works of Metropolitan Kallistos on the internet and it is a remarkable thing. There are ten whole pages in small print. He has covered almost every topic, usually in short and understandable articles: women priests, ecumenism, hesychasm, the Jesus Prayer. It's all there in clear, simple, understandable language.

I will just end with a little final story. We both know a young priest: he is not in England and he is not English. I said one day to Bishop Kallistos, 'He is one of my Tiggers', meaning young people who need a bit of un-bouncing. You remember the un-bouncing of Tigger? A familiar voice at the other end of the telephone said, 'Father Ephrem, do you not find that at our age Tigger's bounce is not what it was?' So I am not going to say anything in Greek or Slavonic; I am just going to wish him many years of bounce for the future.

Bibliography

The Festal Menaion, trans. Mother Mary and Archimandrite Kallistos Ware (London: Faber & Faber, 1969).

King, John, *The Rites and Ceremonies of the Greek Church in Russia* (London, 1772).

6   John King, op. cit., 102.

The Lenten Triodion, trans. Mother Mary and Archimandrite Kallistos Ware (London: Faber & Faber, 1978).

The Philokalia: The Complete Text, trans. G. E. H. Palmer, P. Sherrard and K. Ware, 4 vols (London: Faber & Faber, 1979–95); vol. 5 is shortly to appear.

Ware, Bishop Kallistos, *The Orthodox Way*, 2nd edn (Crestwood, NY: St Vladimir's Seminary Press, 1995).

Ware, Timothy, *The Orthodox Church: An Introduction to Eastern Christianity*, 3rd edn (London: Penguin, 2015).

ANDREW LOUTH

6 The Theologian

These tributes address different aspects of Metropolitan Kallistos's life, work, and influence. And yet it seems to me – as, I am sure, to all of us making our tributes to him – that Bishop Kallistos cannot be divided up into separate categories. We pay tribute to him as a spiritual father, a pastor, a monk, a teacher, a supervisor of research students, and also as a theologian, and yet they cannot be separated. The spiritual father, pastor, monk, teacher, supervisor: all of these are different aspects of the one who is a theologian. Or one could take each of these aspects and see all the others in it. So I cannot but trespass on the tributes of the others. Nor do I apologize for that.

All of these aspects have been constants, and they are all interwoven: interwoven they manifest something unique, some*one* unique. We shall not see his like again. This is true simply at the level of history. When Metropolitan Kallistos was first drawn to Orthodoxy, it was a very unusual thing to do. He was preceded by a few years by one who was to become his great friend, Philip Sherrard, and received into Orthodoxy alongside W. Jardine-Grisbrooke. As he contemplated Orthodoxy, he was warned of the danger of perpetual eccentricity if he pursued such a course. In some way he was abandoning his Englishness, despite the fact that eccentricity has always been an eminently English characteristic. And, of course, he did not abandon his Englishness, even though, when I first met him, he was prone to speak of 'We Orientals'!

This bears on the kind of theologian he has become. While being totally Orthodox, utterly faithful to the tradition, he remains distinctively English. To begin with, he had a superb English classical education: he left school with an intimate knowledge of Latin and Greek, and went up to Magdalen College, Oxford, to read *Literae Humaniores* ('more – or maybe rather – human letters'), better known as 'Greats'. He distinguished himself, gaining a double first in both Classical Moderations and Greats, which then consisted simply of ancient history and philosophy (both ancient and modern, with little in between). He then went on to read the Honour School of Theology. His theological career led to his embarking on research on St Mark the Monk for an Oxford DPhil. His thesis was an edition of texts attributed to Mark the Monk. A very English academic career could have followed, but by this time much had happened. He had become Orthodox, and been ordained as a priest-monk. He had written, while still a layman, what must be his best-known book, *The Orthodox Church* (published as a Pelican Original in 1963, since then reprinted as a Penguin; it has never been out of print), and the following year a study of a Greek theologian of the eighteenth century, Eustratios Argenti: *Eustratios Argenti: A Study of the Greek Church under Turkish Rule* (OUP). What is emerging? A theologian with, in the traditional English mode, a thorough classical background, capable of detailed textual and historical studies, yes, but also, in his book *The Orthodox Church*, a brilliant teacher. The then Archimandrite Kallistos's academic career properly began in 1966 with his appointment as Spalding Lecturer in Eastern Orthodox Studies in succession to Nicolas Zernov. He remained there for thirty-five years until his retirement in 2001.

Already then, on his appointment to the Spalding Lecturership in 1966, Fr Kallistos (let us call him, for short, and affectionately) had all the ways of being a theologian open to him: technically superbly equipped, but with a gift for communicating. He was also a monk, about to found with Nicolas Zernov the Orthodox parish in Oxford on Canterbury Road. Although a convert from Anglicanism to Orthodoxy, he retained a deep appreciation for Anglicanism. We have then a scholar, concerned to communicate what he knows, for whom the Divine Liturgy celebrated among a parish community is paramount, and with a complete lack of defensiveness, manifest in his ecumenical concerns. We can build up a more detailed picture by looking at his publications over the years. We have mentioned the remarkable book he published when he was barely turning thirty. One more book followed, *The Orthodox Way* (1979), which presented Orthodoxy precisely as a way: a way of life, a way of prayer – beautifully written, with many citations from the Fathers (both ancient and modern), the liturgical texts, and various modern writers. It is like a glittering chain of jewels, many facets of which will long linger in the memory of the reader. These two books – *The Orthodox Way*, together with the more 'objective' (historical and doctrinal) *The Orthodox Church* – must have led many people to Orthodoxy over the last half-century.

Then there are translations, and careful introductions to translations made by others: I think particularly of his introduction to *The Art of Prayer*, an anthology drawn from the letters of (mostly) St Theophan the Recluse,[1] or his introduction to the Classics of Western Spirituality translation of *The Ladder of Divine Ascent* by St John Climacus,[2] as well as the work he did in preparing for publication *The Diary of a Russian Priest*, containing writings by Fr Alexander Elchaninov. His translations include the liturgical translations he made together with Mother Maria of the monastery at Bussy-en-Othe – *The Festal Menaion*[3] and *The Lenten Triodion*[4] – a work of translation that went alongside his involvement, together with Gerald Palmer and Philip Sherrard, in the complete translation from the Greek of the *Philokalia*.[5] Translation is laborious and requires immense dedication.

What else? A host of articles, many based on lectures and papers Fr Kallistos has given throughout his life. Still he seems rarely to turn down an invitation to talk to groups here and all over the world. At first sight it seems that it would be difficult to summarize the main themes of Fr Kallistos's thought: there is little on which he has not touched, always with insight and learning. We might, however, trace a thread starting from

---

[1] *The Art of Prayer: an Orthodox Anthology*, compiled by Igumen Chariton of Valamo, trans. E. Kadloubovsky and E. M. Palmer, with introduction by Timothy Ware (ed.) (London: Faber & Faber, 1966), 9–38.

[2] John Climacus, *The Ladder of Divine Ascent*, trans. Colm Luibheid and Norman Russell, Classics of Western Spirituality (London: SPCK, 1982), 1–70.

[3] *The Festal Menaion*, trans. Mother Maria and Archimandrite Kallistos Ware, with an introduction by Professor Georges Florovsky (London: Faber & Faber, 1969).

[4] *The Lenten Triodion*, trans. Mother Maria and Archimandrite Kallistos Ware (London: Faber & Faber, 1978).

[5] *The Philokalia. The Complete Text Compiled by St Nikodimos of the Holy Mountain and St Makarios of Corinth*, trans. G. E. H. Palmer, Philip Sherrard and Kallistos Ware, 4 vols (so far, out of 5) (London: Faber & Faber, 1979–95).

his experience of the Holy Mountain of Athos, where he spent much time in the 1970s and 1980s working with his companions on the translation of the *Philokalia*.[6]

Speaking of what he had learnt from Gerald Palmer during these visits to Athos, Fr Kallistos once had this to say:

> First, he greatly enhanced my sense of the Athonite environment, of the *physical reality* of the Holy Mountain. He made me aware – far more then I had been previously – of the Holy Mountain as in itself a sacrament of the divine presence ... a *Holy Mountain* ... In Fr Nikon's words, which Gerald used to quote, 'Here every stone breathes prayers.' ... Gerald valued the monastic buildings, the icons, the human presence of the monks, the ever-renewed sequence of liturgical prayer. But all of this acquired its full meaning in his eyes because of the sacredness of the very Mountain itself.[7]

Fr Kallistos continued:

> A second thing that Gerald taught me to feel and know more directly was the stillness of the Holy Mountain, its creative silence. By 'stillness' (*hesychia*) I do not mean a total absence of sound, for of course there are always many sounds on the Mountain: of the wind and the sea, of the birds and the insects, of the simantron, the bells, and the chanting. But all these sounds stand out from an omnipresent background of silence – of a silence that is not an emptiness but a fullness, not an absence but a personal presence: 'Be still, and know that I am God' (Psalm 46: 10).[8]

The decision to translate the *Philokalia* grew out of the spiritual experience of being on the Holy Mountain: a sense of the sacredness of the Holy Mountain linked to an experience of stillness, *hesychia*. These give us two themes, or two pathways, to pursue as we seek to explore the theology of Fr Kallistos. It is from the word *hesychia*, stillness, that the term 'hesychasm' is derived. The meaning of *hesychia* has exercised Fr Kallistos throughout his life: there is a long section on the fourteenth-century hesychast controversy

---

[6] Much of what follows is condensed from my chapter on the Bishop in *Modern Orthodox Thinkers: From the 'Philokalia' to the Present* (London: SPCK, 2015) 332–48.

[7] Bishop Kallistos of Diokleia, 'Gerald Palmer, the *Philokalia*, and the Holy Mountain', *Annual Report of the Friends of Mount Athos* (1994), 23–8 (26–7).

[8] Ibid., 27–8. Both these passages are quoted in Graham Speake's contribution to the *Festschrift* for Bishop Kallistos, 'A Friend of Mount Athos', *Abba*, 29–40.

in his first book, *The Orthodox Church*, which also contains a brief, though significant, discussion of the Jesus Prayer;[9] many articles on different aspects of hesychasm and the Jesus Prayer followed, including a series of important articles on Palamism in the *Eastern Churches Review*;[10] and an article on the meaning of *hesychia*, which was included in volume 1 of his Collected Works,[11] to which one must add his pamphlet, *The Power of the Name*.[12] As with all his articles, one is struck by the range of sources on which he draws and the clarity and vividness of what he has to say. Furthermore, although he is clear in his opinions, he is always respectful of the opinions of others, and writes in a constructive way – something not at all characteristic of writing on hesychasm, for despite the fact that the root from which the term is derived means 'quietness' or 'stillness', controversy over hesychasm is more often noisy and acerbic!

It is striking that the Bishop's thought on hesychasm and prayer is both practical and yet at the same time informs his thought on what it is to be human. The practical side can be illustrated in a lecture given in Athens in 1998, and published in a splendid edition in 2004, *The Inner Unity of the Philokalia and its Influence in East and West*.[13] After his opening words, in which he speaks of the influence of the *Philokalia*, and the way in which 'it has become customary to speak of a characteristically "Philokalic" approach

9   Timothy Ware, *The Orthodox Church* (1st edn, 1963), 72–80, 312–14.
10 'Scholasticism and Orthodoxy: Theological Method as a Factor in the Schism', *Eastern Churches Review*, 5: 1 (1973), 16–27; 'God Hidden and Revealed: The Apophatic Way and the Essence-Energies Distinction', *ECR* 7: 2 (1975), 125–36; 'The Debate about Palamism', *ECR* 9: 1–2 (1977), 45–63.
11 'Silence in Prayer: The Meaning of Hesychia', in A. M. Allchin (ed.), *Theology and Prayer*, Studies Supplementary to *Sobornost*, 3 (1975), 8–28; also in *One Yet Two. Monastic Tradition East and West*, ed. M. Basil Pennington, Cistercian Studies 29 (Kalamazoo, MI, 1976), 22–47; and in *The Inner Kingdom*, 89–110.
12 *The Power of the Name*, Fairacres Publication 43 (1974, revised edn 1977). Much translated and reprinted in, for instance, Elisabeth Behr-Sigel, *The Place of the Heart: An Introduction to Orthodox Spirituality*, trans. Fr Stephen Bigham (Torrance, CA: Oakwood Publications, 1992), 133–73.
13 *The Inner Unity of the Philokalia and its Influence in East and West* (Athens: Syndesmos Ypotrofon Koinofelous Idrymatos Alexandros S. Onasis, 2004).

to theology and prayer, and many regard this "Philokalic" standpoint as the most creative element in contemporary Orthodoxy',[14] he goes on to identify what he calls the 'inner unity' of the *Philokalia*. First, it is concerned with 'inner action', that is, 'the guarding of the intellect', which leads to the discovery of the 'kingdom within us', which is characterized by two virtues: 'by *nepsis*, a term denoting sobriety, temperance, lucidity, and above all vigilance and watchfulness; and by *hesychia*, which signifies not so much exterior silence as inner stillness of heart'.[15] The aim of this inner action is deification: '[t]his ideal of *theosis*, of direct, transforming union with the living God, constitutes a unifying thread throughout the *Philokalia* as a whole'.[16] The means to reach this goal is continual invocation of the Name. Such invocation of the name of Jesus in prayer will 'enable us to "return to the perfect grace of the Spirit that was bestowed upon us in the beginning through Baptism"'.[17] This method Nikodimos, in his introduction to the *Philokalia*, even ventures to call 'scientific', and it can be spelt out in these terms: to pray *without ceasing*, in the *depths of the heart, excluding all images and thoughts*, invoking the *Holy Name of Jesus*, and using, if desired, *physical technique* (head bowed on chest; control of breathing; inner exploration).[18] The Bishop's account of the *Philokalia* emphasizes its practical nature, and in this way finds in the *Philokalia* a dimension that is never far from his own theological approach.

However, there is a series of articles in which Fr Kallistos explores the terminology of the *Philokalia* in order to deepen our understanding of the nature of the human.[19] This is, maybe, not very surprising, as what it

---

14   Ibid., 41.
15   Ibid., 49.
16   Ibid., 50.
17   Ibid., 51.
18   Cf. ibid., 52.
19   I have in mind articles such as: 'The Mystery of the Human Person', *Sobornost/ECR*, 3: 1 (1981), 62–9; 'Nous and Noesis in Plato, Aristotle and Evagrius of Pontus', *Diotima*, 13 [Proceedings of the Second International Week on the Philosophy of Greek Culture, Kalamata 1982, Part II] (1985), 158–63; 'The Soul in Greek Christianity', in M. James C. Crabbe (ed.), *From Soul to Self* (London and New York: Routledge, 1999), 49–69; *O Anthropos os «Mysterion»: I Enotita tou Prosopou kata tous Ellenes*

is to be human – how we are constituted – is bound up with the purpose for which we were created, which is union with God, deification, effected through prayer. A good deal of what these articles explore can be found in the glossary of terms, which forms an appendix to each of the volumes of the English translation of the *Philokalia*; the articles spell out what is present there in summary form.

One point Fr Kallistos frequently makes when considering the nature of the human person is that the human person is a mystery: one article begins by quoting various Fathers on the unknowability of the human person and concludes by quoting Carl Gustav Jung, who said that the psyche is 'a foreign, almost unexplored country'.[20] The human is created in the image of God, and stress is laid on the unity of the human person, created in God's image. In his article on 'The Soul in Greek Christianity' (a contribution to a symposium, *From Self to Soul*, that gathered together papers exploring various ways of approaching the notion of what it is to be human), Fr Kallistos sums up his conclusion in these terms:

> First, there is the notion of the heart as the unifying centre of our personhood, open on the [one] side to the abyss of the unconscious, open on the other to the abyss of divine grace. Second, there is the understanding of the *nous* or intellect as a faculty far higher than the reasoning brain – a visionary power, creative and self-transcending, that reaches out beyond time into eternity, beyond words into silence.[21]

We should note Fr Kallistos's openness to the insights of modern psychology, not least to the notion of the unconscious.

Alongside these explorations of the constituents, as it were, of the human, the Bishop also underlines the way in which the human, in virtue of being in the image of God, exercises a role in the cosmos: he is a microcosm, or better a *megalokosmos*, since the human comprehends the cosmos, whereas the reverse is not the case.[22]

Pateres, Bishop Kallistos's inaugural lecture as member of the Academy of Athens (Athens: Akadimia Athinon, 2008).
20 'The Soul', 49.
21 Ibid., 66.
22 *Anthropos*, 38–44.

This cosmic dimension of the human bears a very direct relevance to what we call the 'environmental crisis', although this very way of conceiving it is, the Bishop argues, a misconception:

> The present crisis is not really outside us, a crisis in our physical surroundings, but it is a crisis within us, a crisis in the way we humans think and feel. The fundamental problem lies not in the ecosystem, but in the human heart. It has rightly been said that we are suffering from ecological heart failure.[23]

This concern for the cosmos leads directly back to Fr Kallistos's experience of the Holy Mountain. We have already noticed in his account of the visits he made there with Gerald Palmer that it is his sense of the *sacredness* of the Holy Mountain that he mentions first, that there he realized with utter clarity that, in Blake's words, 'everything that lives is holy'. Fr Kallistos is fond of recalling in this context the words of Fr Amphilochios, an elder of Patmos, whom he knew when he first visited there (he died in 1970). 'Do you know – he used to say – that God gave us one more commandment, which is not recorded in Scripture? It is the commandment *Love the trees...* When you plant a tree, you plant hope, you plant peace, you plant love, and you will receive God's blessing.'[24]

Bibliography

Louth, Andrew, *Modern Orthodox Thinkers: From the 'Philokalia' to the Present* (London: SPCK, 2015), 332–48.

[Ware], Bishop Kallistos of Diokleia, 'Gerald Palmer, the *Philokalia*, and the Holy Mountain', *Annual Report of the Friends of Mount Athos* (1994), 23–8.

---

23   *Ecological Crisis: Ecological Hope. Our Orthodox Vision of Creation*, Orthodoxy in America Lecture Series (Bronx, NY: Fordham University Press, 2005), 10.
24   Cf. e.g. *Through the Creation*, 5.

ANDREAS ANDREOPOULOS

7 An English Orthodox Bishop?

Several years ago, when I had just started the Master's programme in Orthodox Theology at the University of Wales, I proposed that Bishop Kallistos should be awarded the title of University Fellow in Theology, one of the highest honorary awards of the university. Though he did not know me very well back then, Metropolitan Kallistos accepted, not because he needed the honorary title, but because in this way he demonstrated his support for the new programme and the overall development of Orthodox theological studies in the United Kingdom. To make it possible for him to come, as the journey was difficult otherwise, we travelled together by car from Oxford to Lampeter, in the heart of Wales, a five- or six-hour drive. For me it was a great pleasure, as I had the chance to get to know him a little more.

On the way he asked me about my interests, as well as about the theologians who had influenced me and had contributed to my theological thought, and he also spoke to me about the authors who had contributed to the formation of his theological views. If I remember correctly, I mentioned to him some of the names of the theologians I was studying at the time, as I was trying to cover over the many gaps in my theological knowledge, but I was embarrassed to give him the complete answer. I was too shy to tell him that he himself had played a key role in my own turn towards theology and Orthodoxy, not only through his books and articles, but also through his presence, along with a number of theologians of his generation.

This is as true now as it was twenty years ago. Metropolitan Kallistos was a reference point, an inspiration, for a generation of theologians, not only those who had the good fortune to study with him, but also those who struggled with Orthodox theology over the last forty years. Many people have been touched by him in one way or another, even people who have never met him in person. We primarily think of him as a distinguished theologian, and yet his overall contribution far exceeds what can be measured in terms of academic achievement. It is possible to think of Metropolitan Kallistos as a spiritual father, as a monk, as a bishop, as a teacher, as a translator, and as a theologian.

It is certainly not easy, nor is it fair, to attempt to summarize such a rich and complex life, especially when it is itself the account of a generation and its trajectory. Along with the aspects of Metropolitan Kallistos that are more widely known, we could think of Kallistos the storyteller, Kallistos the preacher and public speaker, Kallistos the travel guide and companion. But perhaps one of the most important aspects of his contribution is Kallistos the man who reminds us that it is possible to be English – one could say *very* English – and Orthodox at the same time, as opposed to the more usual flavours of Orthodoxy, which are associated with an ethnic culture (Greek, Russian, Romanian, and so forth), that may strike the average Western Christian as irrelevant, or as somewhat exotic.

I suspect that in the course of time this may prove to be the aspect of Metropolitan Kallistos that has the greatest impact. We can think of several other Orthodox theologians in the twentieth century who left their mark on Christian theology – bishops, priests, lay men and women – not that Metropolitan Kallistos would not have earned his place on this list, as we can see from his inclusion by Fr Andrew Louth in his recent study *Modern Orthodox Thinkers*.[1] Nowadays most British departments of theology and religion include some Orthodox material in their curriculum, and here we can think of theologians such as Vladimir Lossky, Fr Georges Florovsky, Christos Yannaras, and Metropolitan John Zizioulas. We can see a dramatic change of perspective if, for instance, we compare the early twentieth-century version of the *Catholic Encyclopaedia* with its modern counterpart, looking at articles that have to do with Eastern Christianity such as 'hesychasm'. We may also note that some of the scholars who recovered the theology of Gregory Palamas and the Eastern Fathers in the twentieth century were not Orthodox – people such as Robert Sinkiewicz, Paul Blowers, Charles Kannengiesser, or Brian Daley. Similarly, the Anglican

---

[1] Andrew Louth, *Modern Orthodox Thinkers: From the 'Philokalia' to the Present* (London: SPCK, 2015), 332–48.

world has become much more familiar with Orthodoxy than ever before, something that found its foremost expression in the former Archbishop of Canterbury, Rowan Williams. However, the issue of the convergence between Eastern Christianity and Western culture is not just in the field of theoretical theology. Despite the ongoing dialogue with its problems at the theological level, and the increased level of understanding on both sides, it is still difficult to visualize a non-ethnic Orthodoxy in the present, or, failing this, an Orthodoxy completely at ease within Western culture. Beyond the ivory towers of academic theology, where Orthodoxy is considered an increasingly important voice, one of the greatest challenges of modern Orthodoxy, both in the traditionally Orthodox countries as well as in the West, although expressed in different ways in the two places, is its close entanglement with ethnocentricity and ethnic identity. It is precisely this challenge that Metropolitan Kallistos addresses simply with his presence, in a way that could never be done so effectively by an Easterner in the West, such as Fr Georges Florovsky, or by a competent Western Orthodox of lesser prominence in the visible hierarchy of the Orthodox Church.

The problem of ethnophyletism has been repeatedly identified and condemned by several Orthodox Churches, and yet it is far from solved today. Orthodoxy in the West, even in places where it has been present for many generations, tends to hold on to its ethnic roots. It is not unusual to come across Orthodox parishes in the UK with a history of more than a hundred years which still worship in Greek or Russian. In fact, the number of British Orthodox churches that celebrate in English is shockingly low. This poses a great difficulty for non-Orthodox people who would like to find out more about the life of the Orthodox Church, as well as for many of the parishioners who may be of ethnic extraction, but for whom the mother country is a distant memory two or three generations away, and who have adopted the culture and language of the country in which they live more readily than their ancestors did. Orthodoxy in the West in the past has survived mostly in pockets of population that did not have much to do with the surrounding culture, at least in terms of their religious and cultural identity – a model that was perhaps inherited from the closed world many oppressed populations experienced under the Ottomans. This has begun to change in the twentieth century, but it has not been an easy change.

Despite the emergence of the ecumenical dialogue, the World Council of Churches, and the regional conversations between Orthodox and Western theologians, which one would think could have allowed the two worlds to come closer together (if not in a rushed administrative union, at least in greater mutual understanding), a few decades ago it was extremely difficult for an 'outsider' to be accepted in the Orthodox fold. The experience of Metropolitan Kallistos himself, as he recalls his first contact with the Russian and then with the Greek Church in the 1950s, and the reluctance of the Orthodox Church to receive him, is quite revealing of this.[2]

Nevertheless, this is not only relevant to Orthodox converts. What is perhaps even more positive is that in Western Europe and North America, both at the pastoral and at the theological level, Orthodoxy is increasingly less of an exotic oddity and much more integrated in the spiritual concerns of the people and the land than ever before. The Western world is discovering a lost or forgotten version of Christianity, much closer to its roots. Through Orthodox icons it is perhaps easier to appreciate the faded pre-Reformation frescos that we still find in places such as Durham Cathedral, the twelfth-century side chapel in Winchester, or St Alban's, before the overpowering dominance of the written word. Through the liturgical reading of the Bible it is easier to understand the context in which the Gospels were written and the context in which they were meant to be transmitted. Through the continuous dialogue with the Fathers it is easier to engage with the mind of the Church, and to discern the way it has addressed several of the spiritual problems of the modern world, which often echo much older problems (Arianism is still present today in different forms and under different names), or as it has stood up to new challenges in a spiritually based creativity. For all these reasons the West is gradually discovering the Eastern Christian tradition.

And yet there is a significant gap here. It is still difficult to extract these spiritual principles from their cultural shell and to have a meaningful encounter between them and the modern, some would say post-Christian,

---

[2] Metropolitan Kallistos recalls this experience in the chapter entitled 'Strange Yet Familiar: My Journey to the Orthodox Church' in *The Inner Kingdom* (Crestwood, NY: St Vladimir's Seminary Press, 2000), 1–24.

world. This is precisely the need that Metropolitan Kallistos fulfils with his activity as a theologian, as a pastor, and as a person who is at ease with the cultural background, the concerns, and the hopes of modern Western people. It is perhaps easy to look at Gregory Palamas through the literary memory of Papadiamantis or Dostoevsky, but it is much more difficult and important to do so through the heritage of Thomas Carlyle, John Vianney, M. R. James, and Evelyn Underhill. As Metropolitan Kallistos recalls, when he first met Pope John Paul II, the Pope looked at him and said, 'An English Orthodox bishop? How can this be?' Most likely the Pope found this such an unusual occurrence that he forgot all about it, and when they met again, ten years later, John Paul II said, once again, 'An English Orthodox bishop? How can this be?'

Metropolitan Kallistos offers, in the various ways that describe his activity and his personality, a much-needed reconciliation between Western culture and Orthodoxy, that we hope will be followed by other people of his stature in the future. The various aspects of his contribution make up an image that is greater than the sum of its parts. If Orthodoxy has a future in the West, I believe that he has already done a very great deal towards establishing its firm foundation, 'rightly dividing', as the Liturgy of St John Chrysostom says with reference to the Bishop, 'the word of His truth'.

Bibliography

Louth, Andrew, *Modern Orthodox Thinkers: From the 'Philokalia' to the Present* (London: SPCK, 2015).
Ware, Bishop Kallistos, *The Inner Kingdom* (Crestwood, NY: St Vladimir's Seminary Press, 2000).

PART 2

Papers in Honour of Metropolitan Kallistos

SEBASTIAN BROCK

8 An Early Syriac *Exposition of the Holy Mysteries*

On several occasions at the Eastern Christian Studies Seminar which we organized together while we were both still teaching in Oxford, Metropolitan Kallistos gave a paper on Byzantine commentaries on the Divine Liturgy, and so it seems appropriate in this volume in his honour to offer a translation of what must be one of the very earliest commentaries on the Liturgy to survive. Probably dating from around AD 400 or soon after,[1] and antedating the three-way split in Eastern Christianity, it is preserved in Syriac where it was influential in all three different Syriac liturgical traditions, the Chalcedonian (Rum) Orthodox, Syrian Orthodox, and Church of the East. Although there are some general similarities with certain of the collections of Catechetical Homilies that belong to the turn of the fourth to fifth century, no definite connections with any Greek source can be found, and so it is likely that Syriac was also the original language of the short text. The two earliest Syriac manuscripts containing the text belong to the Chalcedonian Orthodox, and both have been preserved in the library of St Catherine's monastery, Mount Sinai. In the Syrian Orthodox Church the brief text was expanded several times, sometimes by known authors such as George, bishop of the Arab Tribes (who died in 724), while in the Church of the East it was translated into Sogdian for the use of Christian communities in Central Asia; an almost complete text of this Sogdian translation is preserved in a manuscript from Turfan, in western China.

Very probably the text was composed for catechetical purposes, for the original form of the text, found in all but one of the witnesses, commences

---

[1] The absence of any reference to a post-baptismal anointing indicates that the text cannot be any later than the early fifth century.

with the baptismal rite and then runs straight into the Eucharistic liturgy. The Syriac was first published, together with a Latin translation,[2] by the learned Syrian Catholic Patriarch Ignatius Ephrem Rahmani who happened also to be an eminent liturgical scholar. He derived the text from a manuscript dated 882, which can now be identified as the 'Codex Syriacus Secundus', which featured in a famous catalogue of oriental manuscripts put out by the Leipzig dealer Hiersemann in 1922.[3] The provenance of almost all the manuscripts in the catalogue is now known to have been St Catherine's library, which in the late nineteenth and early twentieth century suffered many such losses at the hands of unscrupulous visitors. The 'Codex Syriacus Secundus' was written in a monastery near Beirut in 882, and it contains a very miscellaneous collection of texts; Rahmani saw it when it was in the possession of W. A. Neumann, of Vienna, before it was put up for sale. The subsequent fate of the manuscript was traced by W. Strothmann (Göttingen), who also published a photographic edition of it in 1977.[4] Since then it has been sold again and is now in a private collection in the United States.

For the first part of the commentary, dealing with the baptismal rite, a tenth-century Syrian Orthodox witness in the British Library (Add. 14,496) was published in 1980, together with two separate, slightly expanded forms of the text.[5] This article also made use of the Sogdian translation which had been edited in a Cambridge dissertation of 1978;[6] it also drew attention to the use made of the commentary in the later liturgical commentaries by George, bishop of the Arab Tribes, and by Moshe bar Kepha (d.903).

2   For the details, see below.
3   K.W. Hiersemann, *Katalog 500. Orientalische Manuskripte, arabische, syrische, griechische, aremenische, persische Handschriften des 7.-18. Jahrhunderts* (Leipzig: K.W. Hiersemann, 1922).
4   W. Strothmann, *Codex Syriacus Secundus* (Göttinger Orientforschungen, 1. Reihe: Syriaca, 13; Wiesbaden: Harrassowitz, 1977).
5   In S. P. Brock, 'Some Early Syriac Baptismal Commentaries', *Orientalia Christiana Periodica*, 46 (1980), 20–61.
6   By N. Sims-Williams; this was in due course published: *The Christian Sogdian Manuscript C2* (Berlin: Akademie Verlag, 1985); the English translation of the text is on pp. 112–15.

Since the British Library manuscript only covered the first eighteen sections of the text, it was necessary, in a second article, to employ another Syrian Orthodox manuscript with a slightly expanded form of the text for the remaining sections, on the Eucharistic liturgy.[7] There again comparison was made both with Rahmani's text and with the later Syriac and Sogdian witnesses. Subsequently a second old Syrian Orthodox witness to the text has turned up, preserved in the library of Deir al-Surian in Egypt (Syr. 17); in this manuscript, as in the second Rum Orthodox manuscript, Sinai Syr. 10, the full text is to be found.

In the manuscript of 882, which Rahmani used for his edition, the text has the heading 'Interpretation of the Mysteries of the Church, of John of the Golden Mouth', and this attribution is also found in the other Chalcedonian manuscript, Sinai Syr. 10, of a slightly earlier date. By contrast, the work is likewise left anonymous in the two Syrian Orthodox manuscripts and in the Sogdian translation; the attribution to John Chrysostom, however, was known to Moshe bar Kepha. Although a date towards the end of John's life for the work would seem plausible, the attribution to him is hardly likely: there are very few links with his genuine works, and indeed the closest parallels are to be found in Theodore of Mopsuestia's Catechetical Homilies. As the text got expanded in the Syrian Orthodox tradition, new attributions appear: Severus (Charfet 4/1) and Dionysios the Areopagite (London, Add. 14,538); in the later commentators, George, Moshe, and, later still, Dionysios bar Salibi (d.1199), it is simply a case of incorporating materials from it into more extensive commentaries under their own name.

For the present limited purposes, just a translation of Rahmani's edition of the manuscript dated 882 is provided, though any significant variants to be found in the other available witnesses are also given in the footnotes.[8] For the relationship of the text to the various other sources, and for a discussion

---

7   'An Early Syriac Commentary on the Liturgy', *Journal of Theological Studies*, 37 (1986), 387–403; both articles are reprinted in *Fire from Heaven: Studies in Syriac Theology and Liturgy* (Aldershot: Ashgate, 2006), chapters XV and XVI.
8   I have not had the opportunity to collate Deir al-Surian Syr. 17.

of its witness to the structure of the early Syriac baptismal rite, reference should be made to the detailed studies mentioned in notes 4 and 6.

Witnesses to the Original Form of the Work

A = British Library, Add. 14,496, f. 23 (Syrian Orthodox, tenth century): sections 1–18 only.

D = Deir al-Surian Syr. 17, ff. 6v-8r (Syrian Orthodox, ninth/tenth century): full text.

R = I. E. Rahmani (ed.), in *I Fasti della Chiesa patriarcale Antiochena* (Rome, 1920), x-xiii, based on 'Codex Syriacus Secundus' (Rum Orthodox; dated 882): full text.[9]

S = Sinai Syr. 10, ff. 204v-206v (Rum Orthodox, eighth century): full text.

Sog. = Sogdian tr. (Church of the East, ninth century), ed. with English translation, N. Sims-Williams, *The Christian Sogdian Manuscript C2* (Berliner Turfantexte XII, 1985), 110–23: originally the full text, but some has been lost in the beginning sections.

Translation

1. Faith is the path which provides immortal life, without which no one can live a spiritual life.
2. Whoever draws near to baptism first denies Satan; the denial of Satan (means) the keeping away from evil works.

---

9 Rahmani also had access to a Syrian Orthodox manuscript of 1224 with part of the text only.

3. The confession of the Creator means the drawing close to the good things of heaven.
4. The adjuration (is) the battle with Satan and a supplication to the Judge on behalf of the person who seeks to be freed from evil dominion.
5. The surety is the instructor in the ways of the Church and the guide on the road of truth.
6. Now oil is the invincible armour against the Adversary.
7. Being signed is the acknowledgement of the will of the person being baptized, and it is the imprint of the king[10] which is placed (*lit.* falls) on the spiritual soldier.
8. Being imprinted on the forehead – the part of the body that is important, for the person becomes fearful to the demons.
9. The kneeling on one knee (represents) our fall in sin; the[11] rising up from kneeling on one knee is a sign of the resurrection of Jesus Christ[12] in whom[13] our nature[14] rose.
10. The font fulfils the place of the grave. The water in it is the womb which gives birth to life. Baptism is also rebirth.
11. The threefold baptism in water is a symbol of the three days Jesus Christ[15] was in Sheol among the dead.
12. Saying 'N is baptized', and not 'I baptize', shows that this fearful affair is not from himself, but by grace (the priest) has been chosen by the (divine) will to administer these Mysteries.
13. Our going up from the font is a symbol (*raza*)[16] of the resurrection of our Lord[17] Jesus from the grave.

---

10 S: heavenly king.
11 S: our. The Syriac has a play on words, since the term for both 'rising up' and 'resurrection' is the same (*qyamta*). (A has lost some text through homoioteleuton, jumping from the first occurrence of 'knee' to the second.)
12 A: *om* Christ.
13 S: in which.
14 A S: our whole nature.
15 A: *om* Christ.
16 A Sog. sign (*atha*).
17 A Sog.: *om* our Lord.

14. The *oraria*[18] placed on the heads of those baptized signify the freedom which they have received from Christ.
15. The white garments (serve as) a type of the heavenly glories.
16. That they are soft (is) a sign of the rebirth of the body.
17. The incense in front of the baptized indicates the enlightened knowledge they have received from baptism which is in the name of the Father, Son, and Holy Spirit.[19]
18. Their glorious arrival[20] into the church:[21] indicates their spiritual marriage.
19. The hearing of the Scriptures and their understanding[22] is like bread and water by which everyone is nourished.
20. The washing[23] of the priest teaches the catechumens to wash their minds of cares.[24]
21. The covering of the baptized signifies the unchangeability of the hidden power which they have received.
22. The Peace which the faithful give one another removes and extinguishes enmity between them.
23. The altar is the place of Christ's sepulchre.
24. The bread and wine on it are a symbol of the Body[25] of Jesus Christ, (the Body) in which blood was also present.
25. The Veil above the cup and the paten (is) a sign of the stone which was placed above the sepulchre of our Saviour.
26. The curtains, or covering, are a likeness of this firmament between us and the heavenly region.

---

18 S Sog. *singular* (Sog. S+ the veil); A: crowns.
19 A: + just as also [ ] three persons, one nature rose from the dead and ascended to heaven; Sog: + as also the Lord Jesus, by the power of the invocation of these three names, arose from the tomb and ascended to heaven.
20 S: + during the service.
21 A Sog.: + indicates their spiritual marriage.
22 Sog.: the hearing of the words of Scripture.
23 Sog.: + of the hands.
24 Sog.: evil thoughts.
25 S: holy body; for the last half of the section Sog. has: of our Lord Jesus Christ's Body and Blood.

An Early Syriac Exposition of the Holy Mysteries

27. The priest fulfils three (roles):
    – the likeness of the soul of our Saviour which made an offering before its Maker and was raised up;[26]
    – secondly, he is the tongue in the head of the ecclesiastical body;
    – the painter who depicts spiritual things in the Mysteries.
28. The deacon[27] is the likeness of the angels who appeared at the head and foot of Jesus Christ our Saviour.
29. The *oraria*[28] on their left shoulders: because they were indicating that they are subordinate, since he who has authority puts the *orarion* over[29] both his shoulders.
30. The 'Holy' which they cry out three times is a pointer to the return of the Gentiles, and the fulfilment, which we now perform, of this symbol which Isaiah foresaw (Isa. 6: 3).
31. Their bending down to the ground is a likeness of those guards (at the tomb).[30]
32. The 'Our Father' is a prayer containing acknowledgement of the Maker, love of things that are good, and renunciation of those that are evil, as well as hope of forgiveness of sins, and a request for what is useful.[31]
33. 'That which is Holy to the Holy': an acknowledgement to that blessed Nature which has held mortals to be worthy of the sanctification of his name.
34. The partaking of the Mysteries is the receiving of the vision of Christ.[32]

---

26 Sog.: in the place of the soul of the Lord Jesus who did battle with Satan and ascended to heaven.
27 S Sog.: deacons (Sog. + the two by the altar).
28 S Sog.: *singular*.
29 S Sog.: + his head or.
30 S Sog.: + who out of fear fell on the ground at the time of the resurrection of Christ.
31 Sog.: + and for deliverance from temptation and for protection from Satan.
32 Sog.: the receiving of Christ's Body and of the vision of Him which will not pass away.

35. The right hand stretched out, supported by the left, is a sign of the honour of the Gift which is given,[33] which is a pledge of immortal life.[34]
36. The prayer after the holy Mysteries (is) the thanksgiving and worship which a person repays after receiving a gift.

We have put down (lit. done) these things for the understanding of those who encounter our words without any contempt.

Bibliography

Brock, Sebastian P., 'Some Early Syriac Baptismal Commentaries', *Orientalia Christiana Periodica*, 46 (1980), 20–61.

——, 'An Early Syriac Commentary on the Liturgy', *Journal of Theological Studies*, 37 (1986), 387–403. [Both articles are reprinted in *Fire from Heaven: Studies in Syriac Theology and Liturgy* (Aldershot: Ashgate, 2006), chapters XV and XVI].

Géhin, Paul, 'Reconstitution et datation d'un receuil syriaque melkite', *Rivista di studi bizantini e neoellenici*, 42 (2006), 51–68.

Hiersemann, K. W., *Katalog 500. Orientalische Manuskripte, arabische, syrische, griechische, aremenische, persische Handschriften des 7.-18. Jahrhunderts* (Leipzig: K. W. Hiersemann, 1922).

Rahmani, Ignatius Ephrem II, *I Fasti della Chiesa patriarcale Antiochena* (Rome: Tipografia della R. Accademia dei Lincei, 1920).

Sims-Williams, Nicholas, *The Christian Sogdian Manuscript C2* (Berliner Turfantexte XII; Berlin: Akademie Verlag, 1985).

Strothmann, Werner, *Codex Syriacus Secundus* (Göttinger Orientforschungen, 1. Reihe: Syriaca, 13; Wiesbaden: Harrassowitz, 1977).

---

33 Sog.: to that gift of grace which is received.
34 Sog.: + the Consecration on the Eve of the Resurrection is the appearance of our Lord which was to Mary and to her fellow workers at the time of the Resurrection; and that Consecration that they receive by day at the second and third hours is the appearance of our Lord to the disciples.

MAXIMOS CONSTAS

9 'Nothing is Greater than Divine Love': Evagrios of Pontos, St Maximos the Confessor, and the *Philokalia*

The *Philokalia of the Holy Neptic Fathers* (Venice, 1782) is a collection of Orthodox spiritual writings consisting of both extracts and whole works of thirty-six Church Fathers and ecclesiastical writers from the fourth to the fifteenth century. Compiled on Mount Athos in the eighteenth century, it was soon translated into Slavonic (Moscow, 1793) and eventually Russian (1877–89).[1] The *Philokalia* has exerted profound influence on modern Orthodox spirituality – in Russia from the late eighteenth and nineteenth centuries, and in the West especially from the 1950s – and is now generally recognized as a definitive expression of the ascetic and spiritual tradition of the Orthodox Church. Moreover, the *Philokalia* is surely the most significant Orthodox book to have appeared during the four centuries of Turkish rule (1453–1821), and is undoubtedly the most important book published by (if not actually on) Mount Athos. The collection itself is not, however, a creation of eighteenth-century Athonite piety, for it is now well established that its modern editors, St Makarios of Corinth (1735–1805) and St Nikodimos of the Holy Mountain (1749–1809), modelled the *Philokalia* on anthologies of ascetic and mystical writings compiled by late Byzantine hesychasts.[2]

---

[1] For a concordance of editions and translations of the *Philokalia*, see Vassa Conticello and Elia Citterio, 'La Philocalie et ses versions', in Carmelo Giuseppe Conticello and Vassa Conticello (eds), *La Théologie byzantine et sa tradition*, vol. 2 (Turnhout: Brepols, 2002), 999–1021.

[2] On which, see Chrysostomos Savvatos, 'The Contribution of Makarios of Corinth to the Compilation of the *Philokalia*', in Stylianos Papadopoulos (ed.), Ὁ Ἅγιος

After the pioneering translations of the *Philokalia* by Kadloubovsky and Palmer in the early 1950s,[3] Metropolitan Kallistos Ware's work on the English translation of the *Philokalia* (4 vols, 1979–95) has been one of his most ground-breaking and enduring contributions to the areas of theology and spirituality, enriching the lives of English-speaking Orthodox Christians and bringing the *Philokalia* to the attention of an international readership, both lay and academic.[4] At the same time, his numerous ancillary studies on the history of the collection as a whole, on the Jesus Prayer, and on individual philokalic writers (e.g. Mark the Monk, Diadochos of Photike, Gregory the Sinaite), have served to establish the modern study of the *Philokalia* on solid academic and theological foundations.[5]

Μακάριος (Νοταράς), *Γενάρχης τοῦ Φιλοκαλισμοῦ, Μητροπολίτης Κορίνθου* (Athens: Doukas, 2006), 145–58 (in Greek); and Symeon Paschalides, 'Autour de l'histoire d'une collection ascétique: La *Philocalie*, les circonstances de son édition et sa tradition manuscrite', forthcoming in A. Rigo and P. Van Deun (eds), *From Theognostus to Philokalia: Texts and Authors (13th–18th Centuries)* (Turnhout: Brepols, 2015); cf. Vassa Kontouma, 'La Philocalie des saints neptiques: un bilan', *Annuaire EPHE-Sciences religieuses*, 119 (2012), 191–205. Note that in the fourteenth and fifteenth centuries similar collections (*Sborniki*) were circulating among the Slavs; cf. Anthony-Emil Tachiaos, 'Mount Athos and the Slavic Literatures', *Cyrillomethodianum*, 4 (1977), 1–35.

3 E. Kadloubovsky and G. E. H. Palmer, *Writings from the Philokalia on Prayer of the Heart* (London: Faber & Faber, 1951); cf. their *Early Fathers from the Philokalia* (London: Faber & Faber, 1954), both of which present select English translations of the Russian translation of the original Greek edition of the *Philokalia*.

4 Note that these four volumes have been reprinted, and have been published together with the long-awaited fifth volume, in facing-page Malayalam and English translations: *The Philokalia*, 5 vols (Kottayam, India: Roy International Children's Foundation, 2006).

5 Cf. Kallistos Ware, 'Philocalie', *Dictionnaire de Spiritualité*, 12A (Paris: Beauchesne, 1984), cols 1336–52; id., 'The Spirituality of the *Philokalia*', *Sobornost*, 13: 1 (1991), 6–24; id., *The Power of the Name* (Oxford: SLG Press, 1974; new edition, 1986); id., 'The Beginnings of the Jesus Prayer', in Benedicta Ward and Ralph Waller (eds), *Joy of Heaven: Springs of Christian Spirituality* (London: SPCK, 2003), 1–29; id., *The Jesus Prayer* (London: Catholic Truth Society, 2014); id., 'The Sacrament of Baptism and the Ascetic Life in the Teaching of Mark the Monk', *Studia Patristica*, 107 (1970), 441–52; id., 'The Jesus Prayer in St. Diadochus of Photice', in George

In a series of articles Metropolitan Kallistos has argued that, despite the large number of authors and the variety of viewpoints expressed in the *Philokalia*, the 'predominant influence is that of Evagrios and St Maximos', and that the 'Evagrian terminology and classification prevails, and this is apparent particularly in the texts from St Maximos the Confessor, which occupy a central place in the *Philokalia*.'[6] This paper, offered to Metropolitan Kallistos, explores the nature of the *Philokalia*'s 'Evagrian-Maximian orientation',[7] with particular attention to St Maximos's systematic correction and revision of the spirituality of Evagrios.[8] Given the limitations of space, this paper focuses on the Confessor's *Chapters on Love*, a collection of 400 propositions (*kephalaia*) included in the *Philokalia*, and considered one of the Confessor's most popular and beloved works.[9]

Dragas (ed.), *Aksum Thyateira. A Festschrift for Archbishop Methodios of Thyateria* (London: Thyateira House, 1985), 557–68; id., 'The Jesus Prayer in St. Gregory of Sinai', *Eastern Churches Review*, 4: 1 (1972), 3–22.

6 Kallistos Ware, *The Inner Unity of the Philokalia and its Influence in East and West* (Athens: Onassis Foundation, 2004), 53. The same point had been established in id., 'The Spirituality of the Philokalia', 16; and further developed in id., 'St Nikodimos and the *Philokalia*', in Dimitri Conomos and Graham Speake (eds), *Mount Athos the Sacred Bridge: The Spirituality of the Holy Mountain* (Oxford: Peter Lang, 2005), 112–13; cf. id., 'Prayer in Evagrius of Pontus and the Macarian Homilies', in Ralph Waller and Benedicta Ward (eds), *An Introduction to Christian Spirituality* (London: SPCK, 1999), 14–30.

7 The phrase is from Ware, 'St. Nikodemos and the *Philokalia*', 112.

8 Cf. Nicholas (Maximos) Constas, 'Introduction' to *Maximos the Confessor, On Difficulties in the Church Fathers: The Ambigua to Thomas and the Ambigua to John*, Dumbarton Oaks Medieval Library, vol. 1 (Cambridge, MA: Harvard University Press, 2014), viii.

9 A fact that has not entirely served the Confessor well: whereas important writings by St Maximos have never been translated into English, the *Chapters on Love* is currently available in no fewer than four English translations; cf. E. Kadloubovsky and G. E. H. Palmer, *Early Fathers from the Philokalia*, 287–346 (translated from the Russian); Polycarp Sherwood, *St Maximus the Confessor: The Acetic Life, The Four Centuries on Charity* (Mahwah, NJ: Newman Press, 1955), 136–208; G. E. H. Palmer, Philip Sherrard, and Kallistos Ware, *The Philokalia*, vol. 2 (London: Faber & Faber, 1981), 52–113; George Berthold, *Maximus Confessor: Selected Writings* (Mahwah, NJ: Paulist Press, 1985), 35–87.

As is often pointed out, the works of St Maximos are allotted more space than those by any other author in the *Philokalia*.[10] This surely reflects the prestige of St Maximos among the late Byzantine hesychasts, who, beginning with St Gregory Palamas, recognized him as the *par excellence* theological authority on the nature of mystical experience and divinization.[11] As a highly creative and synthetic thinker, the Confessor deftly wove together diverse ascetic anthropologies and theologies into a doctrinally consistent unity, faithful to the witness of the New Testament and the theology of the Ecumenical Councils. In order to do so, as we shall see in what follows, he introduced a critical reformulation of the Evagrian spiritual tradition. If, then, we are to speak of an 'Evagrian-Maximian orientation' of the *Philokalia*, it can only be in light of the Confessor's clarifying vision of the Christian life, which he articulated initially in the *Chapters on Love*.[12]

It is well known that St Maximos the Confessor (c.580–662) studied and made extensive use of the writings of Evagrios of Pontos (c.345–99).

10   The *Philokalia* contains four works by Maximos: (1) the *Chapters on Love* (400 chapters); (2) *On Theology and the Incarnate Dispensation of the Son of God* (200 chapters); (3) *Various Texts on Theology, the Divine Economy, and Virtue and Vice* (500 chapters); and (4) *On the Lord's Prayer*. In the *Philokalia* the *Various Texts on Theology* (3) is presented as a continuation of *On Theology and the Incarnate Dispensation* (2), but is in fact a separate work, being a later Byzantine anthology of Maximos's writings, apparently compiled by Niketas of Herakleia; cf. Peter Van Deun, 'Les *Diversa Capita* du Pseudo-Maxime et la chaîne de Nicétas d'Héraclée sur l'évangile de Matthieu', *Jahrbuch der Österreichischen Byzantinistik*, 45 (1995), 19–36. The Romanian *Philokalia* includes three additional works by St Maximos (i.e. the *Ascetic Discourse*, the *Questions and Doubts*, and the *Questions to Thalassios*), translated by Dumitru Staniloae, *Filocalia*, vols 2–3 (Sibiu: Tipografia Arhidiecezana, 1947–8); cf. Conticello and Citerio, 'La Philocalie et ses versions', 1006–7.
11   Cf. Maximos Constas, 'St Maximus the Confessor: The Reception of his Thought in East and West', in Maxim Vasiljevic (ed.), *Knowing the Purpose of Creation through the Resurrection* (Alhambra, CA: Sebastian Press, 2013), 44–51.
12   It is therefore mistaken to reduce the *Philokalia* to a merely 'Evagrian' compilation, or to consider Evagrios (or any other writer taken in isolation) as somehow 'essential to the philokalic project', cf. Julia Konstantinovsky, 'Evagrius in the *Philokalia* of Sts. Macarius and Nicodemus', in Brock Bingaman and Bradley Nassif (eds), *The Philokalia: A Classic Text of Orthodox Spirituality* (New York: Oxford University Press, 2012), 175–92.

Scholars have debated the degree of Evagrios's influence on Maximos, but these debates have not been entirely conclusive. Much of the discussion has focused on Maximos's *Chapters on Love*, which is generally acknowledged to be the most 'Evagrian' of all the Confessor's works. It is undeniable that the *Chapters on Love* bears a distinctly Evagrian stamp, partly because it reproduces a large number of verbatim passages from the latter's writings, including no fewer than thirty direct borrowings from Evagrios's *Praktikos*.[13] Indeed, the *Chapters on Love* (cited below as *CL*) begins with a direct borrowing from Evagrios's *Kephalaia Gnostica*:

> Maximos: 'Love is a good disposition of the soul, according to which it prefers no being to the knowledge of God' (*CL* I. 1).[14]
>
> Evagrios: 'Love is the surpassing state of the rational soul, according to which it is incapable of loving anything in this world more than the knowledge of God' (*KG* I. 86).[15]

Such seemingly slavish borrowings have led some scholars to characterize Maximos as a mere 'Evagrian', and to dismiss the *Chapters on Love* as a rather artless compilation lacking in originality.[16] To be sure, in the prologue to the *Chapters on Love*, Maximos himself states that 'these are not

13 For a table of correspondences, see Antoine Guillaumont, *Évagre le Pontique, Traité Pratique*, SC 170 (Paris: Cerf, 1971), 309–10. Note, too, that the very genre of the 'century' can be seen as distinctively Evagrian; cf. Endre von Ivánka, 'KEFALAIA. Eine Byzantinische Literaturform und ihre antiken Wurzeln', *Byzantinische Zeitschrift*, 47 (1954), 285–91; the lucid remarks of Guillaumont, op. cit., 113–15; and more recently, Paul Géhin, 'Les collections de *Kephalaia monastique*', in Antonio Rigo (ed.), *Theologica Minora: The Minor Genres of Byzantine Theological Literature* (Turnhout: Brepols, 2013), 1–50.
14 Ἀγάπη μέν ἐστι διάθεσις ψυχῆς ἀγαθή, καθ᾽ ἥν οὐδέν τῶν ὄντων, τῆς τοῦ Θεοῦ γνώσεως προτιμᾷ (ed. Aldo Ceresa-Gastaldo, *Massimo Confessore, Capitoli sulla carità* [Rome: Editrice Studium, 1963], 50).
15 Ἀγάπη ἐστίν ἡ ὑπερβάλλουσα τῆς λογικῆς ψυχῆς κατάστασις καθ᾽ ἥν ἀδύνατον ἀγαπᾶν τι τοῦ κόσμου τούτου μᾶλλον ἤ τήν τοῦ Θεοῦ γνῶσιν (ΒΕΠΕΣ 78, p. 95 = Greek retroversion from the Syriac).
16 For an extreme statement of this view, see Marcel Viller, 'Aux sources de la spiritualité de saint Maxime: les oeuvres d'Évagre le Pontique', *Revue d'ascétique et de mystique*, 11 (1930), 156–84, 239–68, 331–6.

the fruit of my own meditation, for I went through the writings of the holy Fathers and selected from them whatever had reference to my subject'.[17] This candid disclosure, confirmed by the large body of borrowed material, has been cited as proof that the *Chapters on Love* is essentially a compilation, a withering assessment that has served to discourage scholarly interest in the work as a whole.

A new discovery, however, which will be described in what follows, requires us to reconsider and ultimately reject this assessment. In 2007 Paul Géhin published a previously unknown text from a thirteenth-century Byzantine manuscript which had been brought to Greece by refugees from Asia Minor.[18] The manuscript, which is in the collection of the Benaki Museum in Athens, was discovered by Eurydice Lappa-Zizika and catalogued in 1991, although historians of theology have been somewhat slow in recognizing its importance.[19]

The text in question is called the *Chapters of the Disciples of Evagrios*. It is a collection of more than 200 authentic sayings by Evagrios, written down by his immediate disciples.[20] The discovery of this lost work is obviously a find of major importance, but not simply for the study of Evagrios, since it is now clear that Maximos borrowed heavily from this work when

17　Γινωσκέτω…ὅτι οὐδὲ ταῦτα τῆς ἐμῆς εἰσι γεώργια διανοίας· ἀλλὰ τοὺς τῶν ἁγίων πατέρων διελθὼν λόγους κἀκεῖθεν τὸν εἰς τὴν ὑπόθεσιν συντείνοντα νοῦν ἀναλεξάμενος καὶ ἐν ὀλίγοις πολλὰ κεφαλαιωδέστερον συναγαγών, ἵνα εὐσύνοπτα γένωνται διὰ τὸ εὐμνημόνευτον (ed. Ceresa-Gastaldo, 48, lines 5–10).

18　Paul Géhin, *[Évagre le Pontique] Chapitres des disciples d'Évagre*, SC 514 (Paris: Cerf, 2007).

19　Eurydice Lappa-Zizika and Matoula Rizou-Kouroupou, Κατάλογος ἑλληνικῶν χειρογράφων τοῦ Μουσείου Μπενάκη 10ος – 16ος αἰ. (Athens: Benaki Museum, 1991), 103–6 = no. 53 (TA 72), fols. 193ᵛ-204.

20　Among the disciples of Evagrios were Palladios, John Cassian, Herakleides, Arsenios, and the 'Tall Brothers' (Ammonios, Dioskoros, Eusebios, and Euthymios). Evagrios had many more disciples whose names are not known to us, and they constituted a large circle known as the «ἑταιρεία Εὐαγρίου» (*Lausiac History* 35). Following the anti-Origenist persecutions of Theophilos of Alexandria (c.400), the disciples of Evagrios were forced to flee Egypt and established themselves in Palestine, where, it seems, the *Chapters of the Disciples of Evagrios* were committed to writing in the first decades of the fifth century, cf. SC 170: 27–8; and SC 514: 36–7.

composing his *Chapters on Love*. In short, of the 400 chapters that make up Maximos's work, nearly 100 exhibit various degrees of dependency on the *Chapters of the Disciples of Evagrios*.[21] We now have, in other words, a much wider basis on which to study the sources of the *Chapters on Love*, and thus the possibility of attaining a greater degree of clarity regarding Maximos's use of Evagrios. In the space of this brief paper it is not possible to address the full scope and significance of Maximos's use of the *Chapters of the Disciples of Evagrios*, and we shall therefore limit ourselves to a small number of representative examples.

Our first example, taken from the first of the four Maximian centuries, reveals not simply the Confessor's dependence on Evagrios, but, more importantly, the way in which he modified the latter's theology:

1A) Evagrios: 'Just as the eye, when it is healthy, sees the light ... so does the intellect, when it is pure, see objects' (*CDE* 31).[22]

1B) Maximos: 'Just as the light of the sun attracts the healthy eye, so does the knowledge of God draw the pure intellect to itself naturally through love' (*CL* I. 32).[23]

At first glance, Maximos seems to follow Evagrios rather closely, but there are significant differences. The first thing we notice is that Maximos has reversed the basic metaphor: light is no longer the passive object but the active subject, and it is no longer the eye which sees the light, but rather the light which attracts and draws to itself the power of vision. By means of this simple reversal, Maximos has reframed the Evagrian sentence in such a way as to give prominence to passivity and desire, human conditions and capacities (emphasized by the addition of the adverb 'naturally')

---

21 A concordance of around ninety such borrowings may be found in Géhin, SC 514, 301. However, in many instances a single Evagrian chapter provides material or inspiration for multiple chapters in Maximos, so that the total number of Evagrian chapters actually used by Maximos is much smaller than Géhin's concordance suggests.

22 Ὥσπερ ὅταν ὑγιαίνῃ ὁ ὀφθαλμὸς βλέπει τὸ φῶς...οὕτως ὅτε καθαρός ἐστιν ὁ νοῦς ὄψεται τὰ πράγματα (SC 514, 138).

23 Ὥσπερ τὸ φῶς τοῦ ἡλίου τὸν ὑγιῆ ὀφθαλμὸν πρὸς ἑαυτὸν ἐφέλκεται· οὕτω καὶ ἡ γνῶσις τοῦ Θεοῦ τὸν καθαρὸν νοῦν φυσικῶς διὰ τῆς ἀγάπης πρὸς ἑαυτὴν ἐπισπᾶται (ed. Ceresa-Gastaldo, 60).

that are central to his theological anthropology and moral psychology.[24] The most substantive change, however, is the introduction of an element that is not found in the Evagrian source: love. For Maximos, intellection is not a static condition or mechanical function, like turning on a light and seeing an object, but a dynamic process mediated by love. In Maximos's revised version of the Evagrian sentence, the agency of love is critical, since it is the means by which the intellect is attracted to and ascends to God. Knowledge is now a reality conditioned by love.

Our second example is of a more indirect borrowing, but equally demonstrates Maximos's tendency to shift the emphasis of his Evagrian source-text from knowledge to love:

> 2A) Evagrios: 'The intellect must first fight against the passions through self-control, after which it receives with discernment the reward of dispassion, by which it will fight without fatigue; and it must first fight for doctrines through faith, after which it will receive the reward of knowledge, by which it will fight for these (doctrines) without distraction' (*CDE* 47).[25]

> 2B) Maximos: 'The reward of self-control is dispassion, and that of faith is knowledge; and dispassion gives birth to discernment, while knowledge gives birth to love for God' (*CL* II. 25).[26]

For Evagrios, the intellect fights on two fronts: against the passions and against false doctrines. This battle does not cease with the acquisition of dispassion and knowledge, but continues, although without 'fatigue' or 'distraction'. Maximos has greatly simplified this sentence, disregarding

---

24 See, for example, Maximos, *Amb.* 20 (Constas, DOML 1. 408–19). The nature of passivity (passibility, *pathos*) in the theology of Maximos has been well studied by Adam Cooper, *The Body in St Maximus the Confessor: Holy Flesh, Wholly Deified* (Oxford: Oxford University Press, 2005), 143–60.
25 Πρῶτον δεῖ τὸν νοῦν διὰ τῆς ἐγκρατείας πολεμῆσαι πρὸς τὰ πάθη, ἔπειτα μισθὸν λαμβάνειν διακρίσει τὴν ἀπάθειαν, δι' ἧς ἀκόπως αὐτοῖς πολεμήσει· καὶ πρῶτον διὰ πίστεως δεῖ πολεμῆσαι ὑπὲρ τῶν δογμάτων, ἔπειτα μισθὸν τὴν γνῶσιν λήψεται, δι' ἧς ἀπερισπάστως ὑπὲρ αὐτῶν πολεμήσει (SC 514, 150).
26 Μισθὸς τῆς ἐγκρατείας, ἡ ἀπάθεια· τῆς δὲ πίστεως, ἡ γνῶσις· καὶ ἡ μὲν ἀπάθεια τίκτει τὴν διάκρισιν· ἡ δὲ γνῶσις τὴν εἰς Θεὸν ἀγάπην (ed. Ceresa-Gastaldo, 102).

Evagrios's elaborate double-fronted battle of the intellect. At the same time, he has extended the ladder of spiritual ascent so that the goal of human striving is not knowledge but love. Moreover, the reality of love prompts Maximos to abandon Evagrios's economic metaphor of 'reward' (literally, 'payment') in favour of the more natural, organic, and biological language of 'giving birth'.

The same logic is apparent in our next example, in which Maximos simply removes the word 'knowledge' and replaces it with 'love':

> 3A) Evagrios: 'The knowledge of God not only makes him who acquires it spurn every transient pleasure, but also every sorrow and all pain, just as the Apostle says: "The sufferings of this present time are nothing in comparison with the future glory which will be revealed" (Rom. 8: 18)' (*CDE* 55).[27]

> 3B) Maximos: 'Love for God persuades him who shares in it to spurn every transient pleasure and every pain and sorrow. Let all the saints, who suffered joyfully so much for Christ, persuade you of this' (*CL* II. 58).[28]

Evagrios states that 'knowledge' of God induces the one who possesses it to spurn not only transient pleasures but also every pain and sorrow. Evagrios supports this claim with a citation from Romans 8: 18, which Maximos does not cite, perhaps because the eschatology of Romans 8: 18–30 was interpreted by Evagrios in light of his doctrine of the final restoration (*apokatastasis*).[29] Maximos rejects this vaunted view of 'knowledge' and in its place makes love the central element of Christian life and experience. This is a move consistent with his larger reworking of the Evagrian chapters, but in this case it may have been encouraged by the proximity

---

27   Ἡ γνῶσις τοῦ Θεοῦ οὐ μόνον πάσης ἡδονῆς παρερχομένης ποιεῖ τόν κτησάμενον καταφρονεῖν, ἀλλά καί πάσης λύπης καί παντός πόνου, καθώς καί ὁ ἀπόστολος ἔφη· ὅτι οὐκ ἄξια τά παθήματα τοῦ νῦν καιροῦ πρός τήν μέλλουσαν δόξαν ἀποκαλύπτεσθαι (SC 514, 156).

28   Ἡ εἰς Θεόν ἀγάπη πάσης ἡδονῆς παρερχομένης καί παντός πόνου καί λύπης πείθει καταφρονεῖν τόν μέτοχον αὐτῆς. Καί πειθέτωσάν σε οἱ ἅγιοι πάντες, τοσαῦτα πεπονθότες διά Χριστόν μετά χαρᾶς (ed. Ceresa-Gastaldo, 122).

29   Compare the *Kephalaia Gnostica* IV. 8, which cites Romans 8: 17 (συγκληρονόμοι τοῦ Χριστοῦ) (ΒΕΠΕΣ 78, p. 12); and ibid. VI. 35, citing Romans 8: 29 (ibid. 78, 131).

of Paul's words in Romans 8: 35: 'Who shall separate us from the love of Christ?' The same scriptural verse may have also led Maximos to replace Evagrios's main verb 'to make' with 'to persuade' (with the «πειθέτωσαν» of the Maximian sentence reflecting the «πέπεισμαι γὰρ» of Romans 8: 38), which reflects his strong commitment to human freedom in the context of divine–human synergy.

The next two texts provide us with yet another example of how Maximos systematically transformed the Evagrian chapters:

> 4A) Evagrios: 'It is possible to escape an impassioned thought, first by means of a simple mental representation, second by means of contemplation, and third by prayer' (*CDE* 66).[30]

> 4B) Maximos: 'An impassioned mental representation is a thought compounded of passion and a mental representation. If we separate passion from the mental representation, what remains is the simple thought; we can make this separation by means of spiritual love and self-control, if only we have the will' (*CL* III. 43).[31]

Evagrios argues that one can primarily avoid or escape an 'impassioned thought' (ἐμπαθὴς λογισμός) by means of a 'simple mental representation' (ψιλὸν νόημα), but also by means of 'contemplation' (θεωρία), and finally by prayer. For his part, Maximos enters into these concepts much more deeply, and points out that an 'impassioned mental representation' (νόημα ἐμπαθές) is in fact a complex phenomenon, being composed of a mental image to which passionate feeling or energy has become attached. Rather than suggesting how to 'avoid' such representations, Maximos provides us with a formula by which their constituent elements may be isolated and separated. The solution, of course, which falls within the power of human

---

30 Ἔστι καὶ διὰ νοήματος ψιλοῦ ἐκφυγεῖν τὸν ἐμπαθῆ λογισμόν, καὶ δεύτερον διὰ θεωρίας, καὶ τρίτον διὰ προσευχῆς (SC 514, 164).

31 Νόημά ἐστιν ἐμπαθὲς λογισμὸς σύνθετος ἀπὸ πάθους καὶ νοήματος. Χωρίσωμεν τὸ πάθος ἀπὸ τοῦ νοήματος καὶ ἀπομένει ὁ λογισμὸς ψιλός· χωρίζωμεν δὲ δι' ἀγάπης πνευματικῆς καὶ ἐγκρατείας, ἐὰν θέλωμεν (ed. Ceresa-Gastaldo, 162).

volition (ἐὰν θέλωμεν), is 'spiritual love' in conjunction with 'self-control' (πνευματική ἀγάπη καί ἐγράτεια).³²

At this point it will helpful to expand our immediate frame of reference and recall that Maximos borrows from Evagrios in his other works, reworking Evagrios's doctrine in a way that by now will be familiar to us:

> 5A) Evagrios: 'Faith is affirmed by the fear of God, and the fear of God, in turn, is affirmed by self-control, which becomes unbending through patience and hope, from which is born dispassion, whose offspring is love, but love is the door to natural knowledge, which is succeeded by theology and, in turn, the ultimate beatitude' (*Praktikos*).³³

> 6B) Maximos: 'Love is the door through which a man enters into the Holy of Holies and is brought to the vision of the unapproachable beauty of the Holy and Royal Trinity' (*First Century on Various Texts* I. 38).³⁴

In the stages of Evagrian spiritual ascent, love has only a partial, restricted role to play. For Evagrios, love is not the fulfilment of the Christian life as such, but only of the initial, 'practical' stage of spiritual life, and thus he says that love is the 'door to knowledge' – not, however, to the knowledge of God, but merely to an intermediate form of knowledge called 'natural contemplation', after which comes the highest stage of knowledge and contemplation (here called 'theology').³⁵ For Maximos, on the other hand, the practical life, which is the life of love, is the beginning and end of the life of virtue, from which it follows that love is the summit of human striving and experience. As Maximos will affirm in his later works, love contains

---

32 Compare the parallel discussion in Maximos the Confessor, *Questions to Thalassios* 16 (CCSG 7, 105–9).

33 Τήν πίστιν βεβαιοῖ ὁ φόβος ὁ τοῦ Θεοῦ, καί τοῦτον πάλιν ἐγκράτεια, ταύτην δε ἀκλινῆ ποιοῦσιν ὑπομονή καί ἐλπίς, ἀφ' ὧν τίκτεται ἀπάθεια, ἧς ἔγγονον ἡ ἀγάπη, ἀγάπη δέ θύρα γνώσεως φυσικῆς ἥν διαδέχεται θεολογία καί ἡ ἐσχάτη μακαριότης (SC 171, 492, lines 47–51).

34 Αὕτη [ἡ ἀγάπη] ἐστίν ἡ θύρα, δι' ἧς ὁ εἰσερχόμενος εἰς τά Ἅγια γίνεται τῶν ἁγίων καί τοῦ ἀπροσίτου κάλλους τῆς ἁγίας καί βασιλικῆς Τριάδος καθίσταται ἄξιος θεατής γενέσθαι (*PG* 90, 1193A).

35 On which, see Guillaumont, *Évagre le Pontique*, 38–63, 98–112 (cited above, n. 12).

all the virtues in its universal *logos*, and in the experience of divinization it is the *par excellence* force uniting God to man and man to God.[36] We can safely conclude, then, that Maximos is not simply an uncritical 'compiler' of Evagrian sentences, and that the originality of the *Chapters on Love* consists in establishing love at the heart of a system which tended to marginalize it in favour of knowledge.

Here I would like to open up a small parenthesis, and introduce yet another writer who influenced St Maximos the Confessor: St Gregory of Nyssa. I believe that Maximos's theology of love is deeply and directly influenced by St Gregory of Nyssa, who writes that 'knowledge *becomes* love' (ἡ δὲ γνῶσις ἀγάπη γίνεται) when the object of knowledge is also an object of desire.[37] This is an extremely important moment in St Gregory's theology, for it marks the successful integration of love into a theological anthropology which tended to collapse love into animal desire, and then, in a corollary move, to discard both (love and desire) in a gnostic ascent of the mind to God. Indeed, St Gregory makes the desiring or appetitive faculty the prime agent in spiritual ascent, and so like Maximos he places love at the centre and apex of the human experience of God.

St Gregory's basic insight here is that 'knowledge', understood as a relationship to a particular object, has a direct impact on the consciousness

---

[36] Cf. Maximos, Letter 2: 'For nothing is more Godlike than divine love, nothing more mysterious, nothing more sublime for the divinization of human beings, since it has encompassed within itself all good things [...] it is the fulfilment of the law and the prophets, for they are succeeded by the mystery of love, which though we are human beings makes us gods, and reduces the particular principles of the commandments to one universal principle, for what form of good things does not love possess? Love is therefore a great good, and of goods the first and most excellent good, since through itself it conjoins God and human beings, and enables the Creator of human beings to be manifested as a human being' (*PG* 91, 393C, 401D); id., *Amb.* 10. 9: 'For they say that God and man are paradigms of each other, so that as much as man, enabled by his love, has divinized himself for God, to that same extent God is humanized for man by His love for mankind; and as much as man has manifested God who is invisible by nature through the virtues, to that same extent man is rapt by God in mind to the unknowable' (Constas, DOML 1. 165).

[37] Gregory of Nyssa, *Dialogue on the Soul and the Resurrection* (GNO 3/3, 71, line 2).

of the knower. Knowing, in other words, is not simply a gnoseological act, but an ontological one. Like love, such knowledge is a real 'going out' of the knowing subject into the known object (along with the 'going out' of the known into the knower). Moreover, when, as Gregory suggests, the 'known object' is 'that which is beautiful by nature',[38] that is, the Beauty of God, it not only conditions and determines the form of consciousness of the one who experiences it, but transforms him from a knower into a lover.

We may well ask how Gregory and Maximos arrived at such similar positions. The answer is that they were both involved in similar projects, for Maximos stands in virtually the same relationship to Evagrios as Gregory does to Origen, since both were committed to correcting a fragmented, intellectualist view of knowledge in light of a more unified view of the human person, in which love (and the power of desire) could not be excluded from the highest levels of human experience.

The Cappadocian roots of Maximos's theology are well known, including Maximos's devotion to St Gregory the Theologian. (The *Ambigua*, to cite only one example, is an elaborate commentary on seventy difficult passages excerpted from Gregory's writings.) However, much less attention has been paid to Maximos's use of St Gregory of Nyssa, and I should like to bring this parenthesis to a close by suggesting that herein lies a fruitful area of research in the study of St Maximos the Confessor.[39]

38 Καλόν ἐστιν τῇ φύσει τὸ γινωσκόμενον (ibid., lines 2–3).
39 See, for example, George Berthold, 'The Cappadocian Roots of Maximus the Confessor', in Felix Heinzer and Christoph Schönborn (eds), *Maximus Confessor: Actes du Symposium sur Maxime le Confesseur, Fribourg, 2–5 septembre 1980* (Fribourg: Éditions Universitaires Fribourg Suisse, 1982), 52–9, where relatively little is said about Nyssa. Note, too, that Hans urs von Balthasar's influential *Cosmic Liturgy: The Universe according to Maximus the Confessor*, trans. Brian Daley (San Francisco, CA: Ignatius Press, 2003), has virtually nothing to say about the influence of either of the two Gregorys on Maximos. A notable exception is the work of Paul Blowers, especially his 'Maximos the Confessor, Gregory of Nyssa and the Concept of Perpetual Progress', *Vigiliae Christianae*, 46 (1992), 151–71; cf. Maximos Constas, 'A Greater and More Hidden Word: Maximos the Confessor and the Nature of Language', forthcoming in Sotiris Mitralexis et al. (eds), *Maximus the Confessor as a European Philosopher* (Turnhout: Brepols, 2016).

We seem to have reached the end of our inquiry. Yet it is precisely here where we need to exercise some caution. While it is true that Evagrios subordinated love to knowledge, it would be mistaken to conclude that Maximos simply reversed the formula and subordinated knowledge to love. The great importance that Maximos ascribes to love, which he places at the summit of the spiritual life, should not be taken to mean that he minimizes the role of knowledge, or that he wishes to establish a strict hierarchy between knowledge and love. Such an idea is contradicted by a number of sentences in the *Chapters on Love*, where Maximos contends that nothing is greater than love, precisely because it is love that leads to knowledge:

> Maximos: 'If the illumination of knowledge is the life of the intellect, and if love gives birth to this illumination, it is rightly said that nothing is greater than divine love' (*CL* I. 9).[40]

In other places, he repeatedly affirms that divine knowledge operates '*through* divine love',[41] so that love itself is said to be the *means* to knowledge, which latter is presented as the final goal of the spiritual life. In this way, the *Chapters on Love* offers something like parallel formulae in which both love and knowledge rise to the summit of human experience: love of God engenders knowledge of God and such knowledge engenders love. Love and knowledge have a true interdependence, for the believer knows Him whom he loves, and loves Him whom he knows, so that the relation is less hierarchical and more dialectical, in the sense that each term is able to generate and reinforce the other.

---

40   Εἰ ἡ ζωὴ τοῦ νοῦ ὁ φωτισμός ἐστι τῆς γνώσεως, τοῦτον δὲ ἡ εἰς Θεὸν ἀγάπη τίκτει, καλῶς οὐδὲν τῆς θείας ἀγάπης εἴρηται μεῖζον (ed. Ceresa-Gastaldo, 52).

41   Note the use of the preposition 'through' (*dia*) in the following passages, which I have italicized for emphasis: Maximos, Char I. 12: *διὰ τῆς ἀγάπης* ὑπὸ τῆς θείας γνώσεως ὁ νοῦς ἁρπαγῇ; ibid. I. 32: ἡ γνῶσις τοῦ Θεοῦ τὸν καθαρὸν νοῦν *διὰ τῆς ἀγάπης* πρὸς ἑαυτὴν ἐπισπᾶται; ibid. I. 46: ὁ τῆς θείας καταξιωθεὶς γνώσεως καὶ τὸν ταύτης φωτισμὸν *διὰ τῆς ἀγάπης* κτησάμενος; ibid. I. 47: ὁ μήπω τυχὼν τῆς θείας γνώσεως τῆς *δι' ἀγάπης* ἐνεργουμένης; ibid. I. 69: *διὰ τῆς ἀγάπης* εἰς τὴν γνῶσιν; ibid. II. 6: μήτε ἑαυτοῦ, μήτε τινὸς ἄλλου τῶν ὄντων τὸ σύνολον ἐπαισθάνεσθαι, εἰ μὴ μόνου τοῦ *διὰ τῆς ἀγάπης* ἐν αὐτῷ τὴν τοιαύτην ἔλλαμψιν ἐνεργοῦντος.

We find the same relationship in 1 Corinthians 8: 3 ('If one loves God, he is known by Him'), and, above all, in the Gospel of John, where the relationship between the Father and the Son is a mutual 'knowing', as is the relationship of Christ with 'his own' (John 17: 25–6, 10: 14–15). Moreover, the knower is determined by the one who is known, and because God and the Son 'have life' (John 5: 26), it is 'eternal life' to know God and Christ (John 17: 3). Thus 'knowing' is the supreme mode of being, but it is obvious that such knowledge is materially understood to be love. God is Love, and so the person who is related to Him is related as one who loves (1 John 4: 8). It is thus no surprise that Maximos concludes the *Chapters on Love* with references to 1 Corinthians and the First Letter of John, or that his sentences, as he himself says, are grouped in 'four centuries, equal in number to the four Gospels'.[42]

To sum up, love and knowledge are mutually intertwined; each is defined in reference to the other. Their relation cannot be reduced to that of a means to an end, but of a reciprocal causality, a mutual interdependence. We can love only what we know, and we can never know completely what we do not love. And so Maximos invites us to 'unite love with knowledge': 'Inasmuch as *knowledge puffs up, but love builds up* (1 Cor. 8: 2), unite love with knowledge and you will be humble and a spiritual builder, building up both yourself and all who draw near to you' (*CL* IV. 59).[43]

'Knowledge' by itself will always tend to generate a split between the knowing subject and the known object; it will always tend to 'objectify' the other, reaffirming the ego and reducing the other to its own psychological and cognitive dimensions. Knowledge by itself, moreover, will always tend towards a disincarnated gnosticism: 'For the recollection of fire does not warm the body' (*CL* I. 31).[44] And rather than unite love and knowledge, our world has increasingly torn them apart, generating a seemingly

---

42 Εν ἰσαρίθμοις κεφαλαίων τῶν τεσσάρων εὐαγγελίων ἑκατοντάδων (ed. Ceresa-Gastaldo, 48, lines 3–4).
43 Επειδὴ ἡ *γνῶσις φυσιοῖ, ἡ δὲ ἀγάπη οἰκοδομεῖ* σύζευξον τῇ γνώσει τὴν ἀγάπην, καὶ ἔσῃ ἄτυφος καὶ πνευματικὸς οἰκοδόμος καὶ σεαυτὸν οἰκοδομῶν καὶ πάντας τοὺς ἐγγίζοντάς σοι (ed. Ceresa-Gastaldo, 218).
44 Μνήμη πυρὸς οὐ θερμαίνει τὸ σῶμα (ed. Ceresa-Gastaldo, 60).

endless series of polarizing dichotomies: love vs. knowledge, head vs. heart, thought vs. feeling, subjective vs. objective, and dogma vs. mysticism, to mention only a few.

As we have seen, the discovery of the Evagrian chapters offers us a rare and important glimpse into the mind and working methods of Maximos the Confessor. In the *Chapters on Love*, an early work written by 626, Maximos sets forth the Orthodox view of the spiritual life by curbing and correcting Evagrios's overwhelming emphasis on knowledge. The Confessor seems to have realized, however, that the transformation he envisioned required more than a mere revision of isolated passages in random texts. He consequently set out in his next work, *The Ambigua to John* (begun by 628), to transform the theology of Origen and Evagrios, not simply in the flower of its language, but in its deepest roots, effectively securing Christian asceticism and spirituality on solid theological, philosophical, and anthropological foundations.

Bibliography

On the Philokalia

Archimandrite Aimilianos, *Λόγος περὶ Νήψεως. Ἑρμηνεία στὸν ἅγιο Ἡσύχιο* (Athens: Indiktos, 2007). A line-by-line commentary on Hesychios of Sinai, *On Watchfulness and Holiness* (*Philokalia* 1. 162–98), with a foreword by Metropolitan Kallistos Ware.

Basil of Poiana Marului, *Life and Writings*, trans. a Monk of the Prophet Elias Skete (Mt Athos) (Liberty, TN: St John of Kronstadt Press, 1996). Elder Basil (1692–1767) was the spiritual father of Paisy Velichkovsky. This volume contains the Elder's introductions to the writings of Hesychios, Philotheos of Sinai, and Gregory of Sinai.

Deseille, Placide, *Orthodox Spirituality and the Philokalia*, trans. Anthony P. Gythiel (Wichita, KS: Eighth Day Press, 2008).

Kitromilides, Paschalis M., 'Orthodoxy and the West: Reformation to Enlightenment', in Michael Angold (ed.), *The Cambridge History of Christianity*, 5: *Eastern Christianity* (Cambridge: Cambridge University Press, 2006), 187–209.

——, '*Philokalia*'s First Journey?', in *An Orthodox Commonwealth: Symbolic Legacies and Cultural Encounters in Southeastern Europe* (Aldershot: Ashgate, 2007), ch. VIII.

Nikodimos Hagioritis, 'Proem to the *Philokalia*', in *The Philokalia*, vol. 1, trans. Constantine Cavarnos (Belmont, MA: Institute for Byzantine and Modern Greek Studies, 2008), 27–40.

Sherrard, Philip, 'The Revival of Hesychast Spirituality', in Louis Dupre (ed.), *Christian Spirituality: Post-Reformation and Modern* (New York: Crossroad, 1989), 417–31.

Tachiaos, Antonios-Aimilios, *Ο Παΐσιος Βελιτσκόφσκυ (1722–1794) και ή Ασκητοφιλολογική Σχολή του* (Thessaloniki: Institute for Balkan Studies, 1964; reprinted in 1984, with an updated prologue).

——, 'De La *Philokalia* au *Dobrotoljubie*: La creation d'un 'Sbornik', *Cyrillomethodianum*, 5 (1981), 208–13.

On the Jesus Prayer

Brianchaninov, Ignatius, *On The Prayer of Jesus*, with a Foreword by Bishop Kallistos Ware (Boston and London: New Seeds, 2005).

Hausherr, Irénée, *Noms du Christ et voies d'oraison*, Orientalia Christiana Analecta 157 (Rome: Pontifical Institute of Oriental Studies, 1960); English translation: *The Name of Jesus. The Names of Jesus used by Early Christians. The Development of the 'Jesus Prayer'*, trans. Charles Cummings (Kalamazoo, MI: Cistercian Publications, 1978). Readers of this book are encouraged to read the important review by Metropolitan Kallistos, 'Book Review: I. Hausherr, *The Name of Jesus*', *Sobornost*, 2: 2 (1980), 87–96.

Johnson, Christopher D. L., *The Globalization of Hesychasm and the Jesus Prayer* (London: Continuum, 2010).

A Monk of Mount Athos, *The Watchful Mind: Teachings on the Prayer of the Heart*, trans. George Dokos (Crestwood, NY: St Vladimir's Seminary Press, 2014).

Nikodimos, 'Guarding the Mind and the Heart', in id., *A Handbook of Spiritual Counsel*, trans. Peter Chamberas (Mahwah, NJ: Paulist Press, 1989), 153–72.

Ware, Kallistos, 'Praying with the Body: The Hesychast Method and Non-Christian Parallels', *Sobornost*, 14: 2 (1992), 6–35.

On Evagrios of Pontos

See the online bibliography maintained by Joel Kalvesmaki: <http://evagriusponticus.net/bibliography.htm>

On Maximos the Confessor

Berthold, George C., 'Christian Life and Praxis: The Centuries on Love', in Pauline Alan and Bronwen Neil (eds), *The Oxford Handbook of Maximus the Confessor* (Oxford: Oxford University Press, 2015), 397–413.
Blowers, Paul, 'Gentiles of the Soul: Maximos the Confessor on the Substructure and Transformation of the Human Person', *Journal of Early Christian Studies*, 4 (1996), 57–85.
Hausherr, Irénée, *Philautie, de la tendresse pour soi à la charité selon sainte Maxime le Confesseur*, Orientalia Christiana Analecta 137 (Rome: Pontifical Institute of Oriental Studies, 1952).
Larchet, Jean-Claude, *La divinisation de l'homme selon saint Maxime le Confesseur*, Cogitatio fidei 208 (Paris: Cerf, 1988).
Russell, Norman, 'Maximus the Confessor', in id., *The Doctrine of Deification in Greek Patristic Theology* (Oxford: Oxford University Press, 2004), 262–95.
Staniloae, Dumitru, 'Introduction to the Life and Work St. Maximos the Confessor', in *Φιλοσοφικὰ καὶ Θεολογικὰ Ἐρωτήματα (Περὶ Διαφόρων Ἀποριῶν τῶν ἁγίων Διονυσίου καὶ Γρηγορίου) τοῦ ἁγίου Μαξίμου τοῦ Ὁμολογητοῦ* (Athens: Apostolike Diakonia, 3rd edn, 2002), 13–51 (in Greek).
Thunberg, Lars, *Microcosm and Mediator: The Theological Anthropology of Maximos the Confessor* (Lund: C. W. K. Gleerup, 1965; 2nd edn, Chicago, IL: Open Court Publishing, 1995).
Tympas, G. C., *Carl Jung and Maximus the Confessor on Psychic Development: The Dynamics between the 'Psychological' and the 'Spiritual'* (London and New York: Routledge, 2014).
Vasiljevic, Bishop Maxim (ed.), *Knowing the Purpose of Creation through the Resurrection. Proceedings of the Symposium on St Maximus the Confessor, Belgrade, October 18–21, 2012* (Alhambra, CA: Sebastian Press, 2013) = 29 essays.
Wessel, Susan, 'The Theology of Agape in Maximos the Confessor', *SVTQ* 55 (2011), 319–42.

HILARION ALFEYEV

10 St Symeon the New Theologian and the Studite Monastic Tradition

Twenty years have elapsed since, under the supervision of Metropolitan Kallistos of Diokleia, I wrote and defended a thesis on the relationship between St Symeon the New Theologian and the Orthodox Tradition. In this study I made an attempt to determine the place of St Symeon in this Tradition, to find out his spiritual roots, and to compare his teaching with that of the Fathers before him. I focused to a considerable extent on those aspects of Symeon's theology which at that time did not attract sufficient attention. Symeon's biblical approach, that is, his understanding of Scripture, and his exegetical method had never been considered. His attitude towards the liturgy and the influence the liturgical texts made on him were not studied. His place in the Studite tradition was not defined. The personality of his spiritual father, Symeon the Studite, still remained obscure. The connection between Symeon the New Theologian and Patristic tradition as a whole was only partly clarified. Symeon's knowledge of hagiographical literature and its influence on him were not examined. Some important parts of his own doctrine, such as his anthropology and triadology, were left aside by scholars. Some of these gaps I wanted to fill in by my study of the relationship between Symeon and the Orthodox Tradition. In this work I intend to focus specifically on the influence of the Studite on Symeon the New Theologian.

In the *Ascetical Discourse*, which is the only surviving writing of the Studite, we are not dealing with a coherent narration, but with an assortment of disconnected passages. The narrative is intended only for monks, and moreover for those living within the monastery walls and not for solitaries. In manuscripts the work begins with the word *adelphe* [Brother] and the second person singular is employed throughout the discourse: this may mean that it was addressed to a concrete disciple of the Studite. One wonders whether the addressee of the discourse was not Symeon. For us the discourse is of special importance because we find in it several motifs which were to become characteristic of Symeon.

A. Tears and Compunction

This theme is a leitmotif of the whole work: the Studite constantly returns to it. He recommends us to weep when attending church offices[1] and not to partake of Holy Communion without tears.[2] He also speaks of 'many tears' during evening prayer in the cell,[3] and of the necessity to pray in the cell 'with contrition, attention and unceasing weeping'.[4] So the weeping is to be constant: 'Have unceasing weeping, and do not grow satiated with your tears.'[5] One must weep not only for oneself, but also for other people.[6] Through mourning a man purifies himself from passions, says the Studite.[7] Prayer with tears teaches a man all the virtues.[8] At the same time the virtues and ascetical efforts promote compunction and tears.[9]

For the Studite weeping is directly connected with what he calls 'divine illumination', that is, with mystical experience. 'Where there is contrition with spiritual weeping, there is also divine illumination', the Studite emphasizes.[10] 'Try to purify yourself from passions through tears', he advises, 'so that, having been illumined by grace, you ... reach the blessing of the pure

---

1   Syméon le Studite, *Le Discours ascétique*, 8.
2   Ibid. 24.
3   Ibid. 5.
4   Ibid. 16.
5   Ibid. 20.
6   Ibid. 19.
7   Ibid. 11.
8   Ibid. 23.
9   Ibid. 32.
10   Ibid. 9; cf. also 23.

in heart.'[11] If tears cause divine illumination, the illumination itself, in its turn, produces spiritual joy and tears with compunction.[12]

Such frequent repetition of the same motif without doubt testifies that the Studite had his own experience of constant weeping. If one searches for literary parallels, one can easily find them in early monastic texts, particularly in Evagrios, who said: 'First pray for the gift of tears, so that through sorrowing you may tame what is savage in your soul...Pray with tears and all you ask will be heard.'[13] John Klimakos mentions prayer with compunction and tears,[14] unceasing compunction and mourning,[15] tears with spiritual joy,[16] tears as a means for the extermination of passions;[17] divine illumination as a result of mourning.[18] There are also very important texts on tears by Isaac the Syrian, which will be recalled in a later section. In comparison with Isaac and John Klimakos the Studite is much more concise. He does not provide a special theory of tears and compunction, but repeats practical advice concerning them.

B. Prayer

The Studite points to the traditional monastic ideal of unceasing prayer: 'It is necessary to have the mind always with God, both in sleep and in waking hours, during meals and conversations, in manual labour and every other activity, according to the prophet's word: "I have set the Lord always

---

11   Ibid. 11.
12   Ibid. 30.
13   *Prayer* 5–6 [1168 D-1169 A]; cf. ibid. 78 [1184 C].
14   Klimakos, 28 [1132 B]; 28 [1137 B]; 28 [1140 A].
15   Ibid. 7 [801 D]; 7 [804 D]; 7 [808 D]; 7 [816 D].
16   Ibid. 7 [801 C]: 'joy-making mourning'; 7 [804 B]: 'joyful sorrow'; cf. 7 [812 A].
17   Ibid. 7 [808 B]; 8 [823 BC].
18   Ibid. 7 [804 C].

before me"' (Ps. 16: 8).[19] Every part of this passage is in accordance with early ascetical Fathers. Diadochos says that the remembrance of God must not be interrupted even in sleep.[20] The soul which has been engaged with the word of God all day will be occupied with it in sleep too, says John Klimakos.[21] That prayer is to be continued during labour was emphasized by many authors.[22] The verse from Psalm 16 is traditionally understood in ascetical literature as an indication of unceasing prayer; cf. in Theodore of Edessa: 'If a man fixes his intellect without distraction on our Master and God, then the Saviour...[will] deliver such a soul from its impassionate servitude. It is of this that the prophet speaks when he says: "I have set the Lord always before me: because He is at my right hand, I shall not be moved." What is sweeter or safer than always to have the Lord at our right hand?'[23]

Several examples of practical advice concerning evening and night prayer are provided by the Studite. Though he admits that in exceptional cases the evening prayer can be limited to the reciting of the Trisagion,[24] in general he recommends not to shorten evening prayer, even if one is very tired after a lot of labour: 'however much a man gets tired in labour, if he is deprived of prayer, let him know that he has lost something great.'[25] As to night prayer, the Studite suggests the following order of vigil:

> In the hours of vigil it is useful for you to recite some two hours, and to pray two hours in compunction with tears; and then [read] a canon, whichever you want,

19 Syméon le Studite, *Le Discours ascétique*, 20.
20 Diadoque de Photicé, *Oeuvres spirituelles*, ed. E. des Places, SC 5-bis (1955) 32, 5ff. [102].
21 Klimakos, 20 [941 C].
22 The monks in Egypt always worked without ceasing to practise meditation, according to John Cassian, *De institutis coenobiorum*, ed. M.Petschenig, CSEL 17 (Prague – Wien – Leipzig, 1888), 3, 2 [34]. Cf. the recommendation in *Verba seniorum*, PL 73 VII, 24 [897 C]: 'labora manibus tuis et ora Deum incessanter' [work with your hands and pray to God without ceasing]; cf. *Apophthegm.*, Loukios [253 BC]. Cf. A. Guillaumont, *Aux origines du monachisme chrétien* (Paris, 1979), 125–6.
23 *Cent.* 90 [321].
24 Syméon le Studite, *Le Discours ascétique*, 9.
25 Ibid. 16.

and twelve psalms, if you want, and 'the undefiled' (*ton Amomon*), and the prayer of St Eustratios. This is when nights are long. And when they are short, the rule is shorter, according to the strength given to you by God.[26]

So the whole vigil must take some six hours. This means a monk should not sleep at all in the night of vigil: in the Studite monastery the break between compline and morning office must have not been much more than six hours (though it could have depended on seasons and the length of nights, as the remark by the Studite shows). As regards the structure of the recommended vigil, it does not precisely correspond to any church office or traditional rule of prayer: it seems that the Studite created it by himself, using traditional elements, such as the twelve psalms, canon, Psalm 118/119 (indicated as 'the undefiled'), and one prayer from the Saturday *mesonyktikon* (ascribed to St Eustratios).[27] The phrases 'which you want' and 'if you want', referring respectively to the canon and twelve psalms, show that the Studite left to the disciple's discretion whether to shorten or change the structure of the vigil.

What did the Studite mean when speaking of recitation (*anagnosis*) and prayer (*euche*) as two different elements of vigil? The first term in ascetical texts usually means reading psalms, or less commonly other parts of Scripture. The second term in this context may mean both prayer using the repetition of a short formula ('the prayer of the mind'), and prayer using one's own words. That the Studite was in favour of the latter type of prayer is confirmed by another passage, where he gives an example of prayer with one's own words with uplifted hands, and then concludes: 'Adding to this other [words], which God will put into your mind, remain in prayer...'[28]

There are also two cases which may occur during one's prayer which are discussed by the Studite. First, he warns against false visions of light during prayer: 'If, when you are praying, there is any anxiety or knocking, or light flashes up, or something else happens, do not fear, but pray even

26 Ibid. 24.
27 The service of the twelve psalms is one of the most ancient elements of monastic office; it existed in Egyptian monasteries already in the fourth to fifth centuries: see John Cassian, *Inst.* 2, 4–6 [20–2].
28 Syméon le Studite, *Le Discours ascétique*, 20.

more zealously...For it can happen that worry and anxiety and ecstasy are demonic.'[29] Here the Studite follows Evagrios, who in his 153 *Chapters on Prayer*, known in the time of the Studite as a writing by Neilos of Sinai, describes similar occasions: 'Be attentive, so that demons not deceive you by any vision...Who carries on with his prayer, even if he hears noise, knocking, shouts and swearing from demons, will not fall down.'[30]

Another case which is discussed by the Studite is what to do if someone comes when you are praying; you must interrupt your prayer, open the door, speak with him and console him: 'for the consolation of those who come is equal to reconciliation [with God]'.[31] This advice corresponds to what Klimakos says regarding the same circumstances: 'It often happens that we are standing at prayer, and brothers come to us, and we have to do one of two things, either to stop praying, or to grieve the brother by leaving him without answer. Love is greater than prayer, because prayer is a particular virtue but love embraces all the virtues.'[32] The Studite, however, suggests not to open the door to laymen but only to monks: with laymen one ought to speak after finishing prayer.[33] When the visitor leaves, one must pray about him with tears.[34]

C. Spiritual Direction and Confession

When entering the monastery, one must confess everything one has done since infancy to the spiritual father or the abbot, as to God Himself, 'remembering how John baptized with the baptism unto repentance and all came

---

29   Ibid. 30.
30   94–7 [1188 BD].
31   Syméon le Studite, *Le Discours ascétique*, 29.
32   Klimakos, 26 [1028 B].
33   Syméon le Studite, *Le Discours ascétique*, 29.
34   Ibid. 31.

to him, confessing their sins' (Mat. 3: 6).³⁵ The comparison between repentance and baptism, as well as the theme of second baptism (through tears or through mystical illumination), is traditional in ascetical literature: it occurs in Origen, Gregory the Theologian, the *Makarian Homilies*, John Klimakos, and other authors. Another important thing is that the Studite in the passage quoted shows two possibilities for confession: one before the spiritual father and one before the abbot. Let us examine this evidence more precisely.

As was shown above, confession before the abbot was regarded as a norm in the Studite tradition. However, in exceptional cases it was permitted to have another spiritual father. As an example, let us refer to the *typikon* of the monastery of St Mamas (twelfth century?), which has a chapter entitled 'Of the confession of the brothers, and that all must have the abbot as their spiritual father'. The text prescribes confession before the abbot, 'even if he is not a priest'. At the same time, if necessary, another spiritual father may be appointed to someone, yet not by one's own choice, but by the abbot's decision. The text concludes with the following statement: 'But this, let us say at once, we have said with extreme condescension, since the traditions of the fathers do not give the subjects any right whatsoever not to have their abbot as their spiritual father.'³⁶

Now, Symeon the Studite recommends a monk to go for confession to one of the brothers, chosen by the monk himself and not by the abbot. He emphasizes, though, that confession before the abbot still remains the ideal:

> If you have obtained faith and trust in someone from among the brothers, so that you reveal before him your thoughts, never cease to go to him and confess thoughts which come to you every hour and day. Let everyone go to the abbot for this purpose,

---

35 Ibid. 3.
36 A. Dmitriyevsky, *Opisanie liturgicheskikh rukopisey khraniashchikhsya v bibliotekakh pravoslavnogo Vostoka* [The Description of the Liturgical Manuscripts in the Libraries of the Orthodox East], t.1, part 1: *Typika* (Kiyev, 1895), I, 1, 673; also 745ff.; cf. I. Hausherr, *Spiritual Direction in the Early Christian East*, Cistercian Studies 116 (Kalamazoo, MI, 1990), 107.

but since some, by their great weakness and mistrust of the abbot, avoid it, we allow this by condescension.[37]

We see that in this as in other matters the Studite was not a rigorist: referring to the rule, he allows exceptions. Possibly he had in mind his own situation when writing such a recommendation: he was a spiritual father of many people, among whom there was at least one monk, Symeon the younger.

Continuing, the Studite says that a monk must preserve trust in his spiritual father: 'even if you see that he fell into harlotry, do not be scandalized, because this will not harm you.' We must not pass from one spiritual father to another; otherwise neither the first nor the second of them will trust us: 'And we, having become accustomed to passing from one to another, will not cease to enquire about stylites, recluses and hesychasts, and will not trust in anyone...'[38] One must regard one's spiritual father as a saint and not conceal from him any thought, the Studite emphasizes.[39] The obedience to the abbot (spiritual father) must be absolute, 'right up to death, if he commands so'.[40] The revelation of thoughts must be done every day, and what is said by the spiritual father must be received with full confidence, 'as from God's mouth'; a monk should not ask someone else whether his spiritual father is right or wrong.[41]

These recommendations of the Studite reflect an understanding of spiritual fatherhood which is traditional for Eastern monasticism. We find similar recommendations in John Klimakos, Abba Dorotheos, and other masters of monastic life. Klimakos argues as follows against questioning one's spiritual father: 'The moment any thought of judging or condemning your superior occurs to you, leap away from it as from fornication.'[42] Dorotheos draws a portrait of his disciple Dositheos as an example of

37   Syméon le Studite, *Le Discours ascétique*, 35.
38   Ibid. 35.
39   Ibid. 21.
40   Ibid. 18.
41   Ibid. 6. The recommendation to go to the abbot's cell only rarely (ibid. 9) implies that he was available in church every day.
42   Klimakos, 4 [681 A].

absolute obedience: he did not conceal any thought from the spiritual father, revealing them to him on every occasion.[43]

Apart from the revelation of thoughts, the Studite suggests daily self-accusation before sleep:

> When the day has finished and the evening has come, speak to yourself as follows: 'How, with God's help, have I spent this day? Perhaps, I condemned someone, or hurt, or scandalized, or killed [spiritually], or looked passionately at someone's face, or disobeyed the superior over work and neglected it, or was cross with somebody, or, when attending the office, occupied my mind with useless things, or, being oppressed by idleness, left the church and the office.'[44]

This is a kind of confession, but accomplished face to face with God. It was also advised long before the Studite by Basil the Great: 'When the day has finished and every activity, both bodily and spiritual, has come to an end, before sleep, the conscience of everyone must be subjected to an examination in one's own heart.'[45] Dorotheos suggests that such self-accusation should be accomplished not only in the evening, but also in the morning and then every six hours.[46]

In the last chapters of the discourse the Studite provides some recommendations to the spiritual father concerning the direction of his disciples. These chapters demonstrate the practical mind of the Studite, his knowledge of the psychology of monks, and his skill in spiritual direction. The spiritual father must avoid, the Studite says, any thought of distrust towards his disciples, especially if they go for conversation to someone else.[47] If the disciple, in his turn, begins to distrust the spiritual father for any reason, such as jealousy of other disciples or false shame in revelation of thoughts, the father must recognize it by the expression on the disciple's face and by changes in his external appearance. 'The remedy for such [disciples] consists of assiduous prayers with tears, increase of love, frequent

---

43   Dorothée de Gaza, *La vie de saint Dosithée*, ed. P. M. Brun, OC 26 (1932) [122–45].
44   Syméon le Studite, *Le Discours ascétique*, 5.
45   *Disc.* (40), 5 [881 A].
46   *Disc.* II, 117, 7–14 [364].
47   Syméon le Studite, *Le Discours ascétique*, 36.

exhortation, bodily consolation, and frequent conversations, sometimes gentle and sweet, and sometimes severe...'[48] Only the one who has tested these means in practice can write of them in such a manner. The mention of the 'bodily consolation' among other remedies is noteworthy: it shows the realism of the Studite as a spiritual director.

Discussing how to prevent two young monks from falling into so-called 'passionate love', the Studite suggests several means: to invite them separately from each other and speak to the one 'about many and different matters', mentioning among them 'particular friendship with someone'; and then, if there is no success, speak to the other about the first, 'scolding him and exposing him as a pervert and lover of flesh'.[49] This passage and especially the following two demonstrate, strange to say, the Studite's cunning, which he is likely to employ on some occasions:

> Add also the following: 'I have heard from some people that you have love for this [person], and, knowing both of you, I am sure that your love is spiritual. But so that others will not be scandalized.., please do not speak and sit with him alone. Besides, the abbot has a good impression about you and has the intention of ordaining you'... And he will reject this passion either for spiritual reasons, or because of the ordination, if he is possessed by the passion of vanity.[50]

In other words, our author suggests deceiving the disciple by promising him ordination. The Studite refers to such a 'remedy' as a common custom of the spiritual directors of his time: 'For there is a custom among spiritual fathers to give such promises of the ordination to young monks many times, in order to break the habit of passions.'[51]

One can argue whether this is a good way to direct people, but it seems that the Studite was in favour of it. One would not find a similar

---

48 Ibid. 37.
49 Ibid. 39.
50 Ibid. 39.
51 Ibid. 37.

recommendation in early monastic texts, which never encouraged a monk's desire to be ordained priest.[52]

D. Ascetical Practice

The first step of the monastic ladder, according to Klimakos, is renunciation of the world.[53] Since the term 'world' (*kosmos*) means in this context 'the aggregate of the collective noun which is applied to separate passions,'[54] the renunciation of it is in fact the combat against one's own passions, the mortification of one's own will. That is how the Studite understands it:

> Brother, perfect retirement from the world is the complete mortification of self-will, and then dispassion towards your own parents, relatives, and friends, and renunciation of them. Besides, [it is necessary] to be stripped of all property... and forget all faces, which you used to love dearly, whether bodily or spiritually... [It is necessary] to bear in mind that after your entering into the coenobium all your parents and friends died, and to regard only God and the superior as father and mother.[55]

52 Cf. John Klimakos, *Ladder* 22 [952 B]: 'Do not take any notice when [the demon] suggests that you should accept bishopric, abbacy and professorship.' In this respect one passage from Nikitas Stithatos concerning Symeon's life in the Studite monastery is remarkable: '[Evil people] invited him to suppers, drink parties, chatting and to that which they considered respectable. And what is this? Offices, bright cells and ordinations'; I. Hausherr and G. Horn, *Un grand mystique byzantin. Vie de Syméon le Nouveau Théologien (942–1022) par Nicétas Stéthatos*, OC 12 (1928), 17, 12–15. In accordance with tradition and in contrast with the Studite, Nikitas counts the promise of ordination among monastic temptations, which were, however, successfully conquered by Symeon.
53 Klimakos, 1 [632 A], title: *peri apotagis viou* – literally, 'on renunciation of life'. Cf. Dorothée de Gaza, *Oeuvres spirituelles*, eds L. Reignault and J. de Preville, *SC* 92 (1963) 1, title [146].
54 Isaac the Syrian, *Evrethenta Askitika* (Athens, 1895), 30 [131], Mar Isaacus Ninivita, *De perfectione religiosa*, ed. P. Bedjan (Leipzig, 1909), 2 [18].
55 Syméon le Studite, *Le Discours ascétique*, 1, 2, 4.

This passage is nothing else but a summary of the traditional monastic approach. Free will, which is what was given by God to people in the moment of creation, must be completely sacrificed through absolute obedience in order to obtain humility and other spiritual gifts. John Klimakos calls obedience 'a tomb of self-will and the resurrection of humility',[56] stating that 'blessed is he who mortifies his will to the end, and leaves the care of himself to the director in the Lord; for he will be placed at the right hand of the Crucified'.[57] So the mortification of self-will is a kind of imitation of Christ, self-crucifixion, which includes the renunciation of everything that is dear to one.

The theme of renunciation of parents and relatives is also very typical of both ascetical literature and lives of saints. Klimakos is quite definite about this matter: 'Longing for God extinguishes longing for our parents, and so anyone who says he has both is deceiving himself... Do not be moved by the tears of parents and friends; otherwise you will be weeping eternally.'[58] The *Apophthegmata* contain a story about a monk who did not want to see his mother when she came from afar to visit him.[59] Isaac the Syrian tells us of one monk who did not leave his cell to see his brother, also a monk, even when the latter was dying.[60] To understand such an attitude, which might seem shocking according to our contemporary moral standards, one must take into consideration that monasticism is specifically a complete renunciation of what is dear, and is a literal following of the Gospel's claim: 'Every one that hath forsaken houses, or brethren, or sisters, or father, or mother, or wife, or children, or lands, for My name's sake, shall receive an hundredfold, and shall inherit everlasting life' (Mat. 19: 29).

According to the Studite, a monk must be a stranger not only to his relatives and friends, but also to every brother of the coenobium;[61] he must

---

56   Klimakos, 4 [680 A].
57   Ibid. 4 [704 D].
58   Ibid. 3 [668 AB].
59   Mark of Egypt 3 [296 BC].
60   Isaac the Syrian, *Evrethenta Askitika* (Athens, 1895), *Ep.* 1 [359], Mar Isaacus Ninivita 41 [312].
61   Syméon le Studite, *Le Discours ascétique*, 11.

not have a particular love for anyone, but must regard all the brethren as saints and love them equally.[62] This is again the traditional theme of *xeniteia*, the term which can be translated as 'pilgrimage' or 'exile', and which in monastic literature means 'living as a stranger'. Agathon in the *Apophthegmata* advised a monk who asked him how to live with brothers: 'Spend the whole time of your life among them as if it were the first day when you had just entered [the coenobium]. During the whole of your life keep *xeniteia*.'[63] Evagrios regards *xeniteia* as 'the first of luminous ascetical virtues'.[64] John Klimakos devotes Chapter 3 of the *Ladder* to *xeniteia*, emphasizing that a monk must live 'like one of foreign speech amongst people of another tongue'.[65]

The Studite also follows his predecessors when insisting upon the necessity of non-possessiveness. A monk should not ask from the abbot anything beyond what is permitted; he must have only one set of clothes, and in case he wants to wash them, he must ask some other monk to lend him clothes until his own dry.[66] If a monk's cell seems to become dilapidated, he can remind the abbot about it, but if the latter does not allow him to change it, the monk should be pleased, 'remembering the Lord who had not where to lay His head' (Mat. 8: 20).[67] So non-possessiveness is also an imitation of Christ; according to the Studite, it must be absolute: 'It is not allowed to have in one's cell any material goods, not so much as a thread, except a mat, a sheep skin, a tunic and what you wear; if possible, [do not have] even a podium under your feet.'[68] There is a parallel in the *Rule of Pachomios*: 'No one should allow himself anything beyond what is permitted, either [another] set of clothes, or woollen bed clothes, or a sheep skin, or a prop under his head, or copper money, or anything for

62   Ibid. 10.
63   Agathon 1 [109 A].
64   *Evlog.* 2 [1096 B].
65   Klimakos, 3 [665 C].
66   Syméon le Studite, *Le Discours ascétique*, 15.
67   Ibid. 21.
68   Ibid. 14.

consolation.'⁶⁹ Therefore, when Symeon the Studite recommends a monk to have only one set of clothes, he is closer to the Pachomian rule than to the Studite tradition, since the Studite *Hypotyposis* suggests that each monk should have two sets of clothes.⁷⁰

Several times the Studite mentions humility as an important ascetical virtue. One must do every good deed with humility, remembering the One Who said: 'When you shall have done all those things which are commanded you, say, We are unprofitable servants: we have done that which it was our duty to do' (Luke 17: 10).⁷¹ A monk must feel as one worthless, unknown, and non-existent (cf. reference above).⁷² Regarding all the monks as saints, one should consider oneself as a sinner and think that 'all will be saved, and only I myself will be condemned in the day [of the Last Judgement]'.⁷³ This last phrase reminds us of the words of a certain tanner, who, according to some ancient monastic sources, repeated every day while passing through the town: 'All the people of this town... will go to the kingdom of heaven, and only I will go to eternal punishment for my sins.'⁷⁴

The *Ascetical Discourse* contains occasional suggestions concerning monastic food and drink. 'You may eat everything which is offered to you and also drink wine with abstinence', the Studite recommends.⁷⁵ Especially when a monk is invited to a meal, he should eat everything indiscriminately.⁷⁶ One can mention that, though wine was in general a traditional drink and was even prescribed by monastic *typika*, there was an opposition to drinking wine on the part of several ascetics, just as there was to attending baths and other 'bodily consolations'. Poimin said it was not allowed

69 L. Th. Lefort, 'La règle de S.Pachôme', *Muséon*, 37 (1924), 25.
70 Theodore the Studite, *Hypotyposis* 38 [*PG* 99, 1720 AB].
71 Syméon le Studite, *Le Discours ascétique*, 7.
72 Ibid. 19.
73 Ibid. 8.
74 *Verba seniorum PL* 73, 130 [785 CD]; cf. *Apophthegm.*, Anthony 24 [84 B]; cf. *Histoires des solitaires égyptiens*, ed. F. Nau, *ROC* 12 (1907), 67 [395].
75 Syméon le Studite, *Le Discours ascétique*, 25.
76 Ibid. 25 and 28.

for monks to drink wine at all.[77] Makarios of Egypt, according to the *Apophthegmata*, would drink wine if someone offered it to him, but on the next day he would not drink even water.[78] However, Barsanouphios and John allow monks to drink up to three cups of wine a day.[79]

> The general rule which the Studite gives concerning food is the following:
> A monk should observe the three fasts; during Great Lent [he must] fast with double intensity, except on a great feast, Saturday and Sunday; during the other two fasts he should eat every other day. During the year a monk should eat once a day on weekdays, except Saturday, Sunday and a feast, but not to his heart's content.[80]

In other words, the Studite prescribes eating twice a day only on weekends and feasts, once a day on weekdays during the whole year and on the weekends during Lent; during two long fasts a monk should eat every other day, and in Great Lent he should keep even more severe abstinence. If we compare this prescription with the Pachomian or Studite rules, it may seem more austere. Monks in *Pachomian koinonia* ate twice a day, except Wednesdays and Fridays, when there was presumably only one meal.[81] The Studite *Hypotyposis* also speaks of two meals, even on weekends during Lent; one meal is prescribed only on weekdays during Great Lent and Advent.[82]

Among other practical things, the Studite gives some advice about how to treat people on various occasions. If someone comes to a monk complaining about the superior, the monk should console him, saying that such things happened with him also many times.[83] If a monk is asked by his elder (*kalogiros*) about certain brothers, he should keep silence, and if

---

77 *Apophthegm.*, Poimin 19 [325 D]. Cf. Basil, *Disc.* (40), 4 [877 A]: wine as *vdelyktos* [vile] for monks.
78 Makarios 10 [268 AB]; cf. D. Chitty, *The Desert a City* (Oxford, 1966), 44.
79 *Biblos psychopheletati Barsanouphiou kai Ioannou* (Volos, 1960), 82–3 [72].
80 Syméon le Studite, *Le Discours ascétique*, 22. The three fasts mentioned are Great Lent (seven weeks before Easter), Advent (forty days before Christmas), and the Apostles' Fast of Sts Peter and Paul (several days or weeks before their feast-day, 29 June).
81 H. Rousseau, *Pachomius* (California and London, 1985), 84–5.
82 Theodore the Studite, *Hypotyposis* 29 [*PG* 99, 1713 CD].
83 Syméon le Studite, *Le Discours ascétique*, 26.

the elder insists, answer with humility: 'Believe me, father, I do not know, because I am a private person; I must look after my own negligence. All, by God's grace, are holy and good; however, everyone will reap as he has sown.'[84] If one brother is ill and you have not visited him for a long time, before coming yourself send something as a gift to him, saying: 'Believe me, holy father, I only today learned about your illness and I ask you to excuse me.'[85]

Reference has already been made several times to the Studite's recommendation not to partake without tears. The following suggestion concerning Communion is also indicative: 'You should watch yourself and not receive Communion when feeling something against somebody, even if it is only an assault of thought, before you reach reconciliation through repentance.'[86] This corresponds to the *Rule of Pachomios*: 'The monk who feels hostility towards somebody, before love returns, is not worthy to receive in church either Christ's gift (the *antidoron*), or Communion.'[87]

We see that in his ascetical approach, as well as in his understanding of tears and prayer, the Studite in general adheres to the teaching of ancient monastic writers, especially John Klimakos, whereas in his understanding of spiritual direction he is particularly close to the Studite tradition. He was a practitioner and not a theoretician; this is why in his discourse practical themes predominated.

---

84   Syméon le Studite, *Le Discours ascétique*, 38.
85   Ibid. 27. This recommendation together with the advice to promise ordination to a young monk may suggest that the Studite admitted lies as a means for improving the situation in several circumstances. In connection with this it is not useless to quote here John Klimakos' quite paradoxical saying: 'When we are completely cleansed of lying, then we can occasionally resort to it, though with fear'; Klimakos 12 [856 C].
86   Ibid. 12.
87   *Chapt. Epit.* [*Muséon* 40, 61].

Development of Symeon the Studite's Ascetical Ideas by Symeon the New Theologian

Since the *Ascetical Discourse* is just a collection of disconnected chapters, one cannot make a summary of the Studite's spirituality based on it. Neither can one expect to find there the whole spectrum of ascetical ideas which influenced Symeon. However, it is worth pointing out some features which were later developed by Symeon, who showed himself a faithful disciple and follower of his spiritual father. In *Cat.* 4 Symeon developed the teaching of his spiritual father concerning Communion with tears. Apart from this striking example when the words of the Studite become a starting point for Symeon, there are other examples in which the closeness between the two Symeons seems to be quite considerable.

Symeon inherited from his teacher, and through him from the Studite tradition, the understanding of spiritual fatherhood as a relation between teacher and disciple based on absolute trust on both sides and absolute obedience on the disciple's part. The Studite argues against going to many advisers and searching for 'stylites, hermits, and wonderworkers', and suggests confession to the spiritual father only. Echoing him, Symeon says: 'Do not run searching for monks of renown, and do not scrutinize their life. If by the grace of God you have found a spiritual father, tell him alone your thoughts.'[88]

The Studite identifies the words of the spiritual father with the words of God when declaring that the disciple should regard everything said by the spiritual father as if it came 'from God's mouth'. Symeon many times repeats that the disciple should 'account the words of his teacher as if they came from the mouth of God'.[89] All that the spiritual father orders should be regarded 'as if coming from God's mouth'.[90] The disciple should confess to the spiritual father all thoughts 'as if to God'.[91] Symeon also identifies

---

[88] *Eth.* 6, 399–402.
[89] *Catecheses* 14, 16–17.
[90] *Eth.* 4, 153–4.
[91] *Hymn* 4, 27. Cf. *Cap.* 1, 28; 1, 55; etc.

the spiritual father's will with God's will: 'O Lord, send me a man who knows You, that by entirely submitting myself to his service as to Yours and by fulfilling Your will by doing his, I may please You, the only God.'[92]

If the Studite says that the disciple should not judge his spiritual father even if he sees him 'fallen into harlotry', Symeon almost repeats the Studite when prescribing:

> If you see him eating with harlots and publicans and sinners, do not think anything passionate and human, but rather think of such things as are dispassionate and holy ... With these thoughts see him condescending to human passions. Even if you see with your eyes, do not believe at all, for the eyes too make mistakes, as I have learned through experience.[93]

We see that Symeon slightly modifies the Studite's expressions: instead of 'falling into harlotry' he puts 'eating with harlots', which does not sound so sharp because of parallelism with the Gospel (cf. Mat. 9: 11; Mark 2: 16; Luke 1: 2). It is noteworthy that Symeon refers to his 'experience' of seeing his spiritual father 'condescending to human passions', and confesses that his own eyes made mistakes. One may presume that he refers to the period of his life between twenty and twenty-seven, when he was not so close to the Studite. At least, this suggests that there must have been periods, whether short or long, when he doubted the holiness of his spiritual father.

The Studite refers to confession before the abbot as a norm, but he also allows confession before one of the brothers, presumably one of the simple monks and not necessarily a priest. Symeon also understands the service of the abbot as first of all spiritual fatherhood;[94] however, Symeon is known as a writer who with particular zeal defended the right of non-ordained monks to be spiritual directors and to confess people.[95] There is no need to expound his theory of the power of 'binding and loosing', which,

---

92 *Eth.* 7, 437–44.
93 *Catecheses* 20, 80–7.
94 Especially when speaking of himself as the abbot, Symeon clearly states that his first duty is to 'examine actions and thoughts' of the monks: *Hymn* 14, 86.
95 Cf. his *Ep.* 1.

according to him, passed from bishops to priests and later to monks,[96] not necessarily ordained: this theory has been analysed by scholars many times.[97] What is important for us now is that in his resolute statement, 'we are allowed to confess to a monk who is not a priest, for this was granted from God to his heirs',[98] Symeon is in accord with the Studite and with the monastic practice of his epoch.[99] The personality of the Studite, who was never ordained, stood always before Symeon's eyes as a living confirmation of this theory: 'I too was a disciple of such a father who had not received an ordination from men but who, through the hand of God, that is, the Spirit, enrolled me among [his] disciples.'[100]

In his understanding of monastic life in general Symeon also comes very close to the Studite. Both regard monasticism as renunciation of oneself, which consists of mortification of self-will, deliberate deprivation of all property, renunciation of parents and friends, living as a stranger (*xeniteia*), humility, and abstinence. Symeon, of course, is more precise in discussing these themes simply because of the much greater volume of his literary legacy, but the correspondence in approach is clear. Only more or less direct parallels will be given below.

Whereas the Studite speaks of the complete mortification of self-will as a retirement from the world,[101] Symeon builds a whole theory of 'life-giving mortification' (*zoopoios nekrosis*) on this saying. After quoting literally the Studite's maxim, Symeon continues:

> O blessed voice, or rather blessed soul that was granted to become thus and to be separated from the world! It is to these and to those who are like them that Christ, our Lord, said: 'You are not of the world, but I have chosen you out of the world'

---

96 *Ep.* 1, 12ff. [120ff.].
97 See Holl, 128–37; Krivochéine, 131–40; R. Barringer, 'Ecclesiastical Penance in the Church of Constantinople', DPhil thesis (Oxford, 1979), *passim*.
98 *Ep.* 1, 11, 24–7 [119].
99 Barringer indicates that during the century and a half preceding Symeon's *Ep.* 1 the unordained confessors 'were beginning to think of their activities as being in some way a challenge to the episcopal power of binding and loosing': Barringer, 201.
100 *Ep.* 1, 16, 6–8 [127].
101 Syméon le Studite, *Le Discours ascétique*, 1.

(John 15: 19)... Do you then, [brother], refuse to be humble and submissive, afflicted and dishonoured, despised and reproached? But if [you refuse this], how, tell me, can you become alien to self-will?[102]

Symeon then calls his listeners to imitate his spiritual father, but, if they consider him 'a fool' (*moros*), to imitate Christ Himself.[103] According to Symeon, 'life-giving mortification' is deliberate death through the renunciation of self-will: without this one cannot enter the kingdom of heaven.[104]

The Studite, then, regards the deprivation of all property through its distribution to the poor as a necessary condition for the monastic life;[105] he also suggests that the monk, when he has washed his clothes, should ask for other clothes 'like a beggar and pilgrim'.[106] Symeon says that a monk should bring all his property to the spiritual father and not touch it any more, because from the beginning of his monastic life he must 'be and appear a beggar and pilgrim'.[107] Symeon goes even further when he calls all Christians and not only monks to distribute property and become beggars: 'He who loves his neighbour as himself (Luke 10: 27) does not allow himself to possess more than his neighbour; and if he possesses and does not distribute without jealousy, until he himself becomes a beggar, he has not fulfilled the Lord's commandment.'[108] It is worth reminding ourselves that Symeon not only called for distribution of property, but also put this ideal into practice, refusing his family inheritance when entering the Studite monastery.[109]

The Studite taught his disciples to renounce parents and friends, and to forget all faces which one used to love; instead of parents there must be only one's spiritual father (superior) and God.[110] Symeon put this advice

---

102 *Catecheses* 6, 282–8.
103 *Catecheses* 6, 300–1.
104 *Eth.* 11, 52–60.
105 Syméon le Studite, *Le Discours ascétique*, 2.
106 Ibid. 15.
107 *Cap.* 1, 24–5.
108 *Cap.* 3, 98.
109 Cf. Hausherr and Horn, op. cit., 9, 1–2.
110 Syméon le Studite, *Le Discours ascétique*, 1–2; 4.

into practice, when he rejected his father's admonitions not to hurry to go to the monastery;[111] he also returned to this theme many times in his writings. In the *Chapters* he summarizes the Studite's approach as follows:

> They who prefer in some respect their parents to Christ's commandment, have not obtained faith in Christ ... Renunciation and perfect retirement from the world, accompanied by alienation from all worldly things, customs, opinions, and faces, rejection of one's own body and will, in a short time will bring profit to the one who so hotly left the world ... Seeing the sorrow of your parents, brothers, and friends about you, laugh at the demon which by every means devises this against you. But retire with a great fear and much zeal, and ask God diligently that you may reach the silent harbour of a good [spiritual] father.[112]

In *Cat.* 7 Symeon compares attachment to relatives with a noose which the devil puts around the neck of a monk and by which he drives the monk into the abyss of despair.[113]

Symeon also develops the concept of *xeniteia*, which he understands as 'crucifixion unto the world' (Gal. 6: 14) and 'the desire to be with God alone and the angels, and not to return to anything human'.[114] Following the Studite, who advised the monk not to go to anyone's cell, except the abbot's,[115] Symeon writes: 'Keep silence and detachment from all things, for in this true *xeniteia* consists. Do not enter into the cell of anyone without the permission of your father in God, unless you have been sent by the superior.'[116] Let us notice that Symeon mentions two persons here, the superior and the spiritual father, which directly reflects his experience in the Stoudion, whereas Symeon the Studite is more likely to identify them.

The theme of humility, outlined by the Studite, was also developed by Symeon. After quoting his spiritual father's suggestion that the monk must be 'as one who does not exist',[117] Symeon exclaims in the manner in which he

---

111 Hausherr and Horn, op. cit., 8, 1–20.
112 *Cap.* 1, 12–17.
113 *Catecheses* 7, 59–64.
114 *Cap.* 1, 96.
115 Syméon le Studite, *Le Discours ascétique*, 9.
116 *Catecheses* 26, 77–81.
117 Syméon le Studite, *Le Discours ascétique*, 19.

usually presents the Studite's sayings: 'O blessed words, through which his angelic life is proclaimed, which was above human life!'[118] Symeon understands humility as the imitation of Christ, Who humiliated Himself when people accused Him of being possessed by demons, a deceiver, a glutton and a winebibber (Mat. 27: 63; John 7: 20; Mat. 11: 19). 'Our blessed father, I mean St Symeon [the Studite], heard the same accusations on behalf of us, or rather because of us', Symeon adds.[119] Extreme humility when a man crucifies himself with Christ is nothing else but 'life-giving mortification', through which he becomes a partaker of Christ's glory.[120]

One may notice slight differences between Symeon and the Studite in some details of ascetical practice. As H. Turner points out, the Studite insists on coming to the church before all and leaving it last,[121] whereas Symeon recommends not leaving the church before dismissal (and so not necessarily last).[122] There is a difference between the Studite's order of all-night vigil[123] and Symeon's rule of evening prayer;[124] however, since the question concerns dissimilar cases, one should not expect similarity. Such differences do not provide a sufficient basis to speak of Symeon's 'independence' from his spiritual father.[125] There are, of course, many ascetical themes in Symeon which have not been discussed by the Studite in his discourse, and there are many details which Symeon adds to the themes which have been touched upon. But even on the basis of these points we cannot speak of Symeon's independence, for nobody knows how many ascetical features were discussed by the Studite in conversations, as well as in any writings which have not survived.

[118] *Catecheses* 6, 178–80.
[119] *Catecheses* 6, 301–8.
[120] *Catecheses* 6, 342–68.
[121] Syméon le Studite, *Le Discours ascétique*, 17.
[122] H. J. M. Turner, *Symeon the New Theologian and Spiritual Fatherhood* (Leiden – New York – København – Köln, 1990), 159; cf. *Catecheses* 26, 60–2.
[123] Syméon le Studite, *Le Discours ascétique*, 24.
[124] *Catecheses* 26, 272–85.
[125] Turner, op. cit., 158.

The Mysticism of the Two Symeons Juxtaposed

The *Ascetical Discourse* gives us considerable proofs that the Studite was a mystic with a deep personal experience. There is no systematic discussion of mystical matters in the discourse, but only several passages and remarks; however, they provide sufficient basis for us to state that the Studite was a direct predecessor of Symeon in this most significant aspect of the latter's spirituality. Let us collect these remarks, showing some parallels with Symeon the New Theologian, where applicable.

The following passage from the *Ascetical Discourse* is of great importance:

> When remembrance of this [of God] remains in you for a long time, then in your mind appears a radiance like a ray. The more you search for it, with great attention and concentrated mind, with much effort and tears, the brighter it shines. Shining, it arouses love for itself; being loved, it purifies; purifying, it makes you godlike, enlightening and teaching you to distinguish between good and evil. However, O brother, there is need for much labour... so that this radiance settles in your soul and illuminates it, as the moon [illuminates] the darkness of night.[126]

In fact, the most significant mystical themes of Symeon the New Theologian are outlined in this passage by his spiritual father. The similarity in style and terminology is also considerable. Symeon also uses the images of the moon and of rays when describing the divine light.[127] The theme of the intense search for the divine light is very important for Symeon. He also speaks of different stages of contemplation; of the appearance of the light in the mind; of the love which the divine light causes; of tears which accompany the vision of light; of purification and deification as results of the contemplation of the divine light. Later each of these mystical features in Symeon will be discussed separately; at this stage it is important for us to see the resemblance between him and the Studite.

---

126 Syméon le Studite, *Le Discours ascétique*, 20.
127 Cf. the image of the moon in *Hymn* 29, 9.

The next passage from the *Ascetical Discourse* adds some details to the description of mystical vision: the latter is accompanied by spiritual joy, and it may be brought to an end voluntarily. The Studite says:

> But if in the time of prayer some other light begins to shine upon you, which I am not able to explain, [and because of which] the soul is filled with joy and desire for the best, and tears spring up with compunction, you should know that this is a divine visitation and assistance. But if it continues too long, direct your mind to something bodily... Through this action you will humiliate yourself.[128]

If we compare this passage with what Symeon the New Theologian usually says, we will see that the latter also speaks of divine joy with tears at the time of mystical vision. Like the Studite, Symeon speaks of a voluntary cessation of the vision in order to preserve humility.[129] In most cases, however, he describes this cessation not as a voluntary act, but as what is happening because of the extreme intensity of the experience: 'Being incapable of bearing the sight of such glory, I turned away, and I fled into the darkness of earthly pleasures ... I preferred to go out [of the vision] and to remain in the tomb.'[130]

When speaking of tears in Symeon the Studite, it was mentioned that he regards tears as a means to mystical illumination. The connection between self-purification through repentance and mystical experience is emphasized in the following passage:

> 'It is necessary firstly to purify oneself, and then to converse with the Pure', as it is said.[131] For when the mind becomes purified because of many tears and receives the radiance of the divine light, which will not become less even if one possesses the whole world, then [a man] willingly settles his thoughts in the future and contemplates it, as God shows it to him; and he rejoices spiritually about it, according to

---

128 Syméon le Studite, *Le Discours ascétique*, 30.
129 *Catecheses* 17, 65–7.
130 *Hymn* 11, 81–9.
131 Cf. Grégoire de Nazianze, *Discourses*, eds J. Bernardi, J. Mossay, P. Gallay, C. Moreschini, *SC* 270 (1978–92), 20, 4, 8–9 [62].

the apostle, who said: 'The fruit of the Spirit is love, joy, peace, meekness, temperance' (Gal. 5: 22–3).[132]

In Symeon's system mystical contemplation is also a result of self-purification through tears and repentance: 'For this unceasing repentance... little by little causes us to shed bitter tears and by them wipes away and cleanses the filth and defilement of the soul; then it produces in us pure repentance... and makes us able to see the unsetting radiance.'[133] It is noteworthy that the only Patristic quotation in the *Ascetical Discourse* is from Gregory Nazianzen, the author to whom Symeon refers much more often than to other Church Fathers.

The Studite shows that patience in afflictions may cause mystical experience: '[Let us] every day be ready to bear every affliction, remembering that afflictions are deliverance from many debts ... For that which "eye hath not seen, nor ear heard, neither have entered into the heart of man" (1 Cor. 2: 9) is, according to trustworthy promise, destined for those who show patience in afflictions.'[134]

The same conception we find in Symeon. Those who bear patiently every difficulty and affliction will see 'the promised land', that is, divine light.[135] Symeon confirms this by his own experience: 'When I was in every difficulty and affliction, I saw in myself abundance of joy and happiness through the revelation and manifestation of His face.'[136] The reference to 1 Cor. 2: 9 in the *Ascetical Discourse* is significant: it was one of Symeon's favourite passages, and in his writings he alludes to it over thirty times.

*

Having compared Symeon the Studite's ascetical and mystical approach with that of Symeon, we come nearer to understanding the reason why his influence on Symeon the New Theologian was so profound. It is not

---

132 Syméon le Studite, *Le Discours ascétique*, 32.
133 *Catecheses* 4, 670–7.
134 Syméon le Studite, *Le Discours ascétique*, 13.
135 *Catecheses* 6, 140–2.
136 *Eth.* 10, 285–8.

enough to say that 'his temperament, his methods as a spiritual father and the skills which he possessed were closely attuned to Symeon's needs.'[137] The Studite's methods of direction did indeed assist him in influencing people. But what was much more important for Symeon was that the Studite was a mystic who could share with the disciple his gifts and introduce him into mystical life. And, of course, Symeon the Studite's ascetical approach also influenced Symeon the New Theologian, though this should be put in second place.

A teacher–disciple relationship has always played a pivotal role in the transmission of the Tradition from one generation of spiritual leaders to another. Symeon the New Theologian had his own teacher. In my study on him that I undertook twenty years ago I attempted to prove that all his major ideas are rooted in the Orthodox Tradition and his teaching corresponds to the ideas of such preceding Fathers as Gregory the Theologian, Maximos the Confessor, John Klimakos, Theodore the Studite, and notably Symeon the Studite. I affirmed that Symeon's theology was no more than a continuation and development of the theology of his predecessors. I also asserted that Symeon only repeated what the Church Father taught from age to age, when he preached, in his own time and for his contemporaries, the ideal of 'life according to the Gospel' – this *cantus firmus* of the entire Patristic theology.

Nevertheless, Symeon remains a profoundly original author who made his own unique contribution to the development of Eastern Christian Tradition. What distinguishes Symeon from other Church Fathers is his autobiographical approach to mystical themes and his extraordinary openness in description of his own visions of the divine light and his experience of the presence of God. All the elements of Symeon's theological and mystical doctrine are deeply rooted in the Tradition but he lets it go through himself, integrating it in his own experience. He makes quite traditional mystical themes (tears, ecstasy, dispassion, deification) highly personal.

It can be added that among the Eastern Christian ascetical writers Symeon was the first to emphasize the central place of the Eucharist in

---

[137] Turner, op. cit., 65.

personal spiritual mystical life, giving it the key role in the cause of salvation and journey towards the union of man with God. He was the first to point to the vision of divine light as the main goal of one's ascetical effort. He was the first to speak of dispassion and deification in such a personal manner. Symeon's mystical theology is perfectly 'in harmony' with the common fabric of Patristic tradition, while he remains one of the most original writers the Eastern Church has ever known.

The study of Symeon from the perspective of his 'traditionality' or 'non-traditionality' has led me to come to a key conclusion concerning the very nature of the Orthodox Holy Tradition. His case very convincingly shows that the corner stone of the Holy Tradition lies in none other but the personal mystical experience of a Christian – the experience of direct relationship between God and the human being. The Holy Tradition cannot be true Orthodox if it is not based on the experience of meeting God 'face to face'. Those who try to oppose the formal and rationalistic 'tradition' of the Church majority to the inspired 'mysticism' of particular enthusiasts are deluded because they do not understand the very essence of the Holy Tradition. Such people – regardless of their rank or status in the Church (in case of Symeon, just as in many similar cases, they were representatives of the 'official' Church hierarchy) – seek by all means to preserve and safeguard what they believe to be 'traditional'. Actually, they contribute to the distortion and corruption of the true Tradition. If the Tradition is deprived of its missionary and prophetic heart, it risks turning into narrow 'traditionalism' that has nothing to do with the truly Christian Tradition, inspired and mystical.

In studying Symeon's spiritual legacy, I have come to a very similar conclusion about the nature of mysticism within the Christian Church, namely, genuine mysticism is impossible without the context of the Tradition. A real mystic is not he who sets his own experience above the Church Tradition, but he whose experience is in accord with the experience of the Church in general and her best representatives in particular. The historic role of great Christian mystics was often that of defenders of the Tradition and preachers of the ideal of life according to the Gospel. This is why there was, as a rule, so much maximalism and radicalism in their views. But precisely this maximalism was a source of inspiration for thousands of ordinary Christians as it helped to keep the Orthodox Tradition alive.

In each era of Christian history, the Church has had, or rather has been granted, great mystics who, together with their experience, hand over their inherited ages-long Tradition to their contemporaries and subsequent generations of the faithful. It is in this way that the golden chain of Christian sanctity, so eloquently described by Symeon in one of his works, is preserved and continued: 'The saints in each generation, joined to those who have gone before, and filled like them with light, become a golden chain, in which each saint is a separate link, united to the next by faith, works, and love.'[138]

Bibliography

The writings of St Symeon the New Theologian

Action de grâces 1–2, *SC* 113 (1965), 304–57.
Catéchèses, eds B. Krivochéine and J. Paramelle, t. I (*Cat*. 1–5), *SC* 96 (1963); t. II (*Cat*. 6–22), *SC* 104 (1964); t. III (*Cat*. 23–34), *SC* 113 (1965).
Chapitres théologiques, gnostiques et pratiques, ed. J. Darrouzès, *SC* 51-bis (1980).
The Discourses, trans. C. J. de Catanzaro (Mahwah, NJ, 1980).
Hymnes, eds J. Koder, J. Paramelle and L. Neyrand, t. I (*Hymn* 1–15), *SC* 156 (1969); t. II (*Hymn* 16–40), *SC* 174 (1971); t. III (*Hymn* 41–58), *SC* 196 (1973).
Hymns of Divine Love, trans. G. Maloney (Denville, NJ, *s.a.*).
The Practical and Theological Chapters and Three Theological Discourses, trans. P. McGuckin, Cistercian Studies 41 (Kalamazoo, MI, 1982).
Traités théologiques et éthiques, ed. J. Darrouzès, t. I (*Theol*. 1–3; *Eth*. 1–3), *SC* 122 (1966); t. II (*Eth*. 4–15), *SC* 129 (1967).
Του εν αγίοις πατρός ημών Συμεών ευχή μυστική, *SC* 156, 150–4.
Του οσίου πατρός ημών Συμεών του Νέου Θεολόγου τα ευρισκόμενα, ed. Dionysiou Zagoraiou (Venice, 1790).

---

138 *Cap*. 3, 2–4.

The writing of St Symeon the Studite

Syméon le Studite, *Le Discours ascétique*, eds H. Alfeyev and L. Neyrand. *SC* (forthcoming).

The life of St Symeon the New Theologian

Hausherr, I., and G. Horn, *Un grand mystique byzantin. Vie de Syméon le Nouveau Théologien (942–1022) par Nicétas Stéthatos*, *OC* 12 (1928), 1–128.

Patristic literature

Apophthegmata patrum, collectio alphabetica, *PG* 65, 71–440.
Basil the Great, *Sermo asceticus*, *PG* 31, 869–81.
Βίβλος ψυχωφελεστάτη Βαρσανουφίου καὶ Ἰωάννου (Volos, 1960).
Diadochos of Photike, *Oeuvres spirituelles*, ed. E. des Places, *SC* 5-bis (1955).
Dorotheos of Gaza, *La vie de saint Dosithée*, ed. P. M. Brun, *OC* 26 (1932).
Evagrios of Pontus, *De oratione capitula*, *PG* 79, 1165–1200.
Gregory of Nazianzos, *Discourses*, eds J. Bernardi, J. Mossay, P. Gallay, C. Moreschini, *SC* 270 (1978–92).
Histoires des solitaires égyptiens, ed. F. Nau, *ROC* 12 (1907).
Isaac the Syrian, Εὑρεθέντα Ἀσκητικά (Athens, 1895).
——, *The Ascetical Homilies* (Boston, MA, 1984).
John Cassian, *De institutis coenobiorum*, ed. M. Petschenig, *CSEL* 17 (Prague – Wien – Leipzig, 1888).
John Klimakos, *The Ladder of Divine Ascent* (Boston, MA, 1990).
——, *Scala paradisi* (+ *Liber ad pastorem*), *PG* 88, 631–1210.
Makarios of Egypt, *Reden und Briefe*, ed. H. Berthold, Bd. 1–2 (Berlin, 1973).
Mar Isaacus Ninivita, *De perfectione religiosa*, ed. P. Bedjan (Leipzig, 1909).
Maximus Confessor, *Selected Writings*, trans. G. C. Berthold (Mahwah, NJ, 1985).
The Philokalia, trans. G. E. H. Palmer, P. Sherrard and K. Ware, vols 1–3 (London, 1979–84).
Pseudo-Macarius, *The Fifty Spiritual Homilies and the Great Letter*, trans. G. Maloney (New York, 1992).
Theodore the Studite, *Hypotyposis* [*PG* 99, 1704–20].
Verba seniorum PL 73, 130 [785 CD].

Secondary literature

Barringer, R., 'Ecclesiastical Penance in the Church of Constantinople', DPhil thesis (Oxford, 1979).
Chitty, D., *The Desert, a City* (Oxford, 1966).
Dmitriyevsky, A., *Opisanie liturgicheskikh rukopisey khraniashchikhsya v bibliotekakh pravoslavnogo Vostoka* [The Description of the Liturgical Manuscripts in the Libraries of the Orthodox East], t. 1, part 1: *Typika* (Kiyev, 1895).
Guillaumont, A., *Aux origines du monachisme chrétien* (Paris, 1979).
Hausherr, I., *Spiritual Direction in the Early Christian East*, Cistercian Studies 116 (Kalamazoo, MI, 1990).
Holl, K. *Enthusiasmus und Bussgewalt beim griechischen Mönchtum. Eine Studie zu Symeon dem neuen Theologen* (Leipzig, 1898).
Lefort, L. Th., 'La règle de S.Pachôme', *Muséon* 37 (1924).
Rousseau, H., *Pachomius* (California and London, 1985).
Turner, H. J. M., *Symeon the New Theologian and Spiritual Fatherhood* (Leiden – New York – København – Köln, 1990).

ELIZABETH JEFFREYS

11 On the Annunciation: Manganeios Prodromos, no. 120

This brief discussion of an epigram on the Annunciation to the Theotokos arises out of my recent work on an edition of a collection of twelfth-century Greek verse. It is offered to Metropolitan Kallistos as a small token of esteem.

The text in question reads as follows:[1]

Εἰς τὸν χαιρετισμὸν τῆς ὑπεραγίας Θεοτόκου

Ἔοικε καὶ νοῦς ἐκ μόνης τῆς ἰδέας
ἐπαγγελίαν μηνύειν τῇ Παρθένῳ,
ξένην, ἀνεκλάλητον, ἀπορουμένην,
τὸ χαροπὸν δὲ καὶ τὸ φαιδρὸν τῆς θέας·
καί σοι, δοκῶ, δίδωσιν ἐννοεῖν, Κόρη,   5
Θεοῦ μεγαλεῖόν τι πλὴν ὑπὲρ φύσιν·
σκεῦος γὰρ οὖσα λαμπρότητος ἐνθέου,
ἔχεις παρ' αὑτῇ τῶν ὑπὲρ νοῦν ἐμφάσεις.
Οὐκοῦν ὁρῶσα καὶ Θεοῦ παραστάτην
πρὸς τὴν τοσαύτην ἀτρεμεῖς θεωρίαν,   10
ἀλλ' οἷον ἄρα σοι τὸ πνεῦμα μηνύει
ἐγγάστριον σύλληψιν ὑψίστου Λόγου,
πράγματος ὑπόστασιν οὐ χωρουμένου,

---

[1] The text presented here is taken from the edition of the works of Manganeios Prodromos that has been in preparation for far too long by Elizabeth Jeffreys and Michael Jeffreys. The epigram has been edited previously, without discussion, in: Emmanouel Miller, 'Poèsies inédites de Théodore Prodrome', *Annuaire pour l'association pour l'encouragement des études grecques en France*, 17 (1883), 51–2. All but four of Manganeios's 148 poems are to be found in Marcianus Graecus XI. 22 (= M); poem 120 is on f. 86.

ἐν σῇ δὲ μήτρᾳ καὶ περιγεγραμμένου·
ἀλλ' ὦ χαρὰν ἄρρητον εἰσδεξαμένη,   15
ἐνστερνισαμένη τε τὴν σωτηρίαν,
χαρᾶς ἐκείνης μὴ στερήσαις σοῦ τόκου[2]
τοὺς ὑπὸ τὴν σὴν δεξιὰν κεκλιμένους.

On the salutation to the Most Holy Theotokos

From its appearance alone it seems that the spirit / makes an announcement to the Virgin / that is strange, inexpressible, puzzling, / the joyous and brilliant element of the scene; / [5] and, I think, the spirit makes you consider, Maiden, / that God's greatness surpasses nature; / for being the vessel of divine brilliance, / you have in yourself impressions of matters beyond comprehension. / So, gazing at God's attendant / [10] you are silent before so great a sight, / but the spirit announces, as it were, to you / conception in your womb of the most high Word, / an hypostasis of matter that cannot be contained / yet is circumscribed in your womb; / [15] but, you who have received ineffable joy, / who have embraced salvation within your bosom, / do not deprive of the joy of your birth-giving / those who kneel beneath your right hand.

(trans. Elizabeth Jeffreys and Michael Jeffreys)

This short poem, or epigram, comes from a collection of verse written between about 1142 and 1160 by a writer known to modern scholarship as Manganeios Prodromos.[3] In his career and poetic *oeuvre* Manganeios is a typical member of the group of well-educated men who sought to support themselves by teaching and writing in mid-twelfth-century Constantinople.[4] His more successful counterparts include figures such as Theodore Prodromos (with whom he is often confused), John Tzetzes, Constantine Manasses, and Nicholas Kallikles. There were probably many others who are now lost to view, thanks to the vagaries of manuscript

2   17 σοῦ M: τοῦ Miller.
3   Manganeios's *oeuvre* has suffered a chequered publication history. The catalogue entry for M remains an essential reference tool: Elpidio Mioni, *Biblioteca Divi Marci Venetiarum Codices Graeci Manuscripti*, vol. 3 (Venice: Roma, 1970), 116–31. This has to be supplemented from Paul Magdalino, *The Empire of Manuel Komnenos, 1143–1180* (Cambridge: Cambridge University Press, 1993), 494–500, which has additional bibliography up to 1993. Numbering of Manganeios's poems follows that of Mioni's catalogue.
4   Magdalino, *Empire of Manuel Komnenos*, 440–54.

transmission. Manganeios's extensive *oeuvre* (some 17,000 lines of verse in fifteen- and twelve-syllable lines) is, for example, known only by the chance survival of one thirteenth-century manuscript, while another unique collection of a similar date preserves numbers of anonymous epigrams of largely unascertainable authorship.[5]

While Manganeios wrote for two patrons in particular – the emperor Manuel and for the *Sevastokratorissa* Eirene, the emperor's widowed sister-in-law[6] – he was also employed occasionally by several other men and women from the Constantinopolitan elite. The topics on which he wrote covered lengthy encomia on the emperor which recorded military triumphs and other important events, intended to be performed on state occasions; laments consoling Eirene on her many misfortunes, which included imprisonment on charges of treachery; joyous epithalamia for the marriages of her children and other members of the Komnenian clan; and epigrams to accompany votive offerings in churches and chapels of Constantinople. Praises of, and supplications to, the Theotokos form a noticeable element in Manganeios's corpus, with much written in the persona of the *sevastokratorissa* who had a special devotion to the Theotokos – though the poem under consideration here is not connected to her.

Manganeios, the authorial voice in this text, is contemplating a depiction of the Annunciation and appeals to the Virgin Mary for her support; he speaks on behalf of all those who offer her their devotion. It is an example of an intercessionary appeal of a very usual type, though in this case Manganeios is not framing it as a supplication from a particular

---

[5] Marc. Gr. 524, on which see Spyridon Lambros, 'Ὁ μαρκιανὸς κώδιξ 524, *Neos Hellenomnemon*, 8 (1911), 1–59 and 123–91, but now, importantly, Foteini Spingou, 'Words and Artworks in the Twelfth Century and Beyond: The Thirteenth-Century Manuscript Marcianus Gr. 524 and the Twelfth-Century Dedicatory Epigrams on Works of Art' (unpublished DPhil thesis, University of Oxford, 2012).

[6] On Manuel, see Magdalino, *Empire of Manuel Komnenos*. On Eirene, see most recently Elizabeth Jeffreys, 'The Sevastokratorissa Eirene as Patron', in M. Grünbart, M. Mullett and L. Theis (eds), *Female Founders in Byzantium and Beyond* (Vienna, 2013) [= *Wiener Jahrbuch der Kunstgeschichte*, 60/61 (2011/12)], 175–92.

individual with a particular problem.[7] In this respect it is both like and unlike Manganeios's votive poems 85–88 which also deal with an image of the Annunciation.[8] These are votive poems in that their titles refer to the texts' donor, while the texts themselves are descriptive of the contents of the frescos that are their subject matter (to the extent of naming the artist responsible) but do not make a specific supplication.

This poem is constructed with two clauses of four lines, on the angel and the Virgin respectively, followed by six which report the writer's interpretation of the Virgin's response; and conclude with four lines of the writer's plea for the Virgin's benevolence, that the grace she had received may be bestowed on those who make supplication to her. There is play on the multivalent implications of verbal forms associated with *nous* [spirit/mind]: *ennoein* [line 5: consider], *hyper noun* [line 8: beyond comprehension]. There is resonance between *ideas* [line 1: appearance] and *theas* [line 4: element of the scene]; note too *theorian* [line 10: sight]: all these words are placed prominently at the line end. *Eoike* [line 1: it seems] and *doko* [line 5: I think] indicate the tentative nature of the writer's interpretation of what is before him. There is also a lesser thread to do with speech, or lack of it: note *aneklaleton* [line 3: inexpressible], *arreton* [line 15: ineffable], and the silent calm implied by *atremeis* [line 10: you are silent].

The image that is before Manganeios presents two figures: the angel or spirit, who is not named, and the Virgin. In line 1, *nous*, the word used for the angel, is unusual, but adequately attested elsewhere in this sense[9] and is used by Manganeios in other epigrams on the Annunciation (perhaps prompted by metrical convenience).[10] It is translated here as 'spirit'; in

---

7   For a collection of recent studies on the development of such prayers, see *Presbeia Theotokou: The Intercessory Role of Mary across Times and Places in Byzantium (4th–9th Century)*, Leena Mari Peltomaa, Andreas Kulzer and Pauline Allen (eds) (Vienna: Verlag der Österreichischen Akademie der Wissenschaften, 2015).
8   Previously edited in Miller, 'Poésies inédites de Theodore Prodrome', 32–4, and Nikos Bees, 'Kunstgeschichtliche Untersuchungen über die Eulalios-Frage', *Repertorium für Kunstwissenschaft*, 39 (1916), 103–4.
9   Geoffrey Lampe, *A Patristic Lexicon* (Oxford: Clarendon Press, 1961), s.v. νοῦς, I. E (at p. 925), notably from Dionysios the Areopagite.
10 e.g. Manganeios 85. 1, and cf. 48. 200 in a secular context.

line 11, the angel is referred to as a spirit with the more usual word, *pneuma*. In the standard depictions of the Annunciation, the angel is on the viewer's left and the Virgin on the viewer's right. There is no reason to think that the image suggested by this poem is any different. One might suppose that the phrase 'From its appearance alone' could suggest that the angel has been rushing in at speed to complete his mission – as in the famous twelfth-century icon in St Catherine's at Sinai where the angel's robes flutter in the breeze in a pause before the message is delivered.[11] No words are attributed to the angel, who makes an announcement which amidst its strangeness is also *aneklaleton* [line 4: 'inexpressible', or perhaps 'unspoken'].

The Virgin is also quietly silent during the angel's announcement. This perhaps hints at the idea, widespread from the fourth century but still current in late Byzantium, that the Word entered the Virgin's body through her ear.[12] The presence of 'the most high Word' from that moment in the Virgin's womb was also occasionally given visual expression, again as in the Sinai icon where a faint foetal shape is marked on the Virgin's body. However, the rarity of this motif makes it difficult to suggest it was part of the image that was in front of Manganeios.

Byzantine poems of this sort are with good reason known as epigrams: they were intended to be inscribed on objects, and read – usually aloud – by those who beheld them. Much work has been done recently to explore this

---

11   Henry Maguire, 'The Self-Conscious Angel: Character Study in Byzantine Paintings of the Annunciation', *Harvard Ukrainian Studies*, 7 (1983), 376–92, remains important; see also id., *Art and Eloquence in Byzantium* (Princeton, NJ: Princeton University Press, 1981), 44–56. The Sinai Annunciation icon has been shown, for example, in the exhibition, *The Glory of Byzantium* (New York: Metropolitan Museum of Art, 1997), and is discussed in the exhibition catalogue (Helen Evans and William Wixom (eds)), no. 246, 374–5.

12   As initiated by Proclus (bishop of Constantinople 434/7–446/7); cf. Andrew of Crete, *In Navitatem Mariae* (*PG* 97, col. 820 C), John Geometres, *In Annuntiationem* (*PG* 106, col. 820 BC). See Nicholas Constas, *Proclus of Constantinople and the Cult of the Virgin in Late Antiquity* (Leiden: Brill, 2003), especially chapter 5, 'The Ear of the Virginal Body: The Poetics of Sound in the School of Proclus'.

aspect of Byzantine literary, and artistic, culture.[13] In this case there is no suggestion that an icon is being offered as a votive in a church or chapel of the Theotokos, with or without any of the accoutrements that can adorn an icon: an *encheirion* [icon veil], *podea* [drape], or *kosmos* [metal revetment], all of which were frequently decorated with inscriptions. Nonetheless, despite its length, Manganeios's wording is appropriate to be inscribed, or in the case of the fabric veils embroidered, on any of these objects.[14] This poem of reflection on the image that is before the viewer, and author, would then become the viewer's prayer.

Bibliography

Bees, Nikos, 'Kunstgeschichtliche Untersuchungen über die Eulalios-Frage', *Repertorium für Kunstwissenschaft*, 39 (1916), 97–117.

Bernard, Floris, *Writing and Reading Byzantine Secular Poetry, 1025–1081* (Oxford: Oxford University Press, 2014).

——, and Christoffel Demoen (eds), *Poetry and its Contents in Eleventh-Century Byzantium* (Aldershot: Ashgate, 2012).

Constas, Nicholas, *Proclus of Constantinople and the Cult of the Virgin in Late Antiquity* (Leiden: Brill, 2003).

---

13 Notably in Vienna under the aegis of Wolfram Hörandner, which has resulted in the three volumes edited by Andreas Rhoby, *Byzantinische Epigramme in inschriftlicher Überlieferung* (Vienna: Verlag der Österreichischen Akademie der Wissenschaften, 2011–14). There is much to be learned too from Ivan Drpić, 'Kosmos of Verse: Epigram, Art and Devotion in Later Byzantium' (unpublished PhD thesis, Harvard University, 2011).

14 It is quite surprising how many words can be fitted on an icon frame. On the placement of inscriptions of this type, see Valerie Nunn, 'The Encheirion as Adjunct to the Icon in the Middle Byzantine Period', *Byzantine and Modern Greek Studies*, 10 (1986), 73–102, and Drpić, 'Kosmos of Verse', e.g. 100–2.
I would like to thank Dimitrios Skrekas for a useful discussion and, as always, Michael Jeffreys.

Dripić, Ivan, 'Kosmos of Verse: Epigram, Art and Devotion in Later Byzantium' (unpublished PhD thesis, Harvard University, 2011).
Evans, Helen, and William Wixom (eds), *The Glory of Byzantium* (New York: Metropolitan Museum of Art, 1997).
Jeffreys, Elizabeth, 'The Sevastokratorissa Eirene as Patron', in M. Grünbart, M. Mullett and L. Theis (eds), *Female Founders in Byzantium and Beyond* (Vienna, 2013) [= *Wiener Jahrbuch der Kunstgeschichte*, 60/61 (2011/12)], 175–92.
Lambros, Spyridon, 'Ο μαρκιανὸς κῶδιξ 524' [The Marcianus manuscript 524], *Neos Hellenomnemon*, 8 (1911), 1–59 and 123–91.
Lampe, Geoffrey, *A Patristic Lexicon* (Oxford: Clarendon Press, 1961).
Lauxtermann, Marc, *Byzantine Poetry from Pisides to Geometres* (Vienna: Verlag der Österreichischen Akademie der Wissenschaften, 2003).
Magdalino, Paul, *The Empire of Manuel Komnenos, 1143–1180* (Cambridge: Cambridge University Press, 1993).
Maguire, Henry, *Art and Eloquence in Byzantium* (Princeton, NJ: Princeton University Press, 1981).
——, 'The Self-Conscious Angel: Character Study in Byzantine Paintings of the Annunciation', *Harvard Ukrainian Studies*, 7 (1983), 376–92.
Miller, Emmanuel, 'Poèsies inédites de Théodore Prodrome', *Annuaire pour l'association pour l'encouragement des études grecques en France*, 17 (1883), 19–64.
Mioni, Elpidio, *Biblioteca Divi Marci Venetiarum codices graeci manuscripti*, vol. 3 (Venice: Roma, 1970).
Nunn, Valerie, 'The Encheirion as Adjunt to the Icon in the Middle Byzantine Period', *Byzantine and Modern Greek Studies*, 10 (1986), 73–102.
Patrologia Graeca. Patrologiae cursus completus. Series Graeca. Patrologia Graeca, 161 vols (Paris: Apud J.-P. Migne, 1857–66).
Peltomaa, Leena Mari, Andreas Kulzer and Pauline Allen (eds), *Presbeia Theotokou: The Intercessory Role of Mary across Times and Places in Byzantium (4th–9th Century)* (Vienna: Verlag der Österreichischen Akademie der Wissenschaften, 2015).
Rhoby, Andreas, *Byzantinische Epigramme in inschriftlicher Überlieferung* (Vienna: Verlag der Österreichischen Akademie der Wissenschaften, 2011–14).
Spingou, Foteini, 'Words and Artworks in the Twelfth Century and Beyond: The Thirteenth-Century Manuscript Marcianus Gr. 524 and the Twelfth-Century Dedicatory Epigrams on Works of Art' (unpublished DPhil thesis, University of Oxford, 2012).

JOHN CHRYSSAVGIS

12 *Philokalia*: A Vocabulary for Our Time

A Classic Text: Reclaiming an Ancient Vocabulary

In 1982, along my favourite Athonite route at the time – from the skete of Karoulia to the monastery of Dionysiou – I was stopped by a seemingly elderly, quite dishevelled monk longing for some fleeting conversation. 'I have coffee', he called out from above some crags! 'And raki', he added; 'I'll even give you some old books', he pleaded. That last quip led me straight to temptation without deliverance. They were an early two-volume edition of the *Philokalia*, subsequently deposited safely in a library at New Skete. In 1782, exactly two centuries before quaffing that distilled beverage, a massive Greek folio was published in Venice, with the title Φιλοκαλία τῶν Ἱερῶν Νηπτικῶν, *Philokalia of the Holy Neptics*.[1] It contained a selection of spiritual and mystical texts by thirty-six authors dating from the fourth to the fifteenth centuries, all of them – with the exception of John Cassian – from the Christian East.[2]

---

1   On the original publication of the *Philokalia* and on later editions and translations, see Kallistos Ware, 'Philocalie', *Dictionnaire de Spiritualité*, 12 (1984), 1336–52. See also his 'The Spirituality of the *Philokalia*', *Sobornost incorporating Eastern Churches Review*, 13: 1 (1991), 6–24.
2   For the (as yet incomplete) English edition, see G. E. H. Palmer, Philip Sherrard and Kallistos Ware (London/Boston: Faber & Faber, 1979-). Hereafter: *Philokalia*. A selection of texts from the *Philokalia* was published in 1951 and translated from the Russian by E. Kadloubovsky and G. E. H. Palmer, entitled *Writings from the Philokalia: On Prayer of the Heart* (London and Boston: Faber & Faber). Hereafter: *Writings* [from the 1992 first paperback edition]. For the (third) Greek edition, see Astir/Papadimitriou (Athens, 1957–63). In 1951 T. S. Eliot persuaded his fellow

In his introduction to the *Philokalia*,[3] St Nikodimos is conscious of the fact that 'certain of the texts included in [his] volumes will sound strange to the ears of most people'.[4] It may be helpful, then, to provide some definition – or, at least, clarification – of key theological principles and spiritual practices broached in the *Philokalia*.

It has become fashionable, for Orthodox and non-Orthodox alike, to be infatuated with certain exotic eastern terminology, technical idioms that define foundational dimensions of Orthodox theology and spirituality. Scholars and students alike become enchanted by the mystical implications of such concepts as θέωσις [deification] and νοερά προσευχή [prayer of the intellect, or the Jesus Prayer], or ἡσυχία [silence or stillness] and ἄκτιστον φῶς [uncreated light]. The word 'spirituality' itself is vulnerable to misunderstanding and misuse unless carefully 'unpacked' and nuanced. Some theologians are quick to claim that there is no reference in the classical tradition to 'spirituality' as such and rightly emphasize the connection between the Spirit of God and the Christian life.

Still, words communicate the pregnancy of divine life when approached in a spirit of humility. That is precisely my intention here as I seek to draw on the classics of prayer in the remarkable anthology of the *Philokalia* – from the fourth-century Egyptian desert dwellers, through the sixth-century Maximos the Confessor, to the tenth-century Symeon the New Theologian, and finally the fourteenth-century hesychasts – in order to paint a portrait of desert spirituality worthy of veneration and emulation.

At the time of its first appearance, the *Philokalia* seems to have had only limited inspiration and circulation in the Orthodox world, while in the West it was for a long time virtually unknown. Yet, in some ways, the *Philokalia* is arguably the most significant and influential text published in recent centuries. To this day, not only does it remain in print in the original Greek and in numerous translations, but it has been regularly and repeatedly reprinted throughout the world over the last decades. In some

---

directors of the publishing house Faber & Faber to publish a partial translation into English from the Theophan Russian version.
3   The English translation does not contain the introduction.
4   *Philokalia*, vol. 1, p. xiii [Greek edition].

circles, it is not unusual to speak even of a 'philokalic' or 'neptic' approach to theology and prayer.

In exploring the lives and texts of the *Philokalia* writers, I have discovered that their conventional vocabulary literally comes alive, critically challenging our perception of God and our appreciation of the world in the struggle for personal holiness and social justice. The aim, surely, in any discussion about 'spirituality' is to bring healing to a world that has grown weary of and accustomed to an unholy dissociation between spirituality and morality,[5] a disconnection between life and love. In his *First Century on Love*, Maximos the Confessor writes: 'He who loves God will certainly love his neighbour as well. Such a person cannot hoard money, but will distribute it in a way befitting God, being generous to everyone in need.'[6] So let us explore some fundamental and vital concepts of the *Philokalia*. Metropolitan Kallistos spent four decades translating the text into English; let me venture some preliminary steps in an effort to translate its ancient contents into a vocabulary for our time.

I. Eschatology: 'Dying, yet behold we live'

'I expect ... the life of the age to come.' This is what the fourth-century 'symbol of faith' proclaims and what Orthodox Christians profess during every Divine Liturgy. The technical term for talk of the age to come is 'eschatology'; it is the study of the ἔσχατα ['last events']. The entire purpose of νῆψις [watchfulness][7] is prayerful vigilance in expectation of the kingdom, much like the parable of the wise and foolish virgins (see Matt. 25: 1–13) – themselves an icon of the early monks. It is essentially – if not exclusively – as wakeful and watchful prophets of the age to come that the life and spirituality of monastics can be justified.

---

5   Chapters 16 and 39, *Philokalia*, vol. 2, 54, 56. References are to the volume and page numbers of the English translation by Faber & Faber.
6   Chapter 23, *Philokalia*, vol. 2, 55.
7   The full title of the *Philokalia* is *The Philokalia of the Neptic Fathers*.

Metropolitan Kallistos has observed that our challenge in the spiritual life is:

> not primarily that we are malicious...[but] that we use only a very small part of our spiritual resources. We run our life at five percent of our full potential. We keep going in very low gear. We are not truly present where we are, gathered in the here and now, practising 'the sacrament of the present moment'.[8]

There is a succession of conviction here regarding watchfulness: Metropolitan Kallistos's observation echoes John Cassian's recollection of Antony's understanding of the Gospel teaching that 'the eye is the lamp of the body' (Matt. 6: 22).[9]

Mindfulness (or attentiveness) denotes expectation (or anticipation) of the heavenly kingdom. Most of us assume that the 'last times' or 'last things' imply an apocalyptic or escapist attitude. But we must disabuse ourselves of the medieval legacy that eschatology is somehow the last, perhaps unnecessary – certainly the most irrelevant – chapter in a manual of dogmatics. Eschatology is not primarily the teaching about what *follows* everything else in this world. It is the teaching about *our relationship* to those last things and last times. It is about the quintessential last-ness and lasting-ness of all things – the Omega defining the Alpha; this world interpreted in light of the next.

So it was my friends in the *Philokalia* who plunged me all unwitting into the essence of eschatology. In the early centuries the monastic cell became a laboratory for exploring hidden truths about heaven and earth, and about life and death, as well as a forging ground for drawing connections between the two. For, while the concept of eschatology is not explicitly developed in the desert tradition, the persistent and pronounced emphasis on remembrance of death becomes the context within which a window is opened to eternity. Those hermits of the desert and mystics of the heart observed and tested what it means to be human – with all the tensions and temptations, all of the struggle beyond survival, all of the conflict between

---

[8] From a lecture entitled 'Word and Silence in the *Philokalia*', delivered at North Park University, Chicago, February 2011.

[9] See especially *Philokalia*, vol. 1.

good and evil. And along the way, some of them may have made theological mistakes; others even entirely lost their spiritual bearings. Whoever said that there is a clear and simple answer to life's questions? Yet, these pioneers dared to push the limits, challenging and defying the norms of their age and society.

I think I received further insight into eschatology when I faced my own mortality in the brokenness of my son's cerebral palsy. The word 'eschatology' no longer seemed otherworldly; it did not focus solely on future events. I was intensely faced with the vulnerability of another human being – so intricately caught up in the last things, but here and now. The lie about heaven-being-elsewhere split wide open, something that only occurred after I admitted I was really broken. I think such incarnational self-awareness – even suffering – is part and parcel of watchfulness:

> Prior to the incarnation of the Logos of God, the kingdom of heaven was as far from us as the sky is from the earth; but when the king of heaven came to dwell amongst us and chose to unite Himself with us, the kingdom of heaven drew near to us all. The Logos of God through His descent to us has brought the kingdom of heaven close to us.[10]

Living life to the full comes only when the ultimate concerns – such as meaninglessness and death – have been honestly confronted and openly embraced. What is far more difficult, it seems, and far more important than learning to live is learning to die. Dying and loss are lessons in how to live and how to love. No wonder, then, that remembrance of death is a crucial virtue in the *Philokalia*, a daily and discernible reminder of human imperfection and vulnerability. For Evagrios: 'The monk should always act as if he was going to die tomorrow; yet he should treat his body as if it was going to live for many years.'[11] And John Klimakos is more graphic: 'Let the remembrance of death sleep and wake with you.'[12] The desert monk knew that success lay not in qualified achievement, but in unconditional

---

10 Gregory Palamas, *Topics of Natural and Theological Science* 56–7; *Philokalia*, vol. 4, 373.
11 *Texts on Watchfulness* 1, *Philokalia*, vol. 3, 53.
12 *Ladder*, Step 15, 53.

abandonment to the *eschaton*; it is eternity that enlightens and inspires all of history. If we want to go through life nice and polished, we need simply think of death. There is little outward sense of perfection in nursing homes and hospices.

II. Silence and tears: Learning to listen and love

In the age to come all words are abandoned and a new awareness or intuition arrives; silence awakens us from numbness to responsiveness. For the authors of the *Philokalia* silence is a requirement of life, the first duty of love. Silence is a way of waiting, a way of watching, and a way of noticing – rather than ignoring – what is going on in our heart and our world. It is the glue that binds our attitudes and our actions, our belief and our behaviour. Silence reflects our ultimate surrender to God as well as our gradual awakening to new patterns of learning and new perspectives of living.

In their *Directions to Hesychasts* the monks Kallistos and Ignatios quote Isaac the Syrian: 'Silence is the mystery of the future life.'[13] And they remind readers of the passage in the *Ladder of Divine Ascent*, where John Klimakos writes: 'Just as in the natural order of things, it is impossible to read books if one does not know the alphabet, it is even more impossible to practise ... silence without the work of the heart.'[14] When we are silent, we learn by suffering and undergoing, not by speculating or understanding. Silence confirms our readiness for a counter-cultural way of life, the capacity to choose rather than be led – what the Orthodox Easter service calls ἄλλης βιοτῆς ἀπαρχή [the dawn of an alternative way of life].

What we learn first and foremost in silence is that we are all mutually interdependent, that the entire world is intimately interconnected, far beyond what we could ever imagine. Nothing is self-contained; the brokenness of one person or even of any particle in nature reflects the fragility of the whole world: 'If one member suffers, all suffer together' (1 Cor. 12: 26). Any bifurcation in spirituality and reality is catastrophic.

---

13   *Treatise* 42; cited in E. Kadloubovsky and G. E. H. Palmer, *Writings*, 186.
14   *Step* 27, 46; ibid., 187.

One of the more tangible ways of expressing this vulnerability, this sensitivity, is weeping. Shedding tears is yet another means of surrendering – of dying, albeit always in the context of life and in the hope of resurrection. Tears are a way of embracing darkness in order to receive light. In the cell, monks grappled with human shortcoming and welcomed human failure as the ultimate opportunity for receiving divine grace and the sure strength that is only 'perfected in weakness' (2 Cor. 12: 9). 'First pray for the gift of tears', says Evagrios, 'so that through sorrowing you may tame what is savage in your soul. And having confessed your transgressions to the Lord, you will obtain forgiveness from Him.'[15]

Somewhere on that long trail between childhood and adulthood many of us lose touch with the vital skills that permit us to know ourselves. Part of the problem, I believe, is that we set impossible goals, which can be met only by angels. The spirituality of the *Philokalia* taught its practitioners that perfection is for God alone, that they are called neither to forego nor to forget their imperfection. Strangely, life has a way of finally catching up with us one way or another – so that we can look it in the face! So we remember – or learn – that God is discerned in the very midst of temptation, tension, and turmoil.

In this regard, tears express the beauty and mystery of being all too human. Tears are our closest companions along the way to deification, our sure escape route from death to life. They are an overture to joy and life, to compassion and love. The monks were convinced that one silent tear could advance us further in the spiritual way than any number of louder ascetic feats or more conspicuous achievements. Thus, tears signify our fragility and woundedness, the broken window through which God enters the heart, bringing healing and wholeness. 'Tears refine the dross of the heart', writes Nikitas Stithatos.[16]

They, too, are intimately connected to alertness and awareness. The silence of tears prepares the heart for self-knowledge and compassion, because knowing why we do what we do facilitates the awareness of why other people do what they do and in the end leads to the acceptance of other

---

15   Evagrios the Solitary, *On Prayer* 5–8; *Philokalia*, vol. 1, 58.
16   *On the Inner Nature of Things* 7; *Philokalia*, vol. 4, 109.

people as they are. Narcissism is not too much self, but rather insufficient knowledge of our true self. People who are self-absorbed or self-centred normally suffer from too little rather than too much self.

Silence and tears, then, are the great stabilizers in the spiritual way; they resemble a secret compass in our relationships with God, others, and ourselves. They are about being, and not simply about doing, rendering the heart acutely attentive and uniquely receptive. Through silence and tears the heart is gradually refined in the art of vigilance and virtue. Silence provides the space and the capacity to listen to and soak up what another person is conveying. In brief, it is the skill as well as the instrument whereby we acknowledge that what is going on in someone else's world truly matters. Nikitas Stithatos says: 'Tears fall on the soul like rain from heaven, cultivating love for God and compassion for others.'[17]

To adopt more technical theological jargon, it may be said that silence and tears introduce an apophatic element to the way we live, learn, and love. For through stillness and tears comes the refreshing suggestion – we could say vocation – of approaching and acknowledging others ... by 'not knowing' them. If we are fixed to our limited preconceptions or apprehensions of other people, then we may never enjoy perfect silence. When we claim to 'know' someone, we have already shut our eyes to that person's constant process of change and growth. We ultimately limit ourselves by rooting others in the past and not rejoicing in their present or potential.

III. Passions: Growing through suffering

Through silence and tears, then, we begin to notice what is happening inside us and around us. However, we do not change suddenly, magically becoming new people, our old faults forgotten. We can never run away from who we are; we never escape temptation and passion: our temper or greed, vanity or ambition, our fear or envy, resentment or arrogance. Yet passions are more than just sins, far more than mere vices. In fact, it

---

17 Nikitas Stithatos, *On the Practice of the Virtues* 32; *Philokalia*, vol. 4, 87.

Philokalia: A Vocabulary for Our Time

is hardly acceptable to speak of sin nowadays. Sin fatigue has led to the demotion and demolition of the notion of sin. To quote Richard Dawkins: 'The Christian focus is overwhelmingly on sin sin sin sin sin sin sin. What a nasty little preoccupation to have dominating your life.'[18]

In the spiritual writings of the *Philokalia*, knowing yourself means acknowledging your sins or passions, your wounds and imperfections. It implies awareness of one's behaviour, and in particular one's weaknesses. Metropolitan Kallistos has reminded us that there are two ways of understanding and responding to the passions: whether negatively and pathologically – the Stoic way – whereby passions are regarded as either a disorder or disease; or else positively and objectively – the Aristotelian sense – whereby passions are considered as either neutral or natural.[19] In his *Ascetic Discourses*,[20] Isaiah of Scetis claims that all passions – indeed, even disingenuous vices like jealousy and lascivious ones like lust – are divine gifts with a sacred purpose; they reflect our 'passionate' love for God and reveal our 'compassionate' care for God's creatures. In his *27 Texts on Guarding the Heart*, Abba Isaiah suggests the positive power of anger: 'There is among the passions an anger of the intellect, and this anger is in accordance with nature. Without anger a man cannot attain purity: he *has* to feel angry with all that is sown in him by the enemy.'[21]

Our passions can be neither denied nor concealed; potentially, they are the very resources for any hope of spiritual restoration and revitalization. When they are misdirected or distorted, the soul is divided; we are no longer whole or healed. Passions are neither quashed nor quenched; they are only fulfilled and transformed by God's loving grace. In the tearful

---

18   *The God Delusion* (New York: Bantam Press-Random House, 2006), 285.
19   See K. Ware, 'The Way of the Ascetics: Negative or Positive?', in V. Wimbush and R. Valantasis (eds), *Asceticism* (Oxford and New York: Oxford University Press, 1995), 3–15.
20   See J. Chryssavgis and P. R. Penkett (eds), *Abba Isaiah of Scetis: Ascetic Discourses* (Kalamazoo, MI: Cistercian Publications, 2002). See K. Ware, 'The Meaning of "Pathos" in Abba Isaias and Theodoret of Cyrus', *Studia Patristica*, 20 (Leuven, 1989), 315–22. For more on the healing of passions, see J. Larchet, *The Theology of Illness* (Crestwood: NY: St Vladimir's Seminary Press, 2002).
21   *On Guarding the Intellect* 1, 1; *Philokalia*, vol. 1, 22. Emphasis mine.

solitude of the heart – in our common temptations as well as in our all too human tensions – we become painfully aware of what is lacking. And it is precisely there that we are haunted by the absence of love and begin to yearn for the depth of communion.

Such self-knowledge eventually becomes a fountain of healing. Self-awareness means knowing what you think, understanding how you behave, and finally accepting others without the need to defend yourself. It is assuming responsibility without the least sense of self-justification or self-righteousness. Ultimately, the measure to which we are able to acknowledge and accept others will depend on the degree to which we can understand and tolerate ourselves. This is because we are more united to each other through our weaknesses than through our strengths; we are more like one another through our shortcomings than through our successes. As Evagrios puts it: 'The true monk regards himself as linked with everyone by always seeing himself in each.'[22] And one thousand years later, Gregory of Sinai adds: 'You will also profit if you say this to yourself: how do I know what or how many other people's sins are, or whether they are greater or equal to my own?'[23] Passions connect us to one another; they are the fertile ground for tolerating and embracing one another. Such is the essence of 'dwelling in the same space' with one another, the radical and revolutionary meaning of forgiveness as συγχώρησις.

IV. Obedience: Learning by direction

One way of recognizing the spiritual unity that binds us all is by humbly embracing the reality of our passions and weaknesses. Thus, through the centuries, lay Christians and ordained clergy, novices and monastics alike, travelled long distances in order to visit renowned elders for spiritual direction or 'a word of salvation'. It was precisely the self-knowledge of these

---

[22] *On Prayer* 125; *Philokalia*, vol. 1, 69. Recall the classic Evagrian saying: 'separated from all and united to all', *On Prayer* 124; ibid.

[23] Gregory of Sinai, *On Commandments and Doctrines*; *Philokalia*, vol. 4, 238.

elders that rendered the *abba* [spiritual father] or *amma* [spiritual mother] uniquely skilled to guide the souls of others.

Self-knowledge, then, comes from being known by another person. If there is a recurring and persistent lesson in the *Philokalia*, it is the conviction that, in order to achieve self-knowledge, we need to open ourselves in trust to another person, who comes to know us through the practice of obedience and the process of spiritual direction. Obedience is the act of listening; it is the art of listening attentively or closely (ὑπακοή). 'Listening to the teaching [of spiritual elders] as though it came from the lips of God', says Symeon the New Theologian.[24] 'So let obedience be your guide', enjoin Kallistos and Ignatios; 'or your compass, such as mariners use for plotting their course.'[25]

While the fine balance between isolation and intimacy is ultimately impossible to attain without divine grace, it is extremely difficult to sustain without sharing – or, in fact, baring – everything before a spiritual director. Through someone else's informed conviction in our self, we begin confidently to restore the solid ground within. Sharing our thoughts and temptations enables us to become familiar with the desires and conflicts that drive our behaviour. Expressing and articulating the reality of our self renders us more conscious of and caring towards others. This is why 'bearing one another's burdens' is the goal of obedience. It is also why Galatians 6: 2 is an archetypal principle in the *Philokalia*. And it reveals the art of spiritual direction as a way of love. Kallistos and Ignatios caution: 'A son who is not made to practise [bearing burdens] cannot profitably inherit the riches of his father's house.'[26]

In order to experience such love, it is necessary to allow another person, a qualified other, into the deepest and darkest recesses of the heart and mind, sharing our every thought, emotion, insight, wound, and joy with complete honesty and trust. For most people, however, this is a difficult venture. It is not easy to open up to another person, revealing the vulnerable and darker aspects of our life. Obedience goes against the grain of

---

24 *Practical and Theological Precepts* 44; *Writings*, 106.
25 *Directions to Hesychasts* 15; *Writings*, 178.
26 *Directions to Hesychasts* 16j; *Writings*, 189.

society, which champions such notions as individuality and independence. It involves much discernment and decisiveness, as well as discernment and detachment.

V. Detachment and akedia: Or, discernment and decision

Finally, the 'lovers of inner beauty' or practitioners of *philokalia* have always deeply valued the fundamental virtue of 'detachment'. For us, detachment is a concept that has lost any positive connotation. Nowadays it is predominantly used in a negative sense to signify the opposite of a healthy engagement with the world and others. It conveys a sense of aloofness, a studied remoteness that verges on indifference. Even identifying it with a monastic virtue – the first step of the monastic life – is an unfortunate reduction, which somehow resigns the rest of us to a lifestyle untouched by such abstractions. The original intuition could not be more different. In the desert, detachment meant not allowing secular values to distract us from what is most essential in our relationship with God and the world. In that respect, I would venture to contend that it is a virtue largely missing today from many monastics as well.

In fact, detachment implies paying close attention to details, even – but not limited to – the intake of food and acquisition of possessions. Not primarily for disciplinary or punitive reasons, but ultimately to discern the value of sharing and the intrinsic value of things. This sort of detachment leaves us neither unmoved nor removed; it renders us fully engaged. It is a prayer that absorbs all manner of pain, transforming it into hope. Abba Isaiah writes: 'The first virtue is detachment, that is, death in relation to every person or thing. This produces desire for God.'[27] A few centuries – and a volume of the *Philokalia* – later, Theognostos adds: 'When you are completely detached from the earthly things and when, your conscience clear, you are at any moment ready in your heart to leave this present life,

---

27 *Philokalia*, vol. 1, 27.

then you may recognize that you have acquired true virtue. If you want to be known to God, do all that you can to remain unknown to men.'[28]

For the early desert elders, detachment from everything and everyone only underlined the dignity of everything and everyone. Detachment was the first step of 'renunciation' or 'flight to the desert'. It was not, however, simply spatial or material. For detachment is not the inability to focus on *some* things; it is the spiritual capacity to focus on *all* things. It is primarily spiritual, an attitude of life.[29]

In this respect, detachment is demanding and continual refinement. The desert elders speak of stages in the way of detachment, just as there are steps in the spiritual ladder. Detachment resembles the shedding of garments of skin, until our senses are sharpened, until 'our inner vision becomes keen'.[30] For, when we learn what to *let go of*, we also learn what is worth *holding on to*. The purpose of monastic detachment is not learning how to live *apart from* the social world, but to inspire us all about how to live *in* the world as a responsible *part of* society. As Neilos the Ascetic puts it: 'Detachment is the mark of a perfect soul, whereas it is characteristic of an imperfect soul to be worn down with anxiety about material things. The perfect soul is called a "lily among thorns" (Song 2: 2), meaning that it lives with detachment in the midst of those who are troubled by such anxiety.'[31] The same purpose extends to one's attitude toward spiritual things. We are to let go of our actions, our words and finally ... even our life. The aim of letting go is learning to pray truly,[32] which is also the starting point and ending point of all action. And in this kind of prayer, the way of silence and the way of service coincide. Work is never separated from prayer; rather, prayer frees us for carefree service of others, whereby we are

---

28 *Philokalia*, vol. 2, 359.
29 In the words of Mexican-American folksinger Sixto Diaz Rodriguez: 'You measure for wealth by the things that you hold / And you measure for love by the sweet things you're told / And you want to be held in the highest regard / Your selfishness is your cardinal sin.' Lyrics to the song 'Like Janis'.
30 *Apophthegmata*, Doulas 1.
31 *Philokalia*, vol. 1, 244.
32 Evagrios, *On Prayer* 60; *Philokalia*, vol. 1, 62.

no longer conditioned by the burden of necessity but always prepared for the novelty of grace. Just as silence conditions our words, prayer conditions our works.

Thus, for example, a truly detached person cannot tolerate creating miserable poverty for the sake of accumulating exorbitant wealth. The moral crisis of our global injustice is integrally spiritual; it signals something terribly amiss in our relationship with God, people, and things. Insulated by privilege and by the sin of attachment, so many of us also remain blind to the ecological devastation created by current financial regimes. The same Neilos notes:

> Attachment to worldly things is a grave obstacle to those who are striving after holiness, and often brings ruin to both soul and body...Possessions arouse feelings of jealousy against their owners, cut off their owners from men better than themselves, divide families, and make friends hate one another. Possessions, moreover, have no place in the life to come,[33] and even in this present life have no great use. Why, then, do we abandon the service of God and devote ourselves entirely to empty trivialities?[34]

The detached person is at heart free, uncontrolled by attitudes that use the world, uncompelled by ways that abuse the world.

In light of all this, the *Philokalia* highlights the notion of ἀκηδία [despondency], originally one of the 'eight evil thoughts' of monastic spirituality, but later dropped from the medieval list of 'seven deadly sins'. However, given the historical emphasis in our world – if not also the obsession in our churches – on 'sins of the flesh', we may find it surprising that the early monks regarded lust as a lesser temptation; attachment and *akedia* were considered far worse because the last [i.e. *akedia*] involved lack of concern, which is precisely the etymological root of the word *a-kedia*. This is a fundamental lesson and caution to church leaders, who enthusiastically restrict morality to carnal vices – to sins below the monastic belt – but casually disregard the ethical aspects of politics and markets.

Often translated as 'sloth' or 'despondency', the terms 'spiritual weariness' and 'boredom' actually come closer to the original meaning of *akedia*,

---

33 Evident again is the eschatological dimension.
34 *Philokalia*, vol. 1, 207.

Philokalia: A Vocabulary for Our Time

which frustrates any attempt at translation. It marks a weighing down of mind, heart, and body, whereby one feels helpless or hopeless. The most comprehensive – almost comical – description is found in Evagrios of Pontos, who further identifies it with impatience or compulsion:

> The demon of *akedia*, called the noonday demon, is the most oppressive of all. It attacks at about 10am, tormenting the soul until about 2pm. First, it makes the sun seem to move slowly, or not at all, so that the day appears fifty hours long ... Then it compels us to look outside the window, watching the sun ... wondering if any brothers will visit. It makes us hate our place, our life and our work, imagining that no one loves us, no one can console us ... It makes us desire other places, where things are easier to acquire and where life is simpler ... It employs every device to make us abandon the good fight.[35]

Elsewhere Evagrios notes that *akedia* makes us 'stare constantly at the window; the door creeps and we jump; as we read, we yawn a great deal and soon sink into sleep; we rub our eyes and stretch out our hands; we stare at the wall and then turn away again; we read a book, count the pages and search for the conclusion, in the end snapping the book shut and either falling asleep or feeling hungry'.[36]

Akedia resembles a spiritual dead end; it is the dead point of a midsummer's daydream, when the mind is smothered, the soul slumbers and the heart almost 'suffocates'.[37] It is that time of day, when some people might consider an 'energy drink' at a trendy coffeehouse.

As for healing the 'noonday demon' – and, to adapt a contemporary song, 'it's *always* [noontime] somewhere!' – Thomas Aquinas recommends taking a nap or indulging in a warm bath; this is the supposed panacea of plain old keeping busy, keeping a full schedule! However, the remedy does not lie in *doing* something or *moving* somewhere; while engaging – and even

---

35 *Praktikos* 12. Metropolitan Kallistos has reminded us of the way in which Evagrios' disciple, John Cassian, solidified the sequence of the deadly sins. Introduction to the *Ladder of Divine Ascent* (New York: Paulist Press, 1982), 63.
36 *On the Eight Evil Spirits* 6. 14–15.
37 Evagrios, *Praktikos* 36. Gabriel Bunge speaks of an 'apparent standstill'. See *Despondency: The Spiritual Teaching of Evagrius Ponticus on Acedia* (Crestwood, NY: St Vladimir's Seminary Press, 2011), 117.

entertaining – diversions and distractions merely postpone or prolong the condition. In the ascetic way, they are considered temptations.[38] Abba Isaac the Syrian divulges the lurking dangers of such activism: 'Excessive work leads to despondency and despondency can lead to frenzy.'[39] I prefer the tested remedy of the *Philokalia*, namely patience in prayer and moderation in discipline; nothing in excess and nothing in exaggeration! Maximos the Confessor simply advises us to stand firm (cf. Luke 21: 19)![40] Perhaps above all, there remains the age-old 'philokalic' strategy of remembrance of death: what Evagrios calls becoming a 'holocaust for God'[41] – that breakdown in daily life that can lead to breakthrough in the spiritual life.

The Spiritual Way: A Language of Authenticity

While the end of the spiritual worldview (or *theoria*) in the *Philokalia* may be the vision of God (or *theosis*), the way of its contemplative writers is none other than the ascetic struggle towards self-knowledge or integrity – carved out of the ordinary experience of everyday life and perceived in the extraordinary light of the kingdom to come. It is the gradual – and, due to our stubborn resistance, often painful – process of learning to be who we are and do what we do with all the intensity of life and love.

In his letter *To the Most Reverend Nun Xenia*, Gregory Palamas observes: 'The life of the soul is authentic life.'[42] In this way, the language of the *Philokalia* defines – in a uniquely tangible and concrete manner, but at the same time in a relevant and timely manner – the theological doctrines about the original creation of the world, the divine incarnation of the Word, and the eternal kingdom that we await with fervent expectation.

---

38 Evagrios, *Letter* 27. 2; *Lausiac History*, 18 and 35.
39 *Treatise* 71; *Writings*, 208.
40 *Chapters on Love* 1. 67; *Philokalia*, vol. 2, 60.
41 Evagrios, *Letter* 61. 3.
42 Paragraph 12, *Philokalia*, vol. 4, 444.

Bibliography

Bingaman, Brock, and Bradley Nassif (eds), *The* Philokalia: *A Classic Text of Orthodox Spirituality* (New York: Oxford University Press, 2012).
Coniaris, Anthony, *A Beginner's Introduction to the* Philokalia (Minneapolis, MN: Light and Life, 2004).
Cook, Christopher, *The* Philokalia *and the Inner Life: On Passions and Prayer* (Eugene, OR: Wipf and Stock, 2012).
Smith, Allyne (ed.), Philokalia: *The Eastern Christian Spiritual Texts* (Woodstock, VT: Skylight Paths Publishing, 2006).

NIKOLAOS HATZINIKOLAOU

13 The Desert, *Hesychia*, and Ascesis: Then and Now

Let me begin by expressing my warmest wishes for the eightieth anniversary of Bishop Kallistos's birthday. May God bless you, Your Eminence, and make you worthy of continuing to see 'the light of God's person unaltered' and 'the prosperity of Jerusalem all the days of your life' (Psalm 128: 5).

Allow me also to express my profound gratitude to Dr Graham Speake and the organizers of this symposium for inviting me to honour Bishop Kallistos; yet I feel that I am the one who is being honoured in return, for, according to a Greek saying, 'in special cases, when we honour the person in honour, we actually honour the one who pays the honour'. I am thankful also for one more reason: for the specific theme of my paper. I could have been invited to write as a bishop on a theological or purely ecclesiastical or even a pastoral theme; or as a scientist to elaborate on a contemporary social or scientific subject. Instead, I was invited to write about monasticism, and I believe that the reason behind it is, on the one hand, that you feel that my episcopal office has not overshadowed my monastic vocation, and on the other, that you wish to emphasize the monastic seal of Bishop Kallistos's life, conduct, and mindset. After he became Orthodox, he followed the monastic life and was tonsured a monk on the holy island of Patmos; then he was ordained a priest, and finally he was elected a bishop of the Orthodox Church.

I believe that it is through the monastic quality of Bishop Kallistos that one can discern the fine characteristics of his inner person: those characteristics that urged him to begin his journey in the Orthodox Church with his pilgrimage to the monastery of the Revelation on the island of Patmos; to conceive the ascetic expression of Orthodoxy as this is expressed in his very early writings; to translate the *Philokalia*; to edit the well-known book *The Art of Prayer*, an analysis of the secret man of the heart with reference to the Fathers of the Church and St Theophan the Recluse; and finally to be able to listen to the echo of *hesychia* as a reflection of the Patristic wisdom and tune the Western world to the fine melody of the ascetic desert.

For this reason, I will not write here as a scholar but as a monk, namely not with my mind but with my heart.

The Meaning and Essence of the Monastic Life

Monasticism constitutes the peak of the spiritual life of our Church; it is *par excellence* the way of perfection in Christ. It is based on one's complete dedication to God and it is characterized by the extremity of its ways and aims. A monk is 'he who keeps his body in chastity, his mouth pure and his mind illumined. A monk is one who constantly constrains his nature and unceasingly watches over his senses. A monk is one who holds only to the commands of God in every time and place and matter.'[1]

Monasticism stretches the limits of human nature to the highest possible degree so that we may draw as close to God as possible. It offers man possibilities to discover his depth, to exploit and experience his divine potential, to reveal the imprints of God's image upon him and prove that he can grow according to His likeness, by transcending human measures. St Nikodimos of the Holy Mountain, who composed the beautiful service for the feast of the Athonite saints, writes that 'they were able to safeguard what is according to nature, to escape what is against nature and become worthy of the gifts which are above nature'.[2] The grandeur of human nature is concealed as a treasure within the conditions of living above one's nature. There God can be touched, His grace is revealed, His presence is confirmed, and the God-like image of man is brought to light.

---

1   St John Climacus, *The Ladder of Divine Ascent* (Boston, MA: Holy Transfiguration Monastery, 1991), Step 1, 'On renunciation of the world', 4.
2   Brotherhood of Danilaioi, *Service of the Feast of the Righteous and God-bearing Athonite Fathers* (Holy Mountain: Katounakia, 1986), 62.

This is the true aim of monasticism; it is not just living together with a group of people harmoniously, peacefully, and spiritually for a few years; it is not to learn how to do tasks fastidiously, recite prayers, perform hard ascetic struggles, or offer hospitality and comfort to pilgrims. The task of the monk is prayer of the heart, his vocation is to devote himself wholly to Christ, and his aim is to be united with God, to be deified and sanctified, 'as far as it is possible for human beings'.[3] A monk does not follow the monastic way merely because it is something good, but rather because he is called to do so by God; not because he likes it, but because he loves Him.

The father of monastics is St John the Baptist and their mother is the Mother of God; the fruits of monastic life and conduct are the numerous saints and righteous ascetics, a wonderful community of saints who lived more in heaven than on earth, who are related more to the angels than to humans, who can express themselves better in the realm of eternity than in historical time, and whose souls are more lively than their body and material being.[4]

Monasticism in the Past and in History

The life of monastic ideals is depicted in books on the lives of saintly ascetics, such as the *Gerontikon* (Lives of the Desert Fathers), the history of the monks of Egypt or *Historia Religiosa*,[5] the *Lausiac History*,[6] the *Leimon*

---

3   St John Climacus, *The Ladder of Divine Ascent*, 4.
4   'The angelic orders were amazed at your life in the flesh' (Τὴν ἐν σαρκὶ ζωήν σου κατεπλάγησαν ἀγγέλων τάγματα...), *troparion* for the feast of St Athanasios the Athonite, the father of Athonite monasticism, expressing the extreme ascesis of this Christ-like saint, whose life and grace surpassed even the measures of the angelic orders.
5   Theodoret of Cyrrhus, *Historia Religiosa*, fifth century.
6   Palladios, *The Lausiac History*, fifth century.

(Spiritual Meadow),[7] and the *Evergetinos*.[8] Moreover, the monastic ethos is expressed by the writings of ascetics during the first centuries of the Church's history, such as the works of St Ephraim the Syrian, Abba Dorotheos, and Abba Isaac, the letters of Sts Barsanouphios and John, the teachings of St Makarios of Egypt, Abba Isaiah, St Mark the Ascetic, the *Ladder* of St John of Sinai, the *Philokalia*, etc.

The foundation of cenobitic Orthodox monasticism was established by St Basil the Great in his famous works, *The Longer Monastic Rule*[9] and *The Shorter Monastic Rule*.[10] Large cenobitic monasteries, such as St Sabba, St Theodosios the Cenobiarch, and St Euthymios the Great near the city of Jerusalem, or the Stoudion monastery in Constantinople, the great Russian *lavras*, and various other coenobia on the Holy Mountain and around the world, welcomed the life of numerous monks and nuns who longed to devote themselves wholly to Christ. At the same time, other forms of monastic life also emerged, such as sketes, hermitages, *hesychasteria*, caves, etc., close to or far away from the cenobitic monasteries. Thus monastic states developed in Palestine, the Judean desert, Egypt close to the Nile, Thebais, and Mount Athos. In the Russian tradition we encounter during the second millennium the monastery of the Kiev Caves, Valamo monastery, Optina, and others. In Romania we have nowadays the descendants of Paisy Velichkovsky. At these ascetic places of spiritual struggle, known and unknown saintly ascetics were brought to light through their impressive achievements and reached the highest spiritual measures of human nature.

We, being the Church of the twenty-first century, inherited this ethos and mindset from the saints of previous centuries, such as Sts Seraphim of Sarov and Theophan the Recluse in Russia, Fr Cleopa in Romania, St Justin the New in Serbia, and Elder Joseph the Hesychast, Fr Amphilochios of Patmos, Sts Porphyrios and Paisios the Hagiorites in Greece, Fr Sophrony, the Russian theologian and ascetic, St Silouan, and so many others.

7 John Moschos, *Pratum Spirituale (Leimon)*, sixth century.
8 By monk Paul, 1054.
9 *PG* 31. 332.
10 *PG* 30. 441.

The Desert, *Hesychia*, and Ascesis

Undoubtedly, cenobitic life constitutes the spinal cord of monasticism. Within the cenobium, the ego is diminished, love is cultivated, characters are moulded, the mind is illumined with divine teachings, the soul is enlivened with frequent liturgies and services, and the desire for God is constantly rejuvenated. Through obedience, poverty, and chastity, the new man, the man in the image of Christ, is revealed. The unmarried status of monks, as such, does not designate the monastic vocation, neither does the seclusion within a monastic enclosure; nor does being together with other monks safeguard the monastic conscience and expression. What constitutes the essence of the monastic mindset is the inner life of unceasing prayer, the uncompromising struggle for the acquisition of virtues, the denial of one's own will, the departure from the world, namely the 'denial of nature for the attainment of what is above nature'.[11]

Nevertheless, in order to reach the peak of the monastic life, one has to pass through three very important stages: the desert, *hesychia* (stillness), and ascesis. These three words are set against the world, all kinds of cares and human weaknesses, and reflect the relationship between human nature and the divine in its finest form.

These words do not only refer to the desertion of our souls from our passions and our own will, or to inner stillness, to 'the hidden man of the heart, in that which is not corruptible, even the ornament of a meek and quiet spirit, which is in the sight of God of great price' (1 Peter 3: 4). They also reflect the way of life at a deserted place with absolute external stillness and natural ascesis in the name of God. David refers to this kind of desert in the Book of Psalms: 'then would I wander far off, and remain in the wilderness' (Ps. 55: 7); moreover, Abba Isaac replies to one of his disciples' question on the power of the practice of solitude by saying that 'The

---

[11] St John Climacus, *The Ladder of Divine Ascent*, 4.

practice of solitude mortifies the outward senses and quickens the inward impulses. Intercourse, however, works in the inverse way.'[12]

Throughout the years we see that the monastic tradition of our Orthodox Church is characterized by constant struggles against worldly pleasures, cares, and distractions as well as against human nature with all its weaknesses. All these stand as obstacles to attaining what is above nature, and thus monks resorted to a form of life in the desert under conditions of absolute *hesychia* and uncompromising ascesis. Allow me to refer to a few characteristic examples of such ascetics, in chronological order.

Abba Barsanouphios lived during the fourth century in total seclusion in his cell and, according to St Nikodimos of the Holy Mountain, was not seen by any human being for fifty years.[13] He did not receive visits either from his brothers (answer 346) or from any of the bishops (answer 61) or other ascetics from Egypt who asked persistently to meet him (answer 55). He only accepted visits from Abbot Seridos, who used to bring him three small loaves of bread once a week, water, and Holy Communion (answers 61, 72). One of his letters in his famous book, *Guidance towards Spiritual Life: Answers to the Questions of Disciples*, implies that his prayer encountered the prayer of two other saints before the throne of God – one was John from Rome and the other one Elijah from Corinth – and all three influenced the volition of God (answer 564).

Around the end of the fourth century we read in the *Synaxarion* of St Sara who, despite the fact that she was a woman, lived on a boat for approximately sixty years without taking even one glance at the river's water.[14]

---

12 St Isaac of Nineveh, *Mystic Treatises*, trans. A. J. Wensinck (Amsterdam: Uitgave der Koninklijke Akademie Van Wetenschappen, 1923), Homily 25, 166.
13 St Barsanouphios and St John, *Guidance towards Spiritual Life: Answers to the Questions of Disciples*, vol. 1 (in Greek, Βαρσανουφίου καὶ Ἰωάννου, *Κείμενα διακριτικὰ καὶ ἡσυχαστικά, ἐρωταποκρίσεις*) (Athens: Etoimasia Publications Kareas, 1996), 17.
14 St Nikodimos of the Holy Mountain, *Synaxarisits*, vol. 3, 14 July (in Greek, Συναξαριστής, τόμ. Γ' 14 Ἰουλίου) (Athens: Domos Publications, 2005), 335 n. 2.

In the fifth century St David of Thessaloniki remained for three years in an almond tree, enduring poor weather conditions and trials, but revealing distinct traces of his unique saintliness.[15]

The life of St Mary of Egypt is also worth noting. She lived in the Judean desert during the sixth century and was not seen by anyone for forty-seven years, according to her biographer, St Sophronios of Jerusalem.[16]

St John of the Ladder, another great ascetic of our Church, lived in the cave of Thola on Mount Sinai for forty years at the end of the sixth century. He wrote a unique book on the secret impulses of the soul, describing the virtues and passions, and tracing the path towards unity with God, based on his personal experiences during his stay at the cave.[17]

St Alypios the Stylite lived during the seventh century, standing on a pillar for fifty-three years. His ascesis was so hard that he developed sores underneath his feet, yet the blood dripping from these sores worked miracles.[18]

St Simon the Myrrhbearer, a saint of the thirteenth century, who is the founder of the monastery of Simonos Petra on the Holy Mountain, spent almost seventeen years within a damp cave located next to the monastery.[19]

Moreover, the great neptic saint of the fourteenth century, St Gregory Palamas, lived on the Holy Mountain but also at the skete of Veroia (outside the Holy Mountain) for five years, 'being destitute, afflicted, tormented', abstaining from food and water, being alone with God, praying and secretly communing with the Lord.[20]

15 Bishop Agathangelos of Phanarion, *Synaxarion of the Orthodox Church*, month of June (in Greek, Συναξαριστὴς τῆς Ορθοδόξου Εκκλησίας, Μὴν Ιούνιος) (Athens: Apostoliki Diakonia Publications, 2009), 404.
16 St Sophronios, Patriarch of Jerusalem, *Life of St Mary of Egypt* (*PG* 87C, 3716).
17 St John Climacus, *The Ladder of Divine Ascent*, p. xxxv (*PG* 88. 597).
18 Steven Runciman, *The Byzantine Theocracy* (Cambridge: Cambridge University Press, 1977), 118.
19 *Life and Conduct of our Righteous and God-bearing Father Simon the Athonite* (in Greek, Βίος καὶ Πολιτεία τοῦ Οσίου καὶ Θεοφόρου πατρὸς ἡμῶν Σίμωνος τοῦ Αθωνίτου) (Mount Athos: Holy Monastery of Simonos Petra, 1990). (<http://www.pigizois.net/agiologio/simon.../vios_simonos_athonitou.htm>).
20 Philotheos Kokkinos, *Praising Homily on St Gregory Palamas, Archbishop of Thessaloniki*, *PG* 51. 571.

In the nineteenth century another great saint, Seraphim of Sarov from Russia, prayed for a thousand nights while standing on top of a rock, transcending in this way his nature by God's grace, and receiving the light of the Holy Spirit and the fullness of grace by pleasing God.[21]

I will conclude with St Theophan the Recluse, Bishop of Tabov and then of Vladimir. He resigned after seven years from his position as a bishop and retired to the desert of Vyshen to live in total seclusion for twenty-eight years. His frequent visits to the Pechersky Lavra (monastery of the Caves) in Kiev had a major influence upon him.[22]

The lives of saints, such as those of the Kiev Caves,[23] the stylites, or the fools for Christ, provoke our admiration and amazement, and at the same time reveal the grandeur of human nature, as is shown through the life in the desert, *hesychia*, and ascesis: 'Lord, the desert shall blossom as the lily.' All these saints lived their graceful lives under very hard ascetical conditions for long periods of time, 'bringing forth fruit with patience' (Luke 8: 15) and cultivating 'the good soil'. Their lives generated wisdom, theology, and unique signs of God.

Monasticism Today

There is currently a revival of monasticism after a decline during the twentieth century. In Greece this revival started unexpectedly, after the celebration of the millennium of the Holy Mountain in 1963, whereas in the countries of Eastern Europe and in Russia it started after the fall of communism. In

---

21 Hieromonk Makarios of Simonos Petra, *The Synaxarion: The Lives of the Saints of the Orthodox Church*, vol. 3, January, February (Ormylia: Holy Convent of the Annunciation of Our Lady, 2001), 22–31.
22 Igumen Chariton, *The Art of Prayer: An Orthodox Anthology*, ed. Timothy Ware, trans. E. Kadloubovsky and E. M. Palmer (London: Faber & Faber, 1978), 12.
23 Muriel Heppell (trans.), *The 'Paterik' of the Kievan Caves Monastery* (Cambridge, MA: Ukrainian Reserach Institute of Harvard University, 1989).

these countries there is today an ongoing blossoming of monastic life and of the spiritual life in general.

In parallel, large monastic communities began to emerge in the West at the end of the twentieth century, such as the monastery of St John the Baptist in Essex, the *metochia* (dependencies) of the monastery of Simonos Petra in France, and, most impressively, the twenty monasteries and convents in the USA and Canada which were founded in less than thirty years under the spiritual guidance of Elder Ephraim, the former abbot of the holy monastery of Philotheou on Mount Athos.

Undoubtedly, the statistical findings at first glance declare a significant increase which is a matter of historical importance as well as a sign of God's great blessing. Glory to God! In our times, when the person of Christ is being constantly disputed and faith is being gradually weakened, we never expected such a blessing. Actually, we do not deserve it!

Nevertheless, there is a question that requires a well-considered reply: I wonder whether there is progress in the internal spiritual life that corresponds to this external blossoming of monasticism, which emerged in a very short time during a period of globalized impiety and decline of faith; namely, the numerical increase of monastics, the revival of old monasteries and the founding of new ones, the general enthusiasm for monastic life, the numerous books on monasticism, and the prestigious image of monasteries that impresses even the rulers of this world. How genuine is this revival and in what ways is today's monasticism similar to the traditional one? If, indeed, today's monasticism is inferior to that of the past, does this indicate a deeper change in its ethos or simply a decline in standards? I feel that this subject is very timely and motivates us to search for the truth with a *holy concern*, as Elder Paisios used to say, without being biased by the illusions of external impressions.

At first glance, the points that call for our attention in regard to Greek and Russian monasticism are of a different nature. Our societies are different, our spiritual traditions have different roots, and our history has so far followed a different course. However, we all live in an era which is characterized by a globalized mentality. This means that any social trend or disorder, psychological or whatever, is transmitted from one nation to another and influences the life of the Church, and, ultimately, affects the monastic mindset in a variety of ways, depending on the tradition and individual character of each monastery.

The people who join the monasteries come from this modern world, usually at an age when their personalities have already been formed. Education, social values, the immediate environment in which they have been brought up, the impact of the Church's teachings and principles, all have played a significant role in shaping their mindset, faith, and spiritual experiences.

Based on the above factors, let us try to give a general description of the characteristics, peculiarities, or even pitfalls of contemporary Orthodox monasticism. We will refer to some prevailing characteristics of modern society, which, however, do not absolutely define present-day monasticism; nevertheless, they threaten the future expression of monastic life in general and of ascesis and *hesychia* in particular.

Characteristics of Contemporary Monasticism

The first characteristic is the *quality of faith*. Traditional monasticism developed within a society which was of course sinful and impious but was not unfaithful. There was no question of whether God exists; rather the question was who is God and where is God. People, in general, had a fear of God and were quite open to matters of faith. The government, the structure of education, the social norms, both during Byzantine times and, later on, in the Slavonic countries, in a way respected the Church, which in turn was able to cultivate the faith. As a result, those who followed the monastic life, whether they were ordinary people or intellectuals, being humble and simple in the way they experienced their faith, were fully aware of their calling and could clearly discern their monastic yearning and prospects. Monastic perspective constituted a natural course to follow, since it emerged from a lively spiritual culture.

Today faith is often either unhealthy, or vague, or rationalized, because nowadays we learn about it from books and not from experience. Thus the kind of faith that prevails is the faith of the intellect and not of the heart; the faith of arguments and proofs and not of humble personal experiences. Our relationship with God basically is no longer an existential need but rather an ideology that we should support, a way of life that we choose to follow, or a set of church rituals that we ought to observe (prostrations, specific prayers, fasting, way of dressing, etc). The divine 'signs' have been replaced by narrations or imaginary stories, and God's presence is connected more with questions than confirmations. It is as if holiness belongs to the past; it exists so that we can just admire it and in this way strengthen our faith. It is not part of our life's perspective, and thus we find it difficult to believe that we too can become holy.

In other words, in the past, faith was an indispensable part of culture, it was like a mother tongue, whereas today it becomes like a foreign language. Consequently, monastic life gradually loses its authenticity. It is like a translation or an imitation of an older prototype.

A second characteristic of our times is the uncontrollable *intrusion of technology* in our lives. Worldliness, namely our relationship with the earthly and transient elements of life, has become extremely strong. Technology makes everything easy and desirable, even things that are unnecessary or fake. Ephemeral life has been transformed to an earthly paradise, without eternity and without God, that promises not just many things, but everything; yet, at the same time, it deceives us. This alters the meaning of life and, consequently, has an effect on all of us. At the same time, it weakens our longing for God and distorts the ascetic ethos and heroic mindset.

One of the factors that severely affects monastic mentality and life is the ease and speed of communication: cars, highways, transportation (airplanes), telephones, mobiles, audiovisual communication, internet, Skype, GPS, etc. All these, which are an indispensable part of young people's lives, threaten the conditions of the desert and *hesychia*, which are two basic pillars supporting the monastic ethos. Gradually, we all learn to live in this way. It is easy and fast to reach even the most distant monasteries without making any personal sacrifice. The pilgrims, often unable to detach themselves from the heavy burden of their worldly life, have with them their mobile, which has quick access to the internet through wi-fi, and they visit the monasteries with an iPhone, an iPad, and all kinds of i-machines! Many monasteries turn into places of pilgrimage or tourist attraction and are obliged to offer accommodation with modern facilities. Consequently, monks feel that they ought to become involved with cultural and social matters or with the needs of visitors. In general, there is a great risk that the visitors influence more the life of the monasteries than they themselves are influenced by the spirit of the monks and nuns.

As a result, monasteries lose their atmosphere of *hesychia*; the monks who are responsible for hospitality receive too much information from the outside world; in order to manage their increasing expenses, the monasteries expect the visits of pilgrims, and thus are forced in many ways to adapt their daily programme accordingly. Ultimately, monks and nuns develop a mindset which is directed more to pastoral care and tasks (*diakonia*) and less to the cultivation of inner virtues and prayer. Even hermitages have become easily accessible nowadays, a fact which has a negative effect upon the conditions of *hesychia* and silence.

A third characteristic of our times is the *volume of information* available, which most of the time is useless, sometimes unethical, and often can become even dangerous. The same applies to the form of school education. Today's young people, some of whom will eventually become monastics, have been brought up with mobiles, videos, computers, the internet, Facebook, and Twitter. Their minds are filled with a multitude of images and useless information. They have learned to do everything by just pressing a button and, therefore, are deprived of the reward of their personal accomplishment. They do not use their legs, because they go everywhere by car or use the lift. They do not use their mind, because they rely on machines. They have difficulty in discerning the inner movements of their heart, because they have learned to use only their intellect, which can memorize and rationalize, but cannot think creatively. It is rich in useless information but poor in wisdom and prudence.

This is the youngster that is representative of our times. How can a person addicted to this information culture and mentality conceive the message of the *Philokalia*? How can a dizzy mind experience miracles as signs of God, the spirit of sacrifice as the sole privilege, humility as glory, poverty as incessant wealth, prayer as 'union'[24] with God. He may eventually try the monastic life and be disappointed, or alter its essence by living in extreme ascesis without discretion, full of unhealthy desires and delusions. The whole mentality is changing.

A typical example is the difference between the monastery of the Kiev Caves and the actual caves themselves. The life in the monastery differs a great deal from the life that is reflected by the incorruptible bodies of the heroic saints who were enlightened by the uncreated light when living inside these caves. There is nothing negative about the contemporary Kiev monastery, but it has no relationship with the old caves. Worst of all, nowadays there is nothing that can be compared with the spiritual grandeur of the caves.

The same applies to the Holy Mountain. A visit to the hermitages of Karoulia or Katounakia and a comparison with old photographs convinces us of the spiritual decline of our era. Where one could find small, humble, and poor caves that provoked tears of compunction, today one sees big modern constructions with large rooms for visitors' accommodation and verandas overlooking the sea view. Those caves, that emitted a fragrance from the sweat and tears of the heroic ascetics, are now transformed into places of monastic earthly life. It is tragic to think that not only are we unable to build contemporary hermitages or live ascetically in new caves, but we cannot even respect the old ones so as to be humbled just by looking at them. It is not bad to have some comfort in everyday life or even in a monastery, but it is inappropriate to live comfortably in the most ascetic place on earth. It is totally unfitting to have a mobile communication antenna in the middle of a desert or next to a hermitage.

A fourth characteristic of our era is *consumerism*, amenities, and the variety of food and medication. All these gradually intrude in the life of monasteries and consequently create new needs. The meaning of the word 'necessity' has been altered; the way monastics deal with bodily illnesses and medical treatment has changed; and, at the same time, the meaning of life and death has been distorted. The amount of medication tends to

---

24 St John Climacus, *The Ladder of Divine Ascent*, 212.

exceed the amount of food. Quite a few monasteries on Mount Athos have heliports. This fact creates a feeling of safety: if someone falls ill, he can immediately be transferred to a hospital. And this is not an insignificant detail. Human protection and safety is undesirable in the life of true monks.[25] Death, without our realizing it, is transformed from a desirable dormition into a tragic event.

Moreover, fasting has lost its essential meaning. Large kitchens, huge dining rooms, even during the days of strict fasting, offer a variety of foods whose chemical composition complies with the rules of the Church, but whose artificial flavour contradicts the meaning of abstinence, ascesis, and naturally that of fasting.

How can all this be compared with the exemplary life of the monks in Egypt or in the Caves of Kiev that we read about in the ascetic writings? Nevertheless, many of the present-day monks were inspired by these books and it is through these books that they distinguished the echo of their calling.

The change in the way of living, namely, the *detachment from the natural world*, the lack of contact with nature, and the absence of stamina, all of which result from the urban way of life, have significantly limited the physical endurance of the young monks. They cannot tolerate too much. They cannot stand for long. They easily get tired.

On the other hand, in regard to women's monasticism, monastic life is more centred on social work, handicrafts, or farming production rather than on praying and dedicating time in the cell. What has been kept intact, however, are the services in church which are certainly very important; yet these have to be coupled with inner prayer, personal time in the cell, as well with an honest and close spiritual relationship with the elder or the abbess, in order to bear spiritual fruits in the life of nuns.

There is more to it: *secular education*, ongoing studies and exams which inevitably lead to sedentary life, competition, uncontrollable speed and

---

25   Archim. Aimilianos of Simonos Petra, *Commentary on the Ascetic Discourses of Abba Isaiah* (in Greek, *Λόγοι Ασκητικοί, Ερμηνεία στὸν Ἀββᾶ Ἡσαῖα*) (Athens: Indiktos, 2006), 193.

hastiness, develop anxiety and stress, excessive tiredness from a very young age, as well as limited mental endurance, inner pride, and arrogance.

If we add to all of the above the worldly mentality of a claim to human rights, the total decline of ethical barriers, the prevalence of self-centred attitudes, and the lack of personal sacrifice, we can easily understand why a monk who enters a monastery with these conditions in mind will eventually claim his rights, become mentally tired, and look for a change, since he will be unable to endure the eventual hardships. He will already be exhausted from the very beginning of his monastic struggle, and will find it difficult to practise obedience and come face to face with his sins. Thus he will sink into his thoughts, will start moving from one monastery to the next, will become estranged from his elder and enslaved to his own will. He will be unable to endure life in the desert, ascesis will be too difficult for him, and *hesychia* will distress him.

I will conclude with a final characteristic: *the monastic's relationship with the elder*. In some cases, there is no relationship whatsoever between a monk and his elder and as a result the monk becomes self-sufficient; in other instances, it is based on a psychological dependence on the elder and not on a free spirit of obedience; or the relationship is based on the monk's personal admiration for his elder and not the latter's spiritual guidance. This is a very delicate point and represents a pathological syndrome of contemporary monasticism which emerges from a lack of inner strength and wisdom. So, on the one hand, monks and nuns need more and more spiritual guidance, but on the other hand, there are increasingly fewer wise elders who can carry the load of their problems.

Dealing with the Present Situation

All the characteristics that we have mentioned so far are definitely set against life in the desert and basically destroy the conditions for practising *hesychia* and ascesis. Seeking conveniences and being subjected to one's own will leaves no room for ascetical struggle. Moreover, alienation from natural life is incompatible with the life in the desert. In order to overcome nature's difficulties, first you have to get to know it, to find out its secrets and particularities. In order to struggle, both body and soul ought to be in good shape. Limited endurance, fears, insecurities, along with the harshness of the desert, will be detrimental. That is why our era favours the cenobitic life rather than life in the desert.

Wherever there is easy communication, meaningless verbosity, a plethora of images, constant human interaction, as well as an unceasing flood of information, the desert or *hesychia* is completely absent. Gradually, these concepts fade away from the horizon of modern man and are only preserved in books and historical narrations or in the realm of fantasy. We think that we can understand their meaning but in essence we are totally ignorant. We neither know them, nor can we experience them. Although it seems that cenobitic monasticism is flourishing in our day, fewer monks and nuns choose to live in extreme ascesis.

In addition, worldly education that is founded on arrogance and competitiveness unfortunately 'puffs up' (1 Cor. 8: 1) and leads to the rationalization of faith. As a result, modern people have inflated brains and shrinking souls; their minds easily fill up with useless thoughts, become confused, and cannot find rest in simple faith. They lack the ethos of discipleship or the mentality of a beginner; they find it difficult to seek advice, or obey and live in *hesychia*. Mental and psychological disorders become more and more common. Education, the way of living, technology, the absence of spiritual experiences, have rendered life complex, have increased confusion, have multiplied our desires, but at the same time have weakened our volition and limited our endurance. Consequently, monastic vocations are fewer and elders are harder to find. Our era is swimming in an ocean of knowledge and information but possesses only a few drops of wisdom and prudence.

Nevertheless, although all of the above characteristics demonstrate certain weaknesses of contemporary monasticism, in no way do they affect its value. The calling alone and the decision to join the monastic life in our times have more value than at any other time in the past. For one to hear the calling of God in this noisy era means that one is open to receive spiritual messages. For one to turn one's back on the beauties and challenges of this extremely attractive world means that God dwells in one's heart.

And this is not insignificant. It is true that 'where sin abounded, grace did much more abound' (Rom. 5: 20). It is this grace that exists and that we ought to discover nowadays.

It is important, however, to learn to discern the truth of life as well as the truth of our inner self and not consider ourselves better than we actually are. Elder Paisios, a contemporary saint, used to say: 'If we want to benefit from Abba Isaac, we should not read his writings so as to imitate him. We cannot do so, for we will eventually be disappointed. We read his wise teachings so as to humble ourselves.' Perhaps we do not have the strength to imitate the life of older monks; yet we ought to study their way of living so as to humble ourselves by comparing our own life to theirs, and try to preserve their own ethos: 'Consider the outcome of their way of life, and imitate their faith' (Heb. 13: 7). If this were true, we would not alter the ethos of their conduct and we would specify with greater accuracy our own spiritual limits.

Many people believe that it is not possible to follow the ascetic life in our times. This sounds like a poor excuse that we ought to avoid. I ask your forgiveness for what I am about to say. The traditional way of monastic life, the conditions of desert and *hesychia*, are being preserved with admirable consistency by the Copts in Egypt, as well as in just a few of our monasteries and sketes. Perhaps, instead of finding excuses to ease our conscience or being disappointed, it would be better to be critical of ourselves for compromising with worldly comforts and for being alienated from the life of prayer, stillness, and ascesis. Fr Paisios managed to survive without food, to rest without sleep, to speak without interrupting his silence, to love without discretion, and to pray without distraction. He used to say that 'All monks should avoid as much as possible modern means in the operation of the monastery and should respect the desert by adapting to it. Then the desert will grant us its divine stillness and we shall be assisted in the desertion of our souls from the passions.'[26]

Moreover, we ought to bring to our minds constantly the lives of the older ascetics, which constitute our lost treasure, even if we are unable to

---

26 Elder Paisios of Mount Athos, *Epistles* (Thessaloniki: Holy Monastery of St John the Theologian, Souroti, 2002), 57.

understand it. In the absence of such spiritual experiences, let us resort to reading about them in books. These will help us acquire a correct mindset and desire for such a life, and will cultivate self-criticism and humility, which are indispensable for spiritual life.

In conclusion, let me refer to some Patristic writings on *hesychia*. St Symeon the New Theologian writes: 'Stillness is an undisturbed state of the intellect, the calm of a free and joyful soul, the tranquil unwavering stability of the heart in God, the contemplation of light, the knowledge of the mysteries of God..., the abyss of divine intellections..., intercourse with God, an unsleeping watchfulness, spiritual prayer..., and, finally... union with God.'[27]

Nikitas Stithatos describes the yearning for *hesychia* as follows:

> If you wish to see the blessings 'that God has prepared for those who love Him' (1 Cor. 2: 9), then take up your abode in the desert of the renunciation of your own will and flee the world. What world? The world of the lust of the eyes, of your fallen self (cf. 1 John 2: 16), the presumptuousness of your own thoughts, the deceit of things visible. If you flee from this world, then light will dawn for you, you will see the life that is in God, and the medicine of your soul – that is tears – will swiftly well up in you ... In this way, living in the world and among people, you will be like a man living in the desert and seeing no one.[28]

When our soul is touched by this kind of ascetic life, we may not have the strength to make the decision to flee from this world, yet we may become humbled. Humility is greater than ascesis. The secret meaning of the desert and *hesychia* is described in the *Philokalia*: 'Stillness, which is the basis of the soul's purification, makes the observance of the commandments relatively painless. It has been said: Flee, keep silence, be still, for herein lie the roots of sinlessness.'[29]

---

27   Nikitas Stithatos, *On the Inner Nature of Things* 64; *Philokalia*, trans. G. E. H. Palmer, P. Sherrard, and K. Ware, vol. 4 (London: Faber & Faber, 1995), 125.
28   Nikitas Stithatos, *On the Practice of the Virtues* 75, 98–9.
29   St Peter of Damascus, *Book 1: A Treasury of Divine Knowledge*, 64; *Philokalia*, trans. Palmer, Sherrard, and Ware, vol. 3 (London: Faber & Faber, 1984), 89.

Nevertheless, salvation and sanctification are not achieved only through ascesis and *hesychia* but also through *diakonia* and communion. Living in communion with each other within a monastic community may be equally beneficial.

We read in the writings of Evagrios of Pontos: 'Blessed is the monk who in all joy looks with pleasure upon the salvation and progress of all as he would his own. Blessed is the monk who considers all people as God after God. A monk is one who is separated from all and united with all. A monk is one who esteems himself as one with all people because he ever believes he sees himself in each person.'[30]

A few months ago I came across a small pamphlet issued in 1851 by the monastery of the Caves of Kiev with the title *Small Booklet of Monastic Life*. Reading this practical, simple, well-balanced booklet, one can see how the aim of each monk is clearly defined: he who has renounced such things as marriage, possessions, and other worldly pursuits is outwardly a monk, but may not yet be a monk inwardly.[31] This struggle to become a monk inwardly is summarized in twenty short chapters by the unknown Russian writer, who was obviously a monk, by presenting in a few words and with simple and practical sayings the main principles of the monastic life. Holiness is not only a result of contemplation but is also a fruit of *praxis*.

This was the struggle then, this is the struggle now: it will always be the same, unchangeable. We are also called to fight this struggle today, even if we cannot reach the ascetic achievements and measures of the past. It does not matter. Instead, we can cultivate divine zeal and humility. These virtues apply to every period of time. Abba Ischyrion said that 'In the last days, people will not have the strength to struggle spiritually. But when they will face temptations and fight against them, they will be proven superior

---

30   Evagrios of Pontos, *The Great Ascetic Corpus*, trans. Robert E. Sinkewicz, Oxford Early Christian Studies (Oxford: Oxford University Press, 2006), 206 (*PG* 79. 1193).
31   St Maximos the Confessor, *Four Hundred Chapters on Love*, no. 50; *Philokalia*, trans. Palmer, Sherrard, and Ware, vol. 2 (London: Faber & Faber, 1981), 106 (*PG* 90. 1060A-B).

to us and even to our forefathers.'[32] Therefore, what is worthwhile is not so much ascesis and *hesychia per se*, as it is to have patience and endurance in times of temptations.

I will conclude with some words that Fr Paisios used to repeat quite often: 'The few achievements that the faithful of the last days will manage to accomplish in their spiritual life will be worth more than the many achievements of the faithful in the older times. It is not so necessary to correct our monastic way of life as it is to cultivate inner watchfulness' (my translation).

Bibliography

Chariton, Igumen, *The Art of Prayer, An Orthodox Anthology*, ed. Timothy Ware, trans. E. Kadloubovsky and E. M. Palmer (London: Faber & Faber, 1978).
Evagrios of Pontos, *The Great Ascetic Corpus*, trans. Robert E. Sinkewicz, Oxford Early Christian Studies (Oxford: Oxford University Press, 2006).
Paisios of Mount Athos, Elder, *Epistles* (Thessaloniki: Holy Monastery of St John the Theologian, Souroti, 2002).
Palmer, G. E. H., P. Sherrard, and K. Ware (eds), *The Philokalia*, 4 vols (London: Faber & Faber, 1979–95).
Runciman, Steven, *The Byzantine Theocracy* (Cambridge: Cambridge University Press, 1977).
St Isaac of Nineveh, *Mystic Treatises* (Amsterdam: Uitgave der Koninklijke Akademie).
St John Climacus, *The Ladder of Divine Ascent* (Boston, MA: Holy Transfiguration Monastery, 1991).

---

32   P. V. Paschou, *Sayings of the Desert Fathers* (in Greek, Τὸ Γεροντικόν, ἤτοι Ἀποφθέγματα Ἁγίων Γερόντων) (Athens: Astir Publications, 1970), 58.

JOHN BEHR

14 Patristic Texts as Icons[1]

It is my great pleasure to contribute this essay in honour of Metropolitan Kallistos. There is one particular 'word' of his that I heard during my studies with him which has remained with me ever since, and that I would like to expand upon here: that is, that we should approach the writings of the Fathers, their texts, as icons. I will begin by reflecting on how the Fathers were read during the last century in both Orthodox theology and academic theology more generally, and then suggest how thinking of Patristic texts as icons might take us further in understanding the nature or character of theology itself.

The 'Neo-Patristic Synthesis': Its Genesis and Its Limitations

It would be impossible to think of Orthodox theologians reading the Fathers in the twentieth century and not also to think, immediately, of the 'return to the Fathers' and the 'neo-Patristic synthesis'. This, of course, was one of the expressions in which Orthodox theology (and other areas, such as liturgy, spirituality) was being reborn in the twentieth century, entering a new, creative, and fertile period of life. The pangs of this rebirth involved political upheaval and exile, and problematic relations with various 'others' as a new identity was forged. The account of this rebirth that

[1] Parts of this essay have already appeared in print as 'Reading the Fathers Today', in J. Mihoc and S. Aldea (eds), *A Celebration of Living Theology: Festschrift for Fr Andrew Louth* (London: T. & T. Clark, 2014), 7–19.

became all but canonical for most of late twentieth-century Orthodoxy is one of liberation, struggle, and retrieval, involving a number of émigré theologians, the two main protagonists being, of course, Frs Sergei Bulgakov (1871–1944) and Georges Florovsky (1893–1979). Exiled in the West, the émigré theologians were liberated from the 'Western captivity' of Eastern Orthodox theology and its 'pseudomorphosis'. Along with rejecting their own 'Westernized' past, Florovsky and others also felt compelled to counter the continuing 'Western' influence in Russian religious philosophy, having its roots in the encounter of the nineteenth-century Slavophiles with German Romanticism but manifest contemporaneously, and most dramatically, in the sophiology of Bulgakov.

In and through these struggles, the émigrés in the West saw themselves (just as did their Western counterparts likewise) as returning to the Fathers, to the authentic source of true theology, with the aim that in so doing they themselves would be able to address the existential questions of their own contemporary world. A 'neo-Patristic synthesis' was thus forged, an authentically Orthodox style of theology based upon the Fathers rather than any outside influence. The strength and vitality of this creative approach, as well as the persuasiveness of its self-narrative, is seen in the fact that it has simply been assumed as an unquestioned and unquestionable given by the vast majority of Orthodox theologians in the latter half of the past century: it was taken as the only framework within which to theologize in an Orthodox manner.

But, all the tremendous fruit produced during these years notwithstanding, the persuasive rhetoric of the neo-Patristic synthesis is no longer able to convince as easily as it had done in the past, nor cover over the weaknesses of its own account, methodology, and self-understanding. Looking back now, across the gap of a change in century, we are perhaps in a better position to take a critical re-evaluation of this rebirth, the identity that it constructed, and its limitations. The renewed appreciation for Bulgakov in recent decades has, on the one hand, provided a more sympathetic reading of Bulgakov's sophiology, and his own reading of the Fathers, and, on the other hand, it has opened new insights into the genesis of Florovsky's 'neo-Patristic synthesis', and in so doing, enables a critical assessment of the dominant paradigm.

It has been pointed out that Florovsky's criticism of Russian religious philosophy was in fact only a part of his broader argument against Western theology as a whole following the great schism, which never degenerated, however, into a polemic against the 'West' as it did in others.[2] The common tradition of the undivided Church, Florovsky claimed, was that developed by the Greek Fathers (amongst whom he included Augustine) as a Christian Hellenism, and which remains preserved intact in Eastern Orthodoxy. Already in 1936, the year before his *Ways of Russian Theology* appeared, and building upon themes present even earlier in his pre-theological phase, Florovsky urged those present at the First Pan-Orthodox Congress of Theologians held in Athens to return to their roots, emphasizing that this does not mean a return to dead texts but to the 'creative fire of the Fathers, to restore in ourselves the Patristic spirit', to establish a 'continuity of lives and minds' with the Fathers. Their work, he further claimed, established a 'new Christian Hellenism' which has become a 'standing category of Christian existence', so that any aspiring theologian must enter a 'spiritual Hellenism... Let us be more Greek to be truly Catholic, to be truly Orthodox.'[3]

The return to the Fathers in this way, Florovsky insisted in a number of articles over the following years, should never degenerate into a 'theology of repetition'.[4] 'It is a dangerous habit', he said in a memorable passage, '"*to quote*" the Fathers, that is, their isolated sayings and phrases, outside that of the concrete setting in which only they have their full and proper meaning and are truly alive. "*To follow*" the Fathers does *not* mean just "*to quote*" them. "To follow" the Fathers means to acquire their "mind", their

---

[2] Brandon Gallaher, '"Waiting for the Barbarians": Identity and Polemicism in the Neo-Patristic Synthesis of Georges Flovosky', *Modern Theology*, 27 (2011), 659–91; and, more broadly, Paul L. Gavrilyuk, *Georges Florovsky and the Russian Religious Renaissance*, Changing Paradigms in Historical and Systematic Theology (Oxford: Oxford University Press, 2014).

[3] Georges Florovsky, 'Patristics and Modern Theology', *Diakonia*, 4: 3 (1969), 227–32 (229–30).

[4] Georges Florovsky, 'St Gregory Palamas and the Tradition of the Fathers', in idem, *Bible, Church, Tradition*, Collected Works, 1 (Vaduz: Büchervertriebsanstalt, 1987), 105–20, 127 (notes) (111).

phronema.'[5] In another piece, written towards the end of his life, Florovsky likewise emphasizes how the Fathers themselves, in their own appeal to tradition, were appealing to 'the mind of the Church, her *phronema*', something which could only 'be attested and confirmed by an universal *consensio* of Churches', however difficult this is to establish.[6] Moreover, he says, 'it was precisely the *consensus patrum* which was authoritative and binding, not their private opinions or views ... this *consensus* was much more than just an empirical agreement of individuals. The true and authentic *consensus* was that which reflected the mind of the Catholic and Universal Church.'[7]

It may well have been the sophiologists' own claim to precedent in the Fathers, and especially Palamas, that prompted Florovsky to turn to the Fathers. It is certainly evident that Florovsky deployed his appeal to the 'mind of the Fathers' to construct a neo-Patristic synthesis, his Christian Hellenism, in opposition to the 'Westernized' religious philosophy of Bulgakov and others. It is less evident, but no less the case however, that in doing so Florovsky drew from the same well-spring of Romanticism and Idealism. His habitual recourse to experiential categories (such as 'mind', 'experience', 'vision') attributed to various subjects (especially 'the Fathers' and 'the Church') is not supported by way of a sustained explication of such notions in any particular Father or Fathers,[8] but, as has been pointed

---

5   Florovsky, 'Palamas', 109, italics original.
6   Georges Florovsky, 'The Authority of the Ancient Councils and the Tradition of the Ancient Fathers' [1967], in idem, *Bible, Church, Tradition*, 93–103, 126–7 (notes) (98–9).
7   Florovsky, 'The Authority of the Ancient Councils', 103.
8   The Fathers certainly speak from their experience of Christ, but they do not appeal to this experience to justify their theological assertions. J. Romanides ('Critical Examination of the Applications of Theology', in S. Agouridès (ed.), *Deuxième congrès de théologie orthodoxe* [Athens, 1973], 413–42) appeals to St Gregory the Theologian's words in *Or.* 28 as such an appeal, missing the force of such rhetoric, which Gregory deploys to lead his audience to realize that they cannot do so but 'must start again'. Cf. J. Behr, *The Nicene Faith*, Formation of Christian Theology, 2 (Crestwood, NY: St Vladimir's Seminary Press, 2004), 334–42.

out, derives from the Romanticism of Schelling, mediated through Möhler and Kireevsky.[9]

Not that we therefore need to purge this last remaining trace of supposed Western influence to arrive at an even more purified Orthodoxy. Identity is constructed through difference; difference which need not degenerate into opposition, but rather work though mutual influence, as a symphony of voices, rather than an attempt at monotony. But, being more conscious of the categories deployed in the construction of the 'neo-Patristic synthesis', we can be more alert to the methodological and hermeneutic weakness in the appeal to 'the mind of the Fathers', which is that making such notions the primary point of reference effectively negates any need for careful, disciplined, and patient reading of any actual text of the Fathers: the point is not to quote the Fathers, but to acquire their mind. Their particular differences are not ignored, but neither are they in view: it is the consensus of the Fathers, their *phronema*, that is important. Any differences between them are also likewise elided: differences are recognized, but the particular voice of each Father is not important, for what alone is 'authoritative and binding' is their consensus, expressing 'the mind of the Catholic and Universal Church'.

Already in 1937 Bulgakov had noted that treating the Fathers in this way would be a rather 'rabbinic approach' to their writings, smoothing out and harmonizing differences between them as the Talmud does with different rabbis.[10] Rather than appealing to the 'mind' of the Fathers, Bulgakov himself focused much more explicitly on their 'writings', granting them a 'guiding authority', though not infallibility, and emphasizing that they need to be 'understood within their historical context'. For Bulgakov, this means that the authority of their writings is necessarily bounded by certain limitations, which, he claims, 'is much more greatly felt, of course, when it comes to their scriptural exegesis, which was utterly bereft of the modern

---

9   Gallaher, '"Waiting for the Barbarians"'.
10 Bulgakov, 'Dogma and Dogmatic Theology' [1937], in M. Plekon (ed.), *Tradition Alive: On the Church and the Christian Life in our Time: Readings from the Eastern Church* (Lanham, MD: Rowman and Littlefield, 2003), 67–80 (70).

hermeneutics of textual and historical scholarship'.[11] This is a revealing side comment, a point to which I will return later in a different context.

Florovsky also knew that the words of the Fathers have to be contextualized, and stated his position trenchantly: it is, we have heard him say, 'a dangerous habit *"to quote"* the Fathers, that is, their isolated sayings and phrases, outside of the concrete setting in which only they have the full and proper meaning and are truly alive'. It is indeed a dangerous habit only 'to quote' the Fathers, to repeat the phrases and sayings we all know so well. One must indeed pay careful attention to the context of these words and sayings. But for Florovsky, this context is primarily the 'mind', 'vision', or 'experience' of the Fathers, the 'mind of the Catholic Church', *not* the particular historical situation of each Father, the struggles in which they were engaged, and the unique witness, in all its particularity, that each bore.

Academic Patristic Scholarship

Now, if there is one lesson which academic Patristic scholarship of the past century, especially the last decades, has taught us, it is that disciplined, historical study – the fruit of the enlightenment – is indeed necessary. However, this scholarship has its own genealogy, with its own problematics, especially in the way in which its increasing specialization has corresponded to (or caused) an increasing fragmentation, to the point that it is no longer clear at all that different areas belong to a common discipline of theology, and what such a discipline might be: what is theological about theology?

Borrowing from Edward Farley,[12] one could say, in admittedly broad strokes, that for the first millennium and more, theology was pursued by the contemplative reading of Scripture in the context of the school of liturgy and in the tradition of the Fathers. But during the course of the

11 'Dogma and Dogmatic Theology', 71.
12 E. Farley, *Theologia: The Fragmentation and Unity of Theological Education* (Augsburg: Fortress, 1994).

second millennium, this *paideia* fell apart (East and West): the practice of *sacra pagina* became the discipline of *sacra doctrina*, in which passages of Scripture were accumulated in support of dogmatic points, the *loci communes*, which then took on a life of their own, as the building blocks for dogmatic theology, resulting in handbooks of dogmatic theology, that in turn provided the categories used in the study of Church history and the Fathers, while the study of Scripture proceeded along other lines altogether.

Almost invariably the textbooks of these subjects divide up the early centuries into distinct periods corresponding to modern systematic categories. For instance, the 'Trinitarian' debates of the fourth century were followed by the 'Christological' debates of the following centuries, assuming that 'Trinity' and 'Incarnation', as we now understand these terms, are given categories of theological reflection whose history we can trace as various Fathers worked towards a more perfect understanding of these elements of the Christian faith (or at least, what it is that we think we know). The theological reflection of the Fathers is thus divided into a range of distinct topics – God, Christ, creation, salvation, Mariology, ecclesiology, and so on, each of which is treated as discrete, even if overlapping – so that one can compare or synthesize any of these elements as treated by different Fathers without the necessary task of examining how any given Father held all these elements together, if indeed they were ever thought of as being distinct to begin with.

Under the shadow of Harnack, much work was carried out on the history of dogma, as an overarching narrative of theological development or the Christian tradition; or summaries of this, such as that staple of all students of the early Church in the second half of the last century, J. N. D. Kelly's *Early Christian Doctrine*, which gathers together, thematically, what different writers have to say about any given topic, with the result that the reader is not introduced any particular figure, nor how these different aspects fit together in the thought of any one writer.[13] The manuals of Patrology did introduce the Fathers in their particularity – snapshots of their lives, their

---

13   J. N. D. Kelly, *Early Christian Doctrines*, 5th edn (San Francisco: Harper, 1978 [1958]).

literary remains, and so on – but almost invariably the summary of their theology is presented in terms of the history of dogma.

Of course, one cannot indeed treat everything at once. But dividing up the work in this manner presupposes that the theology of those being presented is amenable to being dissected in this way – what they thought of God, of Christ, of the human being; how they practised scriptural exegesis; etc – what have come to be standard theological loci, without considering the coherence of all this, *as theology*.

A rather glaring example of this problematic in a monograph devoted to a particular locus – that of the Trinity – is evidenced by Richard Hanson in his mammoth tome, *The Search for the Christian Doctrine of God*. In an article written shortly after the publication of this work, summarizing his findings, Hanson asserts that the 'Trinitarian doctrine' elaborated in the fourth century was, in his words, 'a solution, *the* solution, to the intellectual problem which had for so long vexed the church'.[14] The problem perplexing the Church was, thus, an intellectual one: that of establishing the doctrine of the Trinity. Yet this is, for Hanson at least, a task separable from the exegetical practices of those whom he studied, for, as he puts it, in the conclusion to the work itself, 'The expounders of the text of the Bible are incompetent and ill-prepared to expound it. This applies as much to the wooden and unimaginative approach of the Arians as it does to the fixed determination of their opponents to read their doctrine into the Bible by hook or crook.'[15]

He then continues with this even more perplexing statement:

> It was much more the presuppositions with which they approach the Biblical text that clouded their perceptions, the tendency to treat the Bible in an 'atomic' way as if each verse or set of verses was capable of giving direct information about Christian doctrine apart from its context, the 'oracular' concept of the nature of the Bible, the incapacity with a few exceptions to take serious account of the background and

---

14 Richard P. C. Hanson, 'The Achievement of Orthodoxy in the Fourth Century AD', in R. Williams (ed.), *The Making of Orthodoxy: Essays in Honour of Henry Chadwick* (Cambridge: Cambridge University Press, 1989), 142–56 (156).
15 Richard P. C. Hanson, *The Search for the Christian Doctrine of God: The Arian Controversy, 318–381* (Edinburgh: T. & T. Clark, 1988), 848.

circumstances of the writers. *The very reverence with which they honoured the Bible as a sacred book stood in the way of their understanding it.* In this matter they were of course only reproducing the presuppositions of all Christians before them, of the writers of the New Testament itself, of the tradition of Jewish rabbinic piety and scholarship.[16]

Their exegetical practice is simply wrong, even if it a practice going back to the Apostles themselves and their proclamation of the Gospel, a manner of exegesis moreover shared with the rabbis, and which was, in fact, the common approach to sacred texts in antiquity.[17] And, more perplexingly, this was also the exegetical practice within which the doctrine of the Trinity was elaborated and has its meaning.

Hanson clearly has no time for the exegetical practices of the theologians of this period by which they reached their conclusions: reading the Scriptures – the Law, the Psalms, and the Prophets – as speaking of Christ. For Hanson, the doctrine of the Trinity was an 'intellectual problem' that was resolved in the fourth century, and which can now simply be called upon as a given of Christian theology, leaving the following centuries to establish Christological doctrine, the next chapter of modern dogmatic textbooks.

Hanson never, as far as I am aware, addressed the question of what happens when one takes these supposed core theological elements out of the context in which they were composed – the practice of reading Scripture and the celebration of liturgy within which they had meaning – and places them in another context, in this case that of systematic theology and a reading of Scripture that focuses on the historical context of each verse, rather than seeing Scripture as the book of Christ. Neither for that matter was this question addressed by Bulgakov, who, as we saw earlier, while insisting that the Fathers were to be understood in their historical context, lamented the fact that their scriptural exegesis was utterly bereft of the insights of modern historical scholarship.

16   Hanson, *Search*, 848–9, italics mine.
17   Cf. J. L. Kugel, *Traditions of the Bible: A Guide to the Bible as it was at the Start of the Common Era* (Cambridge, MA: Harvard University Press, 1998), 14–19.

With this fragmentation within the study of the Fathers, it is not surprising that over the last decades of the past century the specialized discipline of Patristics became untethered from its moorings in theology to become the study of Late Antiquity, in which all too often the Patristic writings are mined for anything else other than theology.

Reacting to this, and bringing us back to texts, is the book by Elizabeth Clark, *History, Theory, Text: Historians and the Linguistic Turn*,[18] which has become a standard treatment of the discipline of reading historical, especially, Patristic texts, and how that has changed over the past century. After reviewing changes in patterns of historiography over the nineteenth and twentieth centuries, she turns her attention to what these changes mean for the study of pre-modern texts. She notes how, in her own graduate education, '"Patristics" … was a theologically oriented discipline that centered largely on the Church Fathers' Trinitarian and Christological expositions against "heretics". To bring ancient philosophy into relation with theology was as broad a disciplinary reach as I could then imagine would be professionally viable.' But she then notes,

> The social revolutions of the late 1960s merged in the 1970s with social science approaches that were implicitly (and sometimes overtly) aimed at undercutting the dominance of theology in the study of early Christianity – and in the years thereafter, cultural approaches were added in. Social formations, women, the poor, 'heretics', and sexuality now were deemed suitable topics for investigation.[19]

This was not so much an extension of the field of theology, to see how it could change the world, as, in her words, an escape: 'The race for social science provided an escape from a narrow philological and confessionally oriented theological orientation.'

Yet she notes that these changes, intriguingly, remained oblivious to the 'literary/theoretical currents' at work refashioning departments of literature. Looking back several decades later, it has become clear to her that a basic point was neglected in this hasty refocusing on issues deriving from social studies: 'Overlooked in the rush for realignment was a point not then

---

18   Cambridge, MA: Harvard University Press, 2004.
19   Clark, *History*, 160.

Patristic Texts as Icons

so obvious: that we do not possess the types of documents on which social historians of modernity work, but highly literary/philosophical texts that lend themselves well to theoretical analysis.'[20] The opening of new horizons – 'our attention to grids and groups, networks, liminality, and "thick description"' – nevertheless produced new insights and understanding, and so, she adds, 'I would not wish to return Patristics to its traditional disposition.' But, she continues, 'Nonetheless, these social-scientific appropriations obscured the fact that scholars of late ancient Christianity deal not with native informants, nor with masses of data amenable to statistical analysis, but with texts – and texts of a highly literary, rhetorical, and ideological nature.'[21] She thus proposes a return to dealing with the matter in hand – texts; and texts which possess a 'highly literary, rhetorical, and ideological nature'. But, significantly, not texts that evidence a theological concern.

As it is with texts that students of the Fathers deal, these texts 'should be read', she comments, 'first and foremost as literary productions before they are read as sources of social data'. Only, again in her words, by 'joining theoretical to social-scientific and theological-philological analyses' will we be able to 'enrich the field'.[22] As such, 'late ancient Christian studies' must, she argues, 're-envision' themselves as 'a form of the new *intellectual* history, grounded in issues of material production and ideology, that has risen to prominence in the late twentieth century'.[23] Not discounting the insights given by all the other historical disciplines, what should be of most concern for us, Clark asserts, are 'issues of recent theory that pertain to *texts*'. And here she would urge us to concede no ground whatsoever to contemporary theorists – she mentions Jacques Derrida, Fredric Jameson, and Jean-François Lyotard – who 'have lately appropriated for their own purposes the rich texts of late Christian antiquity'.[24] As intellectual historians, scholars of late ancient Christianity enjoy an advantage, she claims,

20   Ibid., 158.
21   Ibid., 159.
22   Ibid., 159.
23   Ibid., italics original.
24   Ibid., 161.

because it is their very profession to 'work with literary texts of a highly rhetorical and ideological nature'.[25]

Now, this call to an 'intellectual history', attuned to the textual nature of its material, is indeed salutary. We can never forget that the material which we study, when reading the Fathers, is literary – texts of different genres, rhetorically structured in diverse ways, serving a multitude of purposes. If 'Patristics' had been mining these texts for particular topics – Trinity, Christology, etc. – we do indeed need to be reminded that we need to learn to read the texts themselves first, paying attention to their concerns, how they work, the rhetoric they employ, how they hold together scriptural exegesis and dogmatic reflection, if one can even speak of the latter as being something distinct from the former.

But what of theology? Clark assures us, in her words, that 'Theology has not been abandoned, but finds a welcome place in this reconfiguration of late ancient Christian studies.'[26] However, in Clark's recounting of the development of the discipline, 'theology' only appears together with philology, as when she notes how the social sciences challenged the 'narrowly philological and confessional oriented theological orientation', and when she urges us to filter everything through critical theory – 'joining theoretical to social scientific and theological-philological analyses' – to enrich the discipline.[27]

'Theology', for Clark, is a matter of Trinitarian and Christological expositions, directed against the 'heretics', and works together with philology and on a philological level (presumably because that is, after all, what the texts speak about). Such theology can still find a place, but it must be subsumed, she argues, under the critical theory that gives a new intellectual history its legitimacy.

But is there indeed room for theology when reading the Fathers in terms of a newly minted, critically attuned, 'intellectual history'? What kind of theology would it be? And what would make it 'theological'?

25 Ibid., 161–2.
26 Ibid., 161.
27 Ibid., 158–9.

The Symphony of the Fathers

Theology, as a unified discipline or *paideia*, has clearly fractured into a number of discrete fields. But, I would suggest, this is not cause for lament, for it also means, in reverse, that within each field a phenomenal amount of scholarship has been expended, erudite volumes produced, and a depth of knowledge attained. And in this way, the spell of a 'harmonization' of history from our own perspective is broken, so that we can begin to 'hear' again each historical witness faithfully.

However, to do so *as theology* requires a creative moment of reintegration. The 're' here, in 'reintegration', is not meant to suggest that we need to return to a lost golden age of (Eastern) theological purity: the past is gone; we stand at this moment of history and no other, and the past was never 'pure' anyway.

One way in which this might be accomplished may well be through a return: returning, now with all of our more historically informed knowledge, to reconsider that which we are perennially tempted to forget – how it was that we first learned the language of Christian theology. For theology does have its own discourse, its own language. But, as Rowan Williams notes, 'Theology ... is perennially tempted to be seduced by the prospect of bypassing the question of how it *learns* its own language.'[28] And here, naturally, the Fathers, especially those of the early centuries, the beginning of the discourse, are in fact of primary help, as those who first began to speak this language, to play this particular language game, as it were, in Wittgensteinian terms, before dogmatic language became detached from exegetical practice, and both from liturgy.

If we are to understand, today, the unity of the (singular) discipline of theology *as theology* – which is, it seems to me, our greatest challenge – the task is before us to learn how to hold together the depth of historical knowledge that we now have *as theology*: not simply as a monolithic consensus ('the mind of the Fathers'), nor the disclosure of a transcendent

---

28 R. Williams, *On Christian Theology* (Oxford: Blackwell, 2000), 131.

subject (the 'mind of the Church'), nor simply as stepping stones to our own systematic theology (whatever that might be), nor as any discourse which happens to use the word 'God' – as if theology were simply speaking *about God*, in a manner analogous to the way in which, for instance, those who study 'geology' speak about the world if for no other reason than God is not subject to our scrutiny, to be merely spoken *about*, described in abstract, uninvolved terms.[29] Nor, less presumptuously, can theology simply be a philological reading of texts in which the word 'God' appears; for if such philological reading is to be subsumed under an intellectual history attuned to critical theory, are its presuppositions such as to allow theology to be *theology*?

Rather what we have before us (or rather behind us) is a history of concrete, historically situated Christians, bearing witness to, and embodying, their faith in Christ until he comes again, a witness embodied in texts and only available to us as texts. The site of the theologian is both undoubtedly historical and inescapably exegetical: standing between the definitive act of God in Christ and his return, patiently and dialogically learning to hear the Word of God, to encounter the risen Christ, in the opening of the Scripture and the breaking of the bread in a history of witnesses to this encounter and a tradition of such practices; hearing how particular Fathers wrote theology, in a variety of contexts – apologetic, anti-heretical, homiletic, poetic – employing a variety of exegetical practices to proclaim Christ in accordance with the Scriptures; making claims *about* creation, human beings, and the work of God, and making claims *upon* their hearers, and bringing all under the sign of the Cross, driven by the tension of the already-but-not-yet.

The history of theology is perhaps best thought of, to adapt an image of Irenaeus, in terms of a symphony, the coming together of many distinct voices in the praise of God; a symphony comprised of different voices throughout time, each lending itself to the melody being played, with

---

[29] Cf. J. Behr, 'What are we doing speaking about God: The Discipline of Theology', in Aristotle Papanikolaou and Elizabeth Prodromou (eds), *Thinking through Faith: New Perspectives from Orthodox Christian Scholars* (Crestwood, NY: SVS Press, 2008), 67–87.

different timbres and tonalities, inflections and themes, and each in turn being shaped by the symphony. In their preaching, bound up as this is with the interpretation of Scripture, these figures were all part of the same symphony, with all the diachronic and synchronic diversity that this entails. This symphony moreover is both public and continuously unfolding, in contrast to those who, from time to time, prefer to play their own tunes. Such discordant voices certainly continue, nevertheless, to influence voices sharing in the symphony; but they do so as ones who have separated themselves from the symphony of the one body of Christ. Speaking theologically, moreover, this symphony is not, therefore, constructed by any individual voice or all the voices together but is governed by its own rhythm and rules, so that, to use Irenaeus' words, it is God who 'harmonizes the human race to the symphony of salvation' (*Haer.* 4. 14. 2).

Reading the Fathers 'symphonically' in this way, then, attunes *us* to the melody that is theology. But rehearsing the symphony, as it has been played to this date, is not yet to do theology; that would only begin when, having read attentively through the score of earlier movements, we take our own part in the only going symphony. It is noteworthy that those who have taken this further step in the twentieth century – such as von Balthasar or more recently Zizioulas – have been accused of transgressing disciplinary boundaries. Balthasar was criticized for being too much influenced by contemporary questions, resulting in a certain 'eclecticism' and 'ahistoricism' in his 'audaciously creative' utilization of Patristic texts.[30] Zizioulas, likewise, has been criticized for being unduly influenced by modern, existential, philosophy, and for giving an inadequate reading of the Fathers, though in his case it would seem to result from a perceived need to stay within the realm of 'Patristic theology', to claim that his understanding of the 'person' is already developed in the work of the Fathers, and so laying claim to legitimacy and authority in this way, rather than clarifying the nature of the discourse of theology within which he would work as a systematic theologian.

---

30   Cf. Brian Daley, 'Balthasar's Reading of the Church Fathers', in Edward T. Oakes, SJ, and David Moss (eds), *The Cambridge Companion to Hans Urs von Balthasar* (Cambridge: Cambridge University Press, 2004), 202.

There is indeed no reason simply to repeat what certain Fathers have said, but if one is not going to rehearse, with care and accuracy, particular movements of this symphony, then one must provide an account of what it is one is in fact doing. In this continuing engagement between the task of reading the Fathers and reading the Fathers *today*, with concern for contemporary questions and philosophical movements, there is, I would suggest, one particularly fruitful area for engagement in addition to hermeneutics: that is, the strain of phenomenology that has undergone a 'theological turn' in recent decades, especially that of Michel Henry, with his 'phenomenology of life',[31] and Jean-Luc Marion and his analysis of saturated phenomena.

Indeed, Marion's analysis of saturated phenomena provides, as recently suggested by Tamsin Jones, an intriguing model for Patristic texts and their reading – received as a pure given, but opening out on to an endless interpretation, as we encounter the phenomenon of God's revelation which exceeds any reduction[32] – *as icon*. The correlation between that which appears and the appearance, between the 'intuition' and one's 'concept' of it, need not only be determined as adequation, in which it is supposed that 'truth' lies, or inadequation, as in the understanding of the phenomenon from Kant to Husserl, but, Marion argues, it can also be encountered as the 'excess' of 'saturation'. And this recognition opens a way to avoid the 'idolatrous' impulse of philosophy to determine and reduce concepts to static formulations, ones which, moreover, take their measure from the capacity of the thinking subject.

The 'nonmetaphysical method of philosophy – phenomenology, but a phenomenology thoroughly secured', as elaborated by Marion[33] – does not impose 'conditions for the possibility of phenomenality, the horizon, the constituting function of the I', whether through Kant's categories

---

31 See Michel Henry, *I am the Truth: Toward a Philosophy of Christianity*, trans. Susan Emanuel (Stanford, CA: Stanford University Press, 2003).
32 Tamsin Jones, *A Genealogy of Marion's Philosophy of Religion: Apparent Darkness* (Bloomington, IN: Indiana University Press, 2011), 158.
33 Jean-Luc Marion, *Being Given: Toward a Phenomenology of Givenness*, trans. J. L. Kosky (Stanford, CA: Stanford University Press, 2002), x.

or Husserl's intentionality;[34] nor does it begin with the subject (even Heidegger's authentic *Dasein*); nor does it privilege Being; but rather it begins with the givenness of what shows itself, and in the case of the saturated phenomenon, to quote Marion: it alone truly appears as itself, of itself, and starting from itself, since it alone appears without the limits of a horizon and without reduction to an *I*. We will therefore call this appearance that is purely of itself and starting from itself, this phenomenon that does not subject its possibility to any preliminary determination, *a revelation*. And – we insist on this – here it is purely and simply a matter of the phenomenon taken in its fullest meaning.[35] Marion's saturated phenomena – the Event, the Idol, the Flesh, the Icon – culminate in the figure of Christ, whose manifestation 'counts as paradigm of the phenomenon of revelation according to the paradox's four modes of saturation':[36] as Event (saturating according to quantity, unable to be accounted); as Idol (saturating according to quality, being unbearable by the look); as Flesh (saturating according to relation, being absolute); and as Icon (saturating to modality, being unable to be looked at), 'precisely because as icon He [Christ] regards me in such a way that He constitutes me as His witness rather than as some transcendental *I* constituting Him to its own liking'.[37]

The subject, the constituting I, has been displaced, however self-aware it has become through contemporary critical theory, to be replaced by one who is given, gifted, called (beyond being?) by Revelation itself. Christ (rather than 'Christology') is once again the subject of revelation, of *theology*, and theology itself is revelatory (rather than 'revelation' being one of the many topics studied by theology), and so perhaps Patristic texts are to be read as themselves saturated phenomena in a *theological* reading, as

---

34 Ibid., 4.
35 Jean-Luc Marion, 'The Saturated Phenomenon', in Dominique Janicaud, Jean-François Coutrine, Jean-Louis Chrétien, Michel Henry, Jean-Luc Marion, and Paul Ricoeur (eds), *Phenomenology and the 'Theological Turn'* (New York: Fordham University Press, 2000), 176–216 (212–13).
36 Marion, *Being Given*, 236.
37 Ibid., 240.

icons that bear witness – that are not reduced to our horizon, but rather open out, saturate, our sight.

There are, needless to say, many unanswered questions: two issues in particular dominate current discussion about Marion's saturated phenomena and the completion of these phenomena in the phenomenon of Revelation. First, who or what is the subject to whom the phenomenon appears, if not to an I, and how does this subject, however understood, receive this revelation without reinscribing the phenomenon in a horizon necessarily subjective? And, second, what is the place of hermeneutics in this analysis of saturated phenomenon, or as Jones puts it: 'What is the actual relation between allowing the given to appear as such without any interpretation by the subject, on the one hand, and the subject's actual experience of this appearance itself, on the other? Or in other words, how can we talk of the appearance itself while totally bracketing out the subject?'[38] Perhaps more careful attention to the symphony of the Fathers (their synchronic and diachronic polyphony), approached now with a keener sense of the saturated character of revelation, may provide some answers.

With regard to the question of the place of the subject addressed by Revelation and the role of hermeneutics, the very development of the discourse of Christian theology has much to offer, inasmuch as answering the call of 'the God who reveals himself through the cross'[39] requires the death of the one who hears: I no longer live, but Christ lives in me (Gal. 2: 20), a death which is alone an entry into life (as in Henry's 'phenomenology of life') and the completion of God's creation of the human being through the creature's own fiat, answering a call that is only heard exegetically (through the opening of the Scriptures), not by another technique or method of reading or exegesis, but by focusing on Christ as the subject, the self-interpreting Word exegeting the Father (cf. John 1: 18), providing the categories and horizons of his own intuition – revelation, rather than being reduced to those of a thinking subject, and heard liturgically, through the breaking of bread, in which his companions, those who share in the broken bread, become his body – so that he disappears from sight.

---

38 Jones, *Genealogy*, 117.
39 Gregory of Nyssa, *Contra Eunomium* 3. 3. 30 (GNO 2. 118. 20–1).

Although Marion reflects on this, beautifully but briefly, in his essay, 'They Recognized Him And He Became Invisible To Them',[40] I am not sure that he (or Henry) has fully appreciated two points. First, the extent to which, and the implications of the fact that, the Christ he speaks of, the Christ of the canonical Gospels, is always already revealed within this hermeneutical structure. Certainly it is Christ himself who grounds or constitutes this revelation, on his own terms: the Gospel is that of God, not of man (to borrow from Paul (Gal. 1: 12), the one whom Luke interpreted). But Christ is not simply there before the disciples' eyes waiting to be recognized by the intuitions he supplies; it is, rather, specifically *in the Gospel of Luke* that he appears on the road to Emmaus. And likewise now to those who stand in the same tradition of opening the scriptures and breaking bread.

The second point is that the excess of this saturated revelation can only be received through the death of the subject, sharing in his passion, to become his body, so that he disappears from sight (rather than remaining to be adored in the Eucharistic gifts, the high point of saturated phenomenon for Marion), for it is alone the death of the subject which breaks down all their attempts to constitute their world, and instead allows them to become clay in the hands of God, to become (finally) flesh, created by God (rather than themselves).

Yet, despite such questions, such theologically attuned phenomenology does, it seems to me, open a space for a theological reading of Patristic texts as icons, rather than as texts which are devoured today in the battle of critical readings, and also offers an approach for explaining what makes such reading theological, and revelatory (phenomenologically), and, indeed, what is *theological* about theology.

---

40 *Modern Theology* 18: 2 (April 2002), 145–52.

Bibliography

Behr, John, *The Mystery of Christ: Life in Death* (Crestwood, NY: St Vladimir's Seminary Press, 2006).

——, 'What are we doing speaking about God? The Discipline of Theology', in Aristotle Papanikolaou and Elizabeth Prodromou (eds), *Thinking through Faith: New Perspectives from Orthodox Christian Scholars* (Crestwood, NY: St Vladimir's Seminary Press, 2008), 67–87.

Farley, Edward, *Theologia: The Fragmentation and Unity of Theological Education* (Augsburg: Fortress, 1994).

Gallaher, Brandon, '"Waiting for the Barbarians": Identity and Polemicism in the Neo-Patristic Synthesis of Georges Florovsky', *Modern Theology*, 27 (2011), 659–91.

Gavrilyuk, Paul L., *Georges Florovsky and the Russian Religious Renaissance*, Changing Paradigms in Historical and Systematic Theology (Oxford: Oxford University Press, 2014).

Hays, Richard, *Reading Backwards: Figural Christology and the Fourfold Gospel Witness* (Waco, TX: Baylor University Press, 2014).

Kugel, James L., *Traditions of the Bible: A Guide to the Bible as it was at the Start of the Common Era* (Cambridge, MA: Harvard University Press, 1998).

Louth, Andrew, *Discerning the Mystery: An Essay on the Nature of Theology* (Oxford: Clarendon Press, 1983).

Williams, Rowan, *On Christian Theology* (Oxford: Blackwell, 2000).

Young, Frances, *Biblical Exegesis and the Formation of Christian Culture* (Cambridge: Cambridge University Press, 1997).

ROWAN WILLIAMS

15 Deification, Hypostatization, and Kenosis

The classical language about participation in the life of God, *theosis*, as the goal of God's saving and restoring work in human beings continues to puzzle and even alienate some, though the number of careful and wide-ranging studies of the subject in the last couple of decades has made such alienation rather more rare, at least among those with any claim to serious familiarity with Christian intellectual history.[1] Part of the difficulty lies in the hybrid conceptual origins of the idea; part lies in an uncertainty about where and how it fits with both fundamental teaching about prayer and its disciplines and central doctrinal themes. This brief reflection on the subject will attempt both to clarify these origins a little and to tease out why the diverse elements need each other and combine to produce what is not only a coherent doctrinal stance but one that illuminates other areas of theology – and practice – in unexpected ways. And to elucidate this, we shall be making use especially of the distinctive perspective of one modern Orthodox teacher, Archimandrite Sophrony (Sakharov), whose analysis of what deification means succeeds in holding the elements of the tradition in an unusually cohesive scheme.

1   The work of Norman Russell deserves special mention here, from his magisterial monograph on *The Doctrine of Deification in the Greek Patristic Tradition* (2nd edn, Oxford: Oxford University Press, 2006) to his overview of more recent theology in *Fellow-Workers with God: Orthodox Thinking on Theosis* (Crestwood, NY: St Vladimir's Seminary Press, 2009). See also Panayiotis Nellas, *Deification in Christ: The Nature of the Human Person* (Crestwood, NY: St Vladimir's Seminary Press, 1987), for an attempt to integrate the theme into a comprehensive Christian anthropology, and Emil Bartos, *Deification in Eastern Orthodox Theology: An Evaluation and Critique of the Theology of Dumitru Staniloae* (Carlisle: Paternoster Press, 1999, for a wide-ranging comparative discussion of a number of twentieth-century Orthodox writers (though not including Fr Sophrony).

The 'hybridity' mentioned can be briefly categorized in these terms: on the one hand, Christian teaching from the very first has taken for granted that the fundamental *novum* in Christian identity is the gift of being able to address God as Jesus did, as 'Abba, Father' (Rom. 8: 15, Gal. 4: 6; and cf. Eph. 2: 18, as well as the Johannine development of the idea, as in John 14: 3, 6–7, 20, 16: 23–4, 17: 24, 20: 17, 1 John 3: 1–2, etc.); on the other hand, Christian practice took for granted a disciplining of the passions that was oriented towards a state of freedom from compulsion by instinct, a state that could be described as godlike, a *mimesis* of divine life involving a share in divine wisdom (e.g. 1 Cor. 2: 13–16, 2 Cor. 4: 4–6, Eph. 2: 4–7, 3: 19, 4: 24, 5: 1–2, Col. 2: 9–10, and, most famously, 2 Peter 1: 4). In the context of the New Testament the disjunction is pretty artificial, since sharing in Christ's relation to the Father is manifestly and explicitly the ground of transformed behaviour and a new mind. However, as Christian reflection developed, the idea of reflecting the *kind* of life lived by God, immortal, stable, and free of passion, drew more and more deeply on available models of such transformation in the intellectual world of late antiquity,[2] and the connection with the basic theme of filiation is sometimes hard to discern. The undeniable difference in focus between emphasizing relation to the Father and emphasizing our accession to a certain 'interior' or 'spiritual' state becomes ever more marked. And so in Christian history these two emphases, which we might call 'filiation' and 'purification', constantly drift apart, recombine, are redefined, and reworked; it is the positive tension between them that gives the doctrine its significance, as we shall see, but that positive tension needs to be repeatedly refreshed by new theological strategies. Such refreshment is part of what this essay aims at.

The more the Church clarifies its belief in Jesus Christ as the unique incarnation of the eternal Word, the more an understanding of filiation moves away from the simple 'imitation' of a paradigm of spiritual practice

---

2   Apart from Russell, *The Doctrine of Deification*, see, for example, D. L. Balas, *Metousia Theou: Man's Participation in God's Perfections* (Rome: Studia Anselmiana 55, 1966); and Richard Sorabji, *Emotion and Peace of Mind: From Stoic Agitation to Christian Temptation* (Oxford: Oxford University Press, 2000, on models of stability and passion-free mental existence.

(calling God what Jesus called God) into a comprehensive reframing or reconfiguring of a finite life in relation to God. Paul's language in Romans 8 already understands the 'Abba' prayer as an act that is not our own but the activity within us of the Spirit: our prayer is immersed in eternal activity, specifically the divine 'repetition' in us by the Spirit of the movement of the Word towards the Father. This prayerful immersion in eternal act, with its expression in the word of address to God the Father, is the manifestation of a comprehensive transformation, since it expresses what we have actually become – adopted children. And while the language is inevitably rooted in and connected in certain ways with our habitual ways of speaking about relations between specific finite agents, the increasing refinement of Nicene theology in East and West makes it clear that we cannot characterize the relation of Father and Word as a *case* of interpersonal intimacy of the sort usually designated by this language of familial intimacy. Various theologies have found various ways of reinforcing the point, from Dionysios's insistence that the Trinity is not either one or three in the sense we are used to,[3] up to Nicolas of Cusa's use of *non aliud* to describe the divine relations.[4] To speak of filiation in the context of a fully developed Trinitarian schema is to speak of induction into a relation with the divine Source that is, crucially, non-dualistic – that is neither an undifferentiated identity nor a confrontation of distinct self-subsisting subjects. And so to pursue an understanding of filiation becomes something that challenges certain models of relation between finite and infinite. It means that we cannot ultimately conceive of our relation to God as that of individual to individual; and our prayer is invited to move out of a simple model of *address* towards what we could call an 'inhabiting', difficult (appropriately) to define within the terms of finite interrelation.

Filiation thus understood implies the dissolution of our familiar models of the religious subject – a human individual having 'religious experiences' or enjoying 'personal relation' with God (in the conventional sense of those words). If our encounter with God the Father is encounter

---

3   Dionysius, *De Divinis Nominibus*, 13. 3 (*PG* 3. 981A).
4   See his treatise, *De Non Aliud*, of 1462; ET by Jasper Hopkins, 3rd edn (Minneapolis, MN: Arthur J. Banning Press, 1987).

with the Trinitarian *non aliud*, then the otherness between myself and God is – to offer a hopelessly but unavoidably clumsy formulation – other to all other forms of otherness; and to assimilate this and live from it thus requires me to strip away in my relation to God all habits and images that potentially reduce God to 'other forms of otherness'. But this in turn is to pose a radical challenge to the entire gamut of human 'passion' – to the defensive and aggressive patterns of relating to what is other to my ego or my will which dominate our humanity and secure its unredeemed state of slavery. To reconceive encounter with God as something beyond a confrontation of 'selves' relativizes what I say, sense, or believe about my 'self' and its supposed needs and wellbeing. And this relativizes all by which I seek to sustain or protect the self I am familiar with; just as those forms of discipline which steadily erode such habits are not aimed at some detached condition of ideal spiritual independence but at filiation in its fullest meaning. The Trinitarian grounding of filiation pushes us to a deeper grasp of purification; the work of purification helps us avoid a model of filiation that leaves the protective/protected self intact. We should expect a certain movement back and forth between the two poles at different points in theological development, but what is important is that they continue to illuminate one another. An orientation towards filiation in simple terms will risk making relation to God a *case* of relation to others, leaving the self's habits intact and untransformed; an orientation towards purification alone may hold our attention to the condition of our 'interior' life in a way that tempts us to forget that it is a process of coming to inhabit divine relatedness. It may indeed issue in what is finally no more than a vastly refined individualism, potentially worse than the unreconstructed individualism of 'naive' filiation.

The category that holds all this together, as several writers of the last century argued,[5] is *kenosis*. The eternal existence of God the Word is 'kenotic'

---

5   Vladimir Lossky, *The Mystical Theology of the Eastern Church* (Cambridge: James Clarke, 1957), especially pp. 144–9; for the theme in Sergii Bulgakov, see, for example, Rowan Williams, *Sergii Bulgakov: Towards a Russian Political Theology* (Edinburgh: T. & T. Clark, 1999), 177, 193–6, and Aidan Nichols, *Wisdom from Above. A Primer in the Theology of Father Sergei Bulgakov* (Leominster: Gracewing, 2005), especially chapter 6, an excellent summary of Bulgakov's handling of this subject. See also

in that it is wholly defined not by any individual intrinsic property located in some autonomous divine subject but by its derivation from and orientation to the Father: what it is to be the Word *is* to be that which is poured out from the eternal Source (which is thus itself kenotically actualized, in being entirely that which spends itself in bestowing life in the Word and Spirit), and that which responsively flows back to the Source. To attempt to put it in the most basic terms, there is nothing for the Word to be or do except to be from the Father and towards the Father (the *pros ton theon* of the first chapter of John's Gospel); the Word has no action or subsistence that is not wholly characterized by relatedness to the Source. The life of God is entirely the *communication* of life; so what we mean by speaking of the divine *hypostaseis* is simply the moment or point from which life is being communicated – the point of the eternal Source, the point of the eternal derived and responsive Word, the point of the inexhaustible 'witness' to the Source and the Word that preserves their relation as open and generative and is nothing but what the Father gives and what the Son gives back, yet is not identical with either or both. To inhabit this reality is to be assimilated to this 'hypostatic' world, where there is nothing that is *possessed*, no solid self that owns, accumulates, gives, or holds back according to will: in this sense 'deification' is the process of becoming hypostatic, personal in the strictest theological sense. Archimandrite Sophrony (Sakharov; 1896–1993), whose writings set this out more explicitly than any other twentieth-century teacher, speaks of the human potential given by God in creation to be not simply a 'created hypostasis', a centre of communication and intercommunication within the world, but a 'universal centre',[6] a place where the boundaryless action of God occurs; the eternal 'I Am' is now uttered in the creaturely 'I'.[7] When the created subject receives the revelation of divine hypostatic being through relation with Christ in the

---

Christos Yannaras, *Person and Eros* (Brookline, MA: Holy Cross Orthodox Press, 2007), for a developed anthropology in which this theme is foregrounded.

6 Archimandrite Sophrony (Sakharov), *We Shall See Him As He Is* (Tolleshunt Knights: Stavropegic Monastery of St John the Baptist, 1988), 201.

7 Ibid., 199, 204–5; cf. Coleridge's often cited remark about the repetition in time of the eternal 'I AM'.

Spirit, that subject is radically altered: our existence begins to become hypostatic in the divine mode, that is, to be structured by, defined by, *kenosis*, the dissolution of the ego's defence and individual interest. This is not, as Fr Sophrony makes plain, a reduction to 'impersonal' life but exactly the contrary: our distinctness becomes not a solid identity but a unique 'point', to use the image again, from which the communication of life radiates. But to become personal in this mode is indeed antithetical to most of what we typically think of as personal, which is in fact to do with the fantasy of the substantive individual over against God and other subjects. The discipline of realizing the gift of deification/hypostatization is precisely that purification from passion which has figured so largely in traditional accounts of deification, but has to be contextualized within the frame of filiation.

Fr Sophrony's perspective becomes still clearer (and more challenging) as he interprets this particularly through the lens of the prayer of Jesus in Gethsemane and in connection with the experience of 'God-forsakenness' – a nexus of insights explored with great precision and perception by Nicholas Sakharov in his monograph on Fr Sophrony.[8] Gethsemane is for Christ the moment when the human realization of his final self-emptying on the cross becomes most immediate, and the abyss of human need and pain opens up with unprecedented clarity. Hence his prayer of 'Abba, Father' in Gethsemane is a kind of summation of 'hypostatic' prayer, a summation of the kenotic intensity of identification with all. As Sakharov brings out in his chapter on Fr Sophrony's teaching on Godforsakenness, the focus here on deification as a participation in the hypostatic life of God allows for the *effect* of kenotic identification to be experienced in a way that is not so obviously intelligible within the more traditional framework which associates deification with the divine energies; or rather, Fr Sophrony's model insists that the life of God *en energeiai* can never be other than hypostatically actualized, and thus kenotic.[9] When God permits the believer to feel the full weight of the world's anguish, without any sustaining awareness

---

8   Nicholas V. Sakharov, *I Love, Therefore I Am: The Theological Legacy of Archimandrite Sophrony* (Crestwood, NY: St Vladimir's Seminary Press, 2002).
9   Ibid., 175–6.

Deification, Hypostatization, and Kenosis

at the affective level of God's presence, this is, according to Fr Sophrony, in order that we may rediscover that we are not so *dominated* by the grace of God that we are no longer free. The sense of being forsaken and at the mercy of the diabolic is an aspect of our growth in 'hypostatic' maturity: we are confronted with the intrinsic emptiness of our 'selfhood' in isolation, and so are redirected to our need to renew our openness to the reality of the threefold God. But to be confronted with that emptiness is to see both in ourselves and in the world the intensity of evil, 'the "curse" of our inheritance'.[10] Hence Fr Sophrony's charting of spiritual growth as a movement of three stages,[11] an initial radical opening to the hypostatic reality of God, a 'descent into hell', in which we are faced with the vacuity of what is not God, in and beyond our own selves, provoking revulsion, a hatred of the illusory self, and finally a realized awareness, a spiritual 'settling' in which God's truth is transparent, not as a content of the intellect but as an unmistakable climate for the life being lived. Fr Sophrony describes[12] the transition from second to third stage as a transformation from anguish over one's own suffering to anguish over the world's suffering: 'My sense of being doomed caused me great agony and this agony cracked the walls of my stony heart. As I was accustomed to apply my experiences to all mankind, I felt pity for all who, like me, were distanced from God. Thus humanity's sufferings became mine, and in the solitude of the desert prayer would come to me for the whole world as for myself.'[13] What is being described, it seems, is the process whereby my sense of desolation is transformed into a Gethsemane-like prayer which takes on the burden of suffering, seeking to 'align' it with the relational life of the threefold God; and in that process the anguish of acknowledging Godlessness within my own soul and in the world becomes a compassion that is aware of its eternal rootedness.

Thus what is distinctive in Fr Sophrony's presentation of deification is that the state of fully inhabiting the divine interaction or interdependence is connected at every level with the personal/hypostatic: deification is

---

10   *We Shall See Him As He Is*, 123.
11   Nicholas Sakharov, op. cit., 177ff. Cf. *We Shall See Him As He Is*, 223–32.
12   *We Shall See Him As He Is*, 229–30.
13   Ibid.

'hypostatization' in its fullest possible sense – growth into a mode of life that is continuous with that of the Word's relation with the Father and as such is radically exposed both to the mystery of divine self-bestowal and to the need and suffering of the world. The 'divinized' subject is the undefended subject; the narrative of deification as outlined by Fr Sophrony is the narrative of losing protection – first through the sheer impact of revelation, then through the consequent exposure to inner and outer meaninglessness and the assaults of the negative and destructive agencies that will afflict a self with its defences down, then through the habitual recognition of alignment with a limitless relatedness which comes to light in the process of desolation or forsakenness. Nicholas Sakharov has a very illuminating discussion of where this scheme does and does not overlap with that of St John of the Cross, noting that in Fr Sophrony and other Eastern authors the equivalent of the 'passive night of the spirit', the most intense phase of desolation, is associated directly with diabolical assault rather than, as in John, with the increasingly consuming pressure on the soul of divine reality itself, the blinding effect of too much light.[14] It might also be noted that John of the Cross does not specifically associate the intensity of desolation with a breakthrough into solidarity with the suffering of others, though a case could well be made that this is an implication of his language about the purification of love involved in the process. As Sakharov rightly notes,[15] there is a nineteenth- and twentieth-century Russian background to Sophrony's stress on Gethsemane, from Metropolitan Philaret of Moscow through Antonii Khrapovitsky to Sergii Bulgakov. Gethsemane exhibits Christ's sharing in human fear and abandonment, but it thus also exhibits the character of God's personal being as free from defence against the world's otherness in its most malign manifestations. This is both a theological insight about *kenosis* and (especially for Khrapovitsky) a model for pastoral engagement;[16] but none of the earlier Russians connect it explicitly with the development of the life of prayer in the way Sophrony

14   Nicholas Sakharov, op. cit., 181–6, 187 ff.
15   Ibid., 186–7.
16   See, for example, Antonii Khrapovitskii, *L'idée morale des dogmes de la Très Sainte Trinité, de la divinité de Jésus-Christ et de la rédemption* (Paris: Welter, 1910), 33-end.

does. For him, Gethsemane represents a specific stage in spiritual growth, when divine personal being breaks through in a new way as a result of an awareness of apparently inexhaustible suffering outside and humiliation, failure, and emptiness within.

As Sakharov stresses, this inscription of Godforsakenness at the heart of the narrative of deification is in marked tension with the approach of some other Orthodox writers, especially Vladimir Lossky,[17] but it is not wholly without Patristic support. What matters, though, is that the connections opened up by this all show an understanding of deification which links it far more deeply and intrinsically to practice as well as to other areas of doctrine. First of all: the fundamental challenge to any picturing of our relation to God as that of finite individual to infinite individual is obviously of a piece with all those elements of the ascetical tradition that insist on the abandonment of images at certain points in the spirit's growth. The Father who is *non aliud* to the Son is likewise not an object or item among others in the mental world of the baptized believer, the person praying in Christ; not 'an' other, yet in no way identical to the self's contents. This 'otherness to all other kinds of otherness', as we called it earlier, requires a complex and self-aware deployment of images and ideas to do with the divine – not a plain rejection (because our notions of what constitutes an absence of images will be as laden with presuppositions as the rest of our imaginative life), but a consistent habit of 'reading' images so as to allow their own tensions and tendings to break open various fixed assumptions about or pictures of the divine. The cross of the incarnate Word is, of course, the primary instance of an image that breaks images and opens a path. But, as we have seen, the challenge to images of the divine entails a challenge also to images of the self, involves a questioning of the solid autonomous or self-subsistent subject. And thus the askesis of denying images of the divine is inseparable from the denial of an illusory selfhood; it is an opening up of the idea of the subject simply as 'place' or 'moment', that from which divine life is communicated in one unrepeatably distinctive mode.

---

17 Nicholas Sakharov, chapter 7, *passim*; cf., for example, Lossky, *Mystical Theology*, 226–7.

The entire ascetical endeavour is thus configured as a dissolution of what is *not yet personal* in the full and theologically determined sense.

Deification understood as 'hypostatization' in Fr Sophrony's sense is the culmination of baptismal identification with and incorporation in Christ: it denotes the change in how we apprehend the self that results from being opened up to the divine agency. Because this divine agency is always irreducibly and fundamentally a kenotic movement, the way in which it modifies our habitual self-image and self-experience is in a kenotic direction; and in the light of the Gospel narrative, especially the account of Christ's agony in Gethsemane, we grasp that the act of *kenosis* in respect of the world we live in is not simply a pouring-out of the self but an opening of the self to the anguish and need of others. Deification is an intensified vulnerability, not some movement into a secure isolation; though at the same time it is important not to see this as some sort of enhanced emotional sensibility, an indulging of 'passion' through the suffering of others (a complex issue which would require longer treatment). Sophrony's analysis of the stages of growth suggests that what happens in the second level of maturation is that my own awareness of my inner emptiness, my utter failure to embody by my own will and strength the self-bestowing love that is God's agency, brings me into solidarity with any and every human situation where the non-appearance of divine love creates pain and fear: not, therefore, a matter of identification with the emotional state of another but the awareness of a *shared* condition of suffering and insecurity, bearable, if at all, through the acknowledgement of what is being broken and remade in this process, that is, the acknowledgement of this as that by which we become 'personal'.[18] Twentieth-century Orthodox theology – Lossky especially, but others too[19] – has laid great stress on the interplay between the one unchanging

---

18   For a modern testimony to the faithful and hopeful handling of extreme spiritual dereliction as intrinsic to sanctification and 'personalization' by means of an unprotected identification with the God-forsaken, we might look to Mother Teresa of Calcutta's letters and journals: *Come Be My Light: The Private Writings of the 'Saint of Calcutta'*, ed. Brian Kolodiejchuk, MC (New York and London: Doubleday, 2007).
19   See, for example, John Zizioulas, *Communion and Otherness; Further Studies in Personhood and the Church* (London: T. and T. Clark, 2006).

form of sanctified life, which is the self-emptying of God the Word, and the infinite diversity of particular lives of faith shaped by the indwelling of Christ's Spirit. From the point of view of Fr Sophrony's account, this duality means simply that each particular human 'location', each site in which the hypostatic life of God will be actualized, will *receive* in an unrepeatable mode that gift of personalization and live it out in the way it also receives the will, need, pressure of the human other. Nicholas Sakharov traces how this shapes Sophrony's understanding of obedience in the believer's life as a realization of divine *perichoresis*, interpenetration; but he also notes that it is grounded in the ascetic practice of first 'taking into oneself' the will and reality of the other through formation in obedience to a spiritual elder:[20] the basic practice of attentive openness to the authority of the elder equips us to enter and be entered by the suffering of the other. In other words, the point of asserting the uniqueness of each particular finite image of God as he or she is deified is not to make what could be a rather routine point about how grace does not extinguish natural human diversity; it is more to say that we are constantly becoming, in the life of deifying grace, ever more uniquely 'personal' precisely in our opening to the otherness of God and our neighbour. Or, put more simply perhaps, it is not that grace simply affirms our existing diversity but that it creates a *deeper* diversity, a spiritual uniqueness, through the reconstruction of our selfhood in *kenosis*.[21]

Summing up the areas of theological discourse that are thus illuminated by such a view of deification, we may point to:

(i) The theology of creation: understanding God's agency as always kenotic means that the difference between God and creation – and most specifically between God and the human subject – is unlike any other difference. It is not a distance between two co-ordinate realities, it is not in any conceivable way a rivalry requiring one to flourish at the

---

20 Nicholas Sakharov, op. cit., 213–16.
21 See the brilliant essay by Verna Harrison, 'Human Uniqueness and Human Unity', in John Behr, Andrew Louth and Dimitri Conomos (eds), *Abba: The Tradition of Orthodoxy in the West. Festschrift for Bishop Kallistos Ware* (Crestwood, NY: St Vladimir's Seminary Press, 2003), 207–20.

other's expense. This is an otherness grounded in the simple freedom of divine agency, the will that there be an other to God; but because it is grounded in this will, it cannot be other, as finite realities are other to each other; that finite otherness is supremely the embodiment of our limitedness, while the otherness between God and the world is the embodiment of God's unlimited freedom.

(ii) The theology of the Trinity: God's unlimited freedom is not the supreme instance of *individual* self-determining – the fantasy that we create out of our misunderstanding or lack of understanding of the personal. It is the freedom of self-bestowal or self-sharing without limit. Nothing constrains the giving of God's agency. The life of God as revealed in the events of the life and death and resurrection of Jesus is neither the story of a divine individual nor the story of a transaction between distinct agents, but the manifestation of the *non aliud* relation of interdependent moments or points from which divine giving occurs – neither assimilation nor separation.

(iii) The theology of the person of Christ: in the life of Jesus, there is a unique and unconditional coincidence of the eternal 'point' of divine agency that we call the Word or son and a point within human history. Thus from this point in human history divine life is communicated in its fullness; but this also means that the form or 'site' of divine life in the world is radically exposed to suffering, since the divine gift or communication can mount no finite defence of itself (John 18: 36). Gethsemane as the manifesting of this exposure in or to the finite awareness of the incarnate Word takes on a particular theological weight in this context.

(iv) The theology of the Church: to be associated with or incorporated into the identity of Jesus through baptism is to be committed to the process whereby Christ's radical exposure takes place in us through the mediating action of the Spirit. This is an exposure both to the non-dual otherness of the God and Father of Jesus and to the otherness of the human neighbour. Our formation in the life of Christ's Body takes place through the variety of ways in which our will is challenged and reconstructed, from the practice of monastic obedience to the elder through to the ordinary pressure of the will and need of any finite other. And Fr Sophrony also insists that the liturgy itself is the recapitulation of the divine act of kenosis, the place where Christ descends again to receive into himself the needs of creation and our prayer moves outwards, away from selfish limits, to expose ourselves to his act and his offering.[22]

In the most immediate and practical terms, all of this means that deification is the vehicle of our solidarity with all. Rather than being in any way a privilege that divides believers from non-believers or the ascetically proficient from 'beginners', it is the evacuation of separateness and worldly security. It is also a challenge to models of solidarity that depend on the simple assimilation of the feelings of others to my own. Fr Sophrony, as we have noted, speaks of being 'accustomed to apply my experiences to all mankind'; but we should not read this as meaning a projection of individual subjective states on to others, but as referring to the conviction that what is most deeply true of my spiritual condition apart from God reveals what is true for all creatures – that they are poised over emptiness. What makes the difference is this awareness of how my particular suffering and desolation genuinely reveals something, so that my own desolation does not become an interesting psychological phenomenon to be explored with fascinated self-absorption. It is the occasion of a sober recognition of the radical groundlessness of any and every inner condition. To see myself as having no intrinsic worth or achievement *as an individual* is precisely the precondition for breaking down barriers between myself and others, so that what I *as an individual* am experiencing (positive or negative) is in some important sense irrelevant to the process going forward in me of becoming 'hypostatic'. This alone makes room for new being to unfold.[23] Our deepest human solidarity, in this perspective, is in our ineradicable need for relatedness to God, in which alone we become personal, and thus distinct in a way that is not exclusive, self-asserting, and self-protecting. What I see when I contemplate the suffering of another is not simply another complex of individual suffering like mine but a unique manifestation of the reality

22   Nicholas Sakharov, op. cit., 112–15.
23   e.g. *We Shall See Him As He Is*, 130, 146, 169.

we share as creatures who *live* only in communion. Sophrony's sharply expressed language about self-loathing, difficult for most contemporary readers, has to be read as having to do with the call to reject an existence cut off from Trinitarian communion – that existence which our individual suffering shows us and which we have to endure and interpret as God's showing to us of what the divine purpose ultimately is in deification. The communion or community which is born out of this solidarity is one in which compassion, the accompaniment of the other in the isolation that characterizes hell, is beyond sentimental fellow feeling; compassion is simply how the divine solidarity with suffering and failing human beings takes flesh and form in this place that is 'me'.

Despite the various ways in which Sophrony's theological scheme departs from that of Lossky, there is one respect in which he echoes Lossky quite closely. Both see Orthodox Christianity as refusing the crude polarization between supposedly personal and supposedly impersonal aspirations in spiritual life. It is possible to see the spiritual and ascetical task as acquiring particular kinds of experience, a particular kind of sensed interiority which can be perceived and in some degree measured as an aspect of individual awareness. It is possible to see the task as the shedding of all specificity, of difference itself, and negating the particular. Lossky spoke[24] of 'two monotheisms', mythologically hyper-personalist on the one hand and monistic on the other; Fr Sophrony, recalling[25] his own youthful fascination with the idea of 'the Supra-personal Absolute' and his absorption in styles of transcendentalist mysticism, identifies his problem as never having grasped the distinction between the individual and the hypostatic. It is true that the

---

24 *Orthodox Theology: An Introduction* (Crestwood, NY: St Vladimir's Seminary Press, 1989), chapter 1. This book is a digest of unpublished lectures given in Paris by Lossky in the last years of his life, in which the theme of Christian theology as a *via media* between mythology and monist abstraction became a dominant and shaping motif, applied at one level to Christianity in the context of world religions, and at another to the 'mediating' position of Orthodoxy within Christian thought, between what he saw as the individualism of Protestant theology and the repressive collectivism of the Catholic Church. Ironically, some of the closest parallels to this, as many have noted, are with the thinking of French Catholic writers like Henri de Lubac.
25 *We Shall See Him As He Is*, 195–6; cf. Nicholas Sakharov, 17–18.

imagined individual self is an obstacle, a restriction of fullness; what is not true, dangerously not true, is that this must entail a rejection of the 'personal', because this would mean rejection of two fundamental realities – the eternal interdependence in giving that constitutes the Trinitarian life, and the dependence on eternal gift that constitutes the finite world. We need here something like the Buddhist language which denies both the affirmation and the denial of 'self'.[26] But – to extrapolate from Fr Sophrony's own presentation a little – making such an observation in the abstract is going to be no more than point-scoring; the definition of a practice that is not reducible to either of the 'two monotheisms' is indeed simply that – the definition of a practice *by* practice, of the kind that Fr Sophrony describes.

Nonetheless, this essay has attempted to show how the implications of the practice as expounded by Sophrony make it clear why deification in the sense of adoption into the relatedness of the Word to the Father and the creation is a theme that has the capacity to draw together the widest imaginable range of Christian reflection and – in its reconfiguring of what the call to solidarity might mean – also to direct us to a new imagining of Christian ethics. Our world is, for Fr Sophrony, irreducibly a world in which the gift of life in joy and reconciliation is bestowed from multiple points or in multiple moments; being itself is relational – a familiar enough theme in modern Orthodox dogmatics.[27] But this entails understanding our being as – in God's purposes – on the way to a mutual transparency which deeply relativizes and problematizes all we might want to say in our habitual modes of speech about selfhood. We are left with the uncompromising repudiation of the myth of *individual* autonomy – but not in the name of some elevation of collective dignities over the particularity of human agencies.

---

26 Buddhist meditation requires a passage beyond the dualism of any theory that tries to decide whether there is in the world such a thing as a self. Quite clearly there is no thing that corresponds to this word; equally clearly, the denial that there is such a thing is spiritually vacuous if it leaves in position a catalogue of other fixed things that confront an individual knowing subject as objects. What matters is the practice of 'emptying' and the full appropriation of one's absolute relatedness.

27 Classically articulated in John Zizioulas, *Being as Communion* (Crestwood, NY: St Vladimir's Seminary Press, 1985; new edn, London: Darton, Longman and Todd, 2004).

The profound theological affirmation of the uniqueness and dignity of the person, so characteristic of many Orthodox theologies, is given by Fr Sophrony a further critical edge by being linked with the conviction that a theologically significant personal distinctness or uniqueness is the fruit of ascetical practice rather than some sort of given. It is arrived at when and only when our uniqueness, our singularity as irreducibly distinct images of God, is understood as radical receptivity – that which can transform our occupation of a unique place in the complex of created interaction into a single and unrepeatable 'site' for God's relation-making liberty to occur. It is of course equally important to stress that, in the context of the spiritual discipline Fr Sophrony and others advocate, this receptivity and obedience (in the sense Sophrony gives to this concept) is not passive or uncritical, a rejection of the call to act and to make a difference: our action in the world is properly and lastingly transforming to the degree that it is united with the hypostatic act of God, the mutual self-giving of Father, Son, and Spirit in which we are 'immersed' and which alone liberates us decisively from the protective individualism which blocks relation with God and creation alike. So long as we assume the individualist stance, we are in fact preventing ourselves from genuinely *acting*: we remain in the realm of passion, and so of reactive behaviour. To become 'personal' is to become a point from which transforming communication acts – a created reflection of what it is to be 'hypostatic' in the life of the Trinity.

Deification understood simply – as it sometimes is in the Fathers – as the acquisition in some degree of divine *attributes* is a concept that does less than justice to the genesis of the notion in the belief that in Christ believers are given a new form of relation to the divine Source, the relation we call that of adopted children. Equally a stress on this relatedness which refuses to ask about ontological and qualitative transformation in the finite subject will do less than justice to the mature Trinitarian understanding of Christ's relation to the Father. The argument of this essay has been that the kind of approach outlined by Fr Sophrony, building on much of the 'personalist' concern of other modern Eastern theologians, and by clarifying and deepening what it means to become 'personal' in Christ, gives us the elements of a theology of deification which not only avoids the risks noted but provides significant resources for a deeper apprehension of both theology and ethics – suggesting indeed that a theology or ethics which ignores this theme is likely to be seriously impoverished.

Bibliography

Bartos, Emil, *Deification in Eastern Orthodox Theology: An Evaluation and Critique of the Theology of Dumitru Staniloae* (Carlisle: Paternoster Press, 1999).

Lossky, Vladimir, *The Mystical Theology of the Eastern Church* (London: James Clarke, 1957).

Russell, Norman, *The Doctrine of Deification in the Greek Patristic Tradition* (Oxford: Oxford University Press, 2006).

Sakharov, Nicholas, *I Love, Therefore I Am: The Theological Legacy of Archimandrite Sophrony* (Crestwood, NY: St Vladimir's Seminary Press, 2002).

Sophrony (Sakharov), Archimandrite, *We Shall See Him As He Is* (Tolleshunt Knights: Stavropegic Monastery of St John the Baptist, 1988).

ELIZABETH THEOKRITOFF

16 Priest of Creation or Cosmic Liturgy?

It is some fifty years now since Christians began exploring theological responses to a looming environmental crisis, a crisis that raises searching questions about the relationship between humans and the rest of material creation. The initial concern was to distinguish the 'dominion over the earth' to which humans are appointed according to Christian tradition from the increasingly humanistic ideas of dominating nature in the modern era. One outcome of this has been the generation of new labels for the human role – first 'stewardship', and more recently 'care for creation'.[1]

Orthodox contributions to this discussion have from the beginning had a strong liturgical and sacramental flavour. In recent years, however, the rich variety of images for man's role in creation, both personal (king, mediator, priest, worshipper ...) and organic or structural (microcosm, link, workshop ...), has increasingly been narrowed down to focus on 'man as priest of creation'. A prime catalyst in this process, I suspect, was the desire to find a label to offer as an alternative to 'steward'[2] – one that gives humans a more elevated and inspiring role than that of managers or caretakers, while affirming the spiritual value and meaning of the rest of material creation.

---

1   For a brief summary of the development of 'stewardship' thinking, see Willis Jenkins, *Ecologies of Grace: Environmental Ethics and Christian Theology* (Oxford: Oxford University Press, 2008), 77–92. For the shift to 'care for creation' and the embrace of this language by some Orthodox, see John Chryssavgis, 'Stewardship as Creation Care' (2013): <http://www.pravmir.com/stewardship-as-creation-care/> (accessed 1 March 2016).
2   See Metropolitan John Zizioulas, 'Proprietors or Priests of Creation?' (Keynote address, Baltic Symposium, June 2003) <http://www.orthodoxytoday.org/articles2/MetJohnCreation.php> (accessed 15 September 2015).

How satisfactory this image has proved will be the subject of this paper. I have argued elsewhere,[3] against critics of Orthodox 'priest of creation' language, that such language needs to be understood within a broader context and does not express a cosmic clericalism which devalues non-human creatures. I would still maintain that 'priestly' imagery is defensible, if carefully defined, and indeed has potentials that Orthodox writers could profitably develop further. I would also agree with most of what Orthodox writers want to convey when they use 'priest of creation' language. But as the idea that 'man is priest of creation' becomes popularized and increasingly treated as received Orthodox teaching, its nuances are ever less likely to be carefully defined. And if we are looking for a single, overarching image to express the cosmological vision of Orthodoxy, and not only its anthropology, I have grave doubts that 'man as priest of creation' is the most suitable choice.

The intention here is to look at the development of modern Orthodox language of human 'priesthood' as well as some of the problems it raises, and suggest ways in which an Orthodox cosmic vision might be better expressed.

Antecedents

As Metropolitan John of Pergamon cautiously puts it,[4] the notion of man as priest of creation 'seems to emerge naturally from' Orthodox Patristic and liturgical tradition. He chooses his words carefully, because such language is not actually *in* that tradition explicitly. Let me make clear: in no way am I suggesting that it is illegitimate or suspect to develop imagery that is not drawn directly from the Church Fathers. But the recognition

---

[3] Elizabeth Theokritoff, 'Creation and Priesthood in Modern Orthodox Thinking', *Ecotheology*, 10: 3 (December 2005), 344–63.
[4] Zizioulas, 'Proprietors or Priests of Creation?' (Keynote address, Baltic Symposium, June 2003) <http://www.orthodoxytoday.org/articles2/MetJohnCreation.php> (accessed 15 September 2015).

that a particular image is not traditional should give us greater freedom to judge it on its merits, and be prepared to drop it if it does not seem helpful.

Patristic tradition has many insights into man's role in creation, but few neat labels. A classic description of what man is comes from St Gregory the Theologian, who speaks of a being compounded of visible and invisible natures, a cosmos placed on earth, 'a "hybrid" worshipper ... a king of things on earth, but subject to the King above; earthly and heavenly, transient and immortal, visible and intelligible, midway between greatness and insignificance, and once spirit and flesh ...' – a creature *en route* to somewhere else, destined for deification.[5] The image of 'priest' may be seen as a cross between 'worshipper' and 'intermediate' (which is implicit in all Gregory's paradoxes). But the prime source claimed for 'priest of creation' language is Maximos the Confessor, who develops to a high degree the notion of man as intermediary. He sees man as related to all the 'extremes' in creation so as to be a 'natural bond', a 'workshop' in which all the divisions of nature were intended to be brought into unity, first with each other and finally with God;[6] and all this set within a vision pervaded with eucharistic imagery. We will return later to St Maximos and consider briefly how his use of such imagery compares with that of modern writers.

The Language of Human Priesthood

Some of the earliest uses of the language of priesthood and mediation connect it with the Jesus Prayer. Thus Nadejda Gorodetzky, writing in 1942, speaks rather tentatively of an exercise of 'the priesthood of all believers'

---

[5] St Gregory the Theologian, *Second Hom. on Easter*, 7–8, *PG* 36: 632.
[6] See Maximos Confessor, *Ambiguum* 41, *PG* 91: 1304D–1312B. See further Andrew Louth, 'The Cosmic Vision of Saint Maximos the Confessor', in Philip Clayton and Arthur Peacocke (eds), *In whom we live and move and have our being: Panentheistic Reflections on God's Presence in a Scientific World* (Grand Rapids/Cambridge: Eerdmans, 2004), 184–96.

through applying the name of Jesus to 'people, books, flowers, to all things we meet, see or think', so that it becomes 'a mystical key to the world, an instrument of the hidden offering of everything and everyone, setting the divine seal on the world'.[7] Fr Lev Gillet, who quotes this passage at length, explicitly speaks of the Prayer as a 'spiritual Eucharist', an 'offering of thanksgiving'.[8]

Mrs Gorodetzky's explicit invocation of the 'priesthood of all believers' is quite atypical. Orthodox 'priest of creation' discourse has generally taken a different path, focusing much more on the ministerial priesthood and celebration of the Divine Liturgy as the root metaphor. But it is highly plausible that the prominence of the idea of the royal priesthood in Western (especially Protestant) thought is reflected in the readiness of these Orthodox writers to apply the image of 'priesthood' so freely to the general human task of offering.[9]

In Fr Lev's case at least, it is quite clear that the background to the human offering of the 'spiritual Eucharist' is a vivid awareness of a world 'evolving towards the total Christ' (a Teilhardian echo here?), of the relatedness of all things to Christ, of God's infinite love for every thing, so he can speak in terms of 'integrating our spiritual life with the life of the universe'.[10] Compared with many later writers, this is an approach that gives far more emphasis to God's presence in and through other creatures, the role of creation itself in guiding our human offering: 'All creation mysteriously utters the Name of Jesus ... It is the utterance of this Name that Christians should hear in nature.' In this way, by invoking the Name of Jesus we 'speak aloud the secret of these things' and 'give [the animals] back their primitive dignity which we so easily forget'.[11]

---

7 N. Gorodetzky, 'The Prayer of Jesus', *Blackfriars*, 23 (1942), 76.
8 A Monk of the Eastern Church, *The Jesus Prayer*, revised edn (Crestwood, NY: St Vladimir's Seminary Press, 1987), 102.
9 I am indebted to Dr Andreas Andreopoulos for this very interesting suggestion.
10 Fr Lev Gillet, *The Burning Bush* (Springfield, IL: Templegate, no date), 19–20.
11 A Monk of the Eastern Church, *On the Invocation of the Name of Jesus* (London: Fellowship of St Alban and St Sergius, no date), 15–16.

Similar insights are found in Paul Evdokimov, who speaks of the calling of each person 'to act as priest *of his whole life*' (my emphasis) – to take all that is human and turn it into a hymn of glory.[12] Note how the 'priestly' role is limited here: the 'offering' is the totality of one's own interactions with other things (and people), so that we are not left to wonder how it can encompass the entire universe. Sacramental and ecclesial language pervades Evdokimov's seminal article 'Nature';[13] through the Church, 'the matter of the cosmos becomes the conductor of grace'. He quotes Metropolitan Philaret of Moscow, saying that man enters the cosmos as king and priest, but seems to see humans as primarily communicants in the cosmic Eucharist.[14] And, incidentally, the dignity of Adam to which man is restored is that of kingship.

A key figure in the popularization of priesthood language was Fr Alexander Schmemann. Already in 1964 he was exploring themes to which he would keep returning: 'Man was created as a priest; the world was created as the matter of a sacrament';[15] and again, 'the world was God's gift to us, existing not for its own sake but to be transformed, to become life, and so to be offered back as man's gift to God.' There is always a sharp distinction between the 'priest' – the 'first basic definition' of man – and the world as the '*matter* [my emphasis] of an all-embracing cosmic Eucharist'.[16] But he speaks in a powerful and compelling way of a *sacramental* use of the world, of how such basic actions as eating to sustain our physical life become communion with God who is our life.

Schmemann speaks of a need to transform the world, but, unlike some other writers, he does not pursue the idea of a 'transformation' performed by man. 'Priest' for Schmemann means above all *homo adorans* – compare

---

12 Quoted in Bishop Kallistos of Diokleia, *The Orthodox Way* (Crestwood, NY: St Vladimir's Seminary Press, 2002), 65.
13 Evdokimov, 'Nature', *Scottish Journal of Theology*, 18 (March 1965), 1–22.
14 Ibid., 17, 22.
15 'The World as Sacrament', reprinted in Alexander Schmemann, *Church, World, Mission* (Crestwood, NY: St Vladimir's Seminary Press, 1979), 223.
16 Alexander Schmemann, *For the Life of the World* (Crestwood, NY: St Vladimir's Seminary Press, 1973), 15.

St Gregory's characterization of man as 'worshipper'. Our priestly offering, therefore, is above all praise. It is in offering praise that man becomes himself; and equally, it is in being offered, being blessed, that created things become *them*selves. 'Thanksgiving is the experience of paradise',[17] in that the world becomes once more 'the means of man's communion with God'.[18] The actual 'transformation', it seems, is not in the non-human world but in the way we apprehend and receive it. Hence Schmemann insists that consecration does not turn things into 'sacred objects' distinct from the profane world, but rather 'refer[s] things to their original and at the same time ultimate meaning – God's conception of them'.[19]

One of many theologians to take up Schmemann's priestly imagery is Fr Dumitru Staniloae.[20] He does so only in passing, but deserves mention here because his sacramental language and his (highly activist) idea of how man offers the world back to God have influenced later proponents of 'priest of creation'. His cosmology is profoundly shaped by St Maximos, especially Maximos's doctrine of the *logoi* which define each thing according to God's intention for it and are also words addressed to us, defining how we offer the world back to God. According to Staniloae, man is to return the gift of creation 'with interest'; the seal on the *prosphora* symbolizes the 'seal' of human understanding and intellectual work whereby creation is 'humanized'. Yet, despite having perhaps the strongest emphasis of any Orthodox writer on working, transforming, and moulding the world,[21] he has a powerful sense of the inseparable unity of all creation, in its ultimate transfiguration and also in its journey – the world is transformed by us, but also transforms us as it nourishes us with divine rationality. Ever faithful

---

17 Alexander Schmemann, *The Eucharist* (Crestwood, NY: St Vladimir's Seminary Press, 1987), 174.
18 Schmemann, *For the Life of the World*, 73, cf. 93.
19 Schmemann, *Eucharist*, 61.
20 e.g. Staniloae, 'The World as Gift and Sacrament of God's Love', *Sobornost*, 5: 9 (Summer 1969), 668–9.
21 See the discussion, with some trenchant criticism, in Jenkins, *Ecologies of Grace*, 196–201.

to St Maximos, Staniloae holds his exalted view of human activity firmly within a framework of a 'cosmic liturgy' centred on Christ.

Metropolitan Paulos mar Gregorios was an eclectic and rather idiosyncratic thinker, but he was writing about man and the cosmos at a time when few other Orthodox were. Influenced especially by Gregory of Nyssa and Maximos, he speaks of man as mediator, one who unites.[22] He does use 'priest' language, though not extensively or exclusively; and it is closely bound up with 'eternal priesthood of Christ', who lifts creation up to God 'in His created body'.[23]

Note the nuanced way mar Gregorios expresses man's relationship with the rest of creation: humanity has 'a special vocation as priest of creation', but 'is not totally discontinuous with creation', and this by the logic of the metaphor itself: 'a priest has to be an integral part of the people he represents.'[24] Such explicit rejections of cosmic clericalism are common, but their implications for the status of creation as a whole are rarely worked out.

How does mar Gregorios envisage human 'priesthood' being exercised? One of his most enduring ideas concerns the balance between *mastery* and *mystery*. This means that priesthood is expressed not only in praise and worship, but also in human use and manipulation of the world. It also means that 'mastery' of the universe has a clearly defined goal – not of having it for our own use, but 'giving nature as our extended body' into God's hands 'in the great mystery of eucharistic *self*-offering'[25] (my emphasis). This way of speaking certainly depends on a certain sense of solidarity with nature as a whole. Clearly it does not coincide exactly with the usual modern understanding of 'man's mastery over nature' – indeed, mar Gregorios describes mastery for our own sake as the 'original sin'. Even so, his hopes for technology as a way of 'humanizing' the world of matter are unlikely to strike many today as either attractive or realistic.

22 See Metropolitan Paulos mar Gregorios, *The Human Presence* (Madras: The Christian Literature Society, 1980).
23 Ibid., 85.
24 Ibid.
25 Ibid., 89.

Olivier Clément, who is an important source for mar Gregorios, speaks of 'humanizing' in a less alarming way; it has to do with the way we 'live the great cosmic eucharist…in our transformation of nature no less than in our understanding of it'.[26] 'The creature expresses the divine glory after its own fashion and by its very existence'; our task is 'to interpret it creatively, to give conscious utterance to the ontological praise of things'. And he illustrates how this is attainable in practice: 'Whereas in new countries nature is either virgin or violated … nature in the old Christian countries shows the marks of grace, almost as if it had a face …'[27]

In a way quite reminiscent of St Maximos, Clément has a very strong doctrine of the mediating role of man, within a cosmos permeated by divine presence. But he speaks almost in passing of man as 'priest as well as king'[28] among several images, both personal and impersonal; it is not priesthood but the Eucharist and worship more generally that provide his primary framework.

Another writer who early on explored 'priesthood' imagery is Philip Sherrard. Well known for his profound mistrust of technology, he sees man's priestly and mediating role as best expressed in the artist. He also stresses an all-important point that is often eclipsed later on: the crucial movement is not 'humanization' of the world but 'God's enhumanization [which] has taken the whole world into God'. With his overwhelming sense of nature as sacramental and indeed 'intrinsically sacred', he will provide a sharp counterpoint to Zizioulas; yet he can also talk, confusingly, of man 'bestow[ing] divine love and beauty on the world'.[29]

Metropolitan Kallistos of Diokleia has also long been using the language of human 'priesthood', often drawing on Schmemann's writings

---

26 Olivier Clément, *On Human Being: A Spiritual Anthropology* (London: New City, 2000), 118.
27 Ibid., 109, 120.
28 Ibid., 110.
29 Philip Sherrard, *The Rape of Man and Nature* (Ipswich: Golgonooza Press, 1987), 42, 40–1, 92, 40.

about worship and thanksgiving.[30] He continues to balance this imagery with other images such as microcosm, king, and mediator. He associates human creativity with the kingly role, so that the eucharistic offering of manmade bread and wine manifests both the kingly and the priestly.[31] In the same vein as Sherrard, Metropolitan Kallistos reminds us that the immeasurably greater eucharistic transformation is performed not by us but by Christ, the true offerer, priest, celebrant, and mediator; humans perform these roles only by virtue of their unity with Christ.[32]

'Priestly' and creative activity are associated principally with the human vocation 'not only to contemplate creation, but to act within it';[33] art and scientific enquiry can both be ways of exercising this vocation. In a move that seems to go beyond Schmemann's 'making things what they are', Metropolitan Kallistos sees creative use of the world as the way man 'gives natural things a voice and renders creation articulate in praise of God'.[34] In support of this, Metropolitan Kallistos quotes Leontios of Cyprus: 'Creation does not venerate the Maker directly and by itself, but it is through me that the heavens declare the glory of God; through me the moon worships God, through me the stars glorify Him, through me the waters and showers of rain, the dew and all creation, venerate God and give Him glory.'[35] This is a very strong statement, because it seems to extend man's role in creation so that his mediation is required not only for its ultimate unity with God, but also for the praise that it offers Him in the interim. On the other hand, any suspicion of human arrogance is allayed by the insistence on the kenotic and ascetic requirements for the task of offering. Eucharist cannot be separated from sacrifice, or 'priesthood of creation'

---

30   e.g. Archimandrite Kallistos Ware, 'The Value of the Material Creation', *Sobornost*, 6: 3 (1971), 154–65.
31   e.g. Kallistos, *The Orthodox Way*, 54.
32   Bishop Kallistos of Diokleia, *Through the Creation to the Creator* (Pallis Memorial Lecture 1995) (London: Friends of the Centre, 1996), 20.
33   Ibid., 15.
34   Kallistos, *The Orthodox Way*, 54.
35   Leontios of Cyprus, *Fifth Homily of Christian Apologetic against the Jews, and on the Icons*, PG 93: 1604B.

from sacrificial love.[36] Orthodox theologians often mention sacrifice in the context of the human role in creation, but rarely develop the theme.[37]

The most enthusiastic and systematic exponent of 'priest of creation' language is undoubtedly Metropolitan John (Zizioulas) of Pergamon. He has elaborated this idea in great detail over the years, and it is not possible to do justice to all the nuances of his position in a brief summary. Many of the key features of his understanding of human priesthood are already familiar. He repeatedly underlines that 'human beings are part of the natural cosmos, and thus their salvation is part of the salvation of the cosmos.'[38] Indeed, he argues for the image of 'priest' in preference to 'steward' precisely because this image presents man as related to nature not functionally but ontologically;[39] this underlines the connection between 'priesthood' language and the Patristic language of microcosm, mid-point, etc. which underlies it. Human 'priesthood' has to do above all with *making a connection* between creation and God, referring His creation back to Him. This precisely reverses the attitude of Adam, who 'makes himself the ultimate point of reference'.[40] For Metropolitan John, as for Schmemann and others, anthropocentrism in this sense is the original sin.

It is with Metropolitan John that the identification of 'priesthood' with Maximos's 'natural bond' really takes hold, with all its eschatological

---

36 Kallistos Ware, Bishop of Diokleia, 'Orthodox Theology in the New Millennium: What is the Most Important Question?' (A contribution to the Summer School 'Living Orthodoxy in the 21st Century', Institute of Orthodox Christian Studies, Cambridge, July 2003); cf. Metropolitan John of Pergamon, 'Ethics *versus* Ethos: An Orthodox Approach to the Relation between Ecology and Ethics', in *The Environment and Ethics: Summer Seminar on Halki '95* (Patriarchate of Constantinople, 1995), 26.
37 Contrast discussion in Norman Wirzba, 'A Priestly Approach to Environmental Theology: Learning to Receive and Give Again the Gifts of Creation', *Dialog: A Journal of Theology*, 50: 4 (Winter 2011, December), 356–64, which draws on Zizioulas.
38 Metropolitan John of Pergamon, 'Ethics *versus* Ethos, 26.
39 Metropolitan John, 'Proprietors or Priests'.
40 Metropolitan John of Pergamon, 'Man the Priest of Creation', in A. Walker and C. Carras (eds), *Living Orthodoxy in the Modern World* (London: SPCK, 1996), 184.

implications. He is talking primarily about ontological survival, not just ecological survival – or indeed about an offering of praise. Man has an essential role because he is the only *creature* able to transcend the limitations which apply to all created things (ourselves included) precisely because they are created out of nothing.[41] Here we have a coherent explanation of how creation can both be 'very good', and still stand in need of 'salvation', of eternal life. The goodness of creation is revealed as something dynamic, part of its progress towards an ultimate goal which lies beyond itself. In this dynamic and eschatological perspective, it is impossible to accept that 'nature does not need man.'

Somewhat more puzzling, however, is the importance that Metropolitan John ascribes to creativity. Man is able to transcend the limitations of creaturehood because of the drive to be free of the laws of nature seen in his urge to create out of nothing, his impatience with any 'given'.[42] This sounds more like a desire to *be* God than a longing to be united with Him; it also presents an image of the essence of human nature in which many humans, the present writer included, find it difficult to recognize themselves.

How does man carry out his priestly role? Metropolitan John takes up some familiar themes. The priestly role is exercised first and foremost by the Church, through the sacraments, in which we recognize God rather than ourselves as Lord of creation and refer creation back to Him. Secondly, he refers to artistic creation as a way of elevating things 'transient and ephemeral to a lasting, even eternal value', seeing even the celebrant at the Eucharist as an 'artist' in this sense. And thirdly, the priestly task involves development – not simply for the sake of human needs, but 'because nature itself stands in need of development through us in order to fulfil its own being and acquire a meaning which it would not otherwise have'.[43]

It is easy to come away from these writings with a sense that the rest of creation is, and should be, overwhelmed by human creative activity. But it seems that this is far from Metropolitan John's intention, judging

---

41 Metropolitan John of Pergamon, 'Preserving God's Creation' (Part 3), *Sourozh*, 41 (August 1990), 31 (reprinted from *King's Theological Review*).
42 Ibid.
43 Metropolitan John of Pergamon, 'Proprietors or Priests?', 6–7, 8, 9.

from his more detailed discussions of his key concepts of *relationship* and *otherness*. In developing these concepts, he makes ever more detailed use of St Maximos, and often seems to affirm the dignity of non-human creation more clearly than in his specifically ecological writings. Perhaps not so incidentally, the writings on relationship and otherness also give considerably less prominence to the 'priest' metaphor, though it is certainly present.

Metropolitan John clarifies that the relationships that constitute our identity include the whole of creation,[44] not just other persons; indeed, he is fascinated by the insights from contemporary physics that support a 'relational ontology' of creation, which 'in its very nature... point[s] to a "beyond the self"'.[45] This enables him to tread the fine line between 'personalizing' the world, which he sees as the error of process philosophy, and affirming that the world 'owes its relational being to a personal presence which, although *in* the world, exists in a *dialectical relation with* it'[46] (emphasis original). Human creativity is presented as the way we treat nature as otherness in communion. Implicitly addressing a prime concern raised by the language of 'humanizing', or indeed 'creativity', he emphasizes that the ecological crisis results from a failure to respect the otherness of non-human creation, the human tendency to absorb it into ourselves. Thus he insists that the body of a particular entity should not be treated as a mere object or resource, but 'as possessing its own desires and communion goals'; a eucharistic approach respects these 'goals', unlike the approach of modern technology according to which humans assign their own goals to things.[47] Another fine line is being trodden here, because the foregoing might well seem to preclude human creativity, at least in the sense of giving things a meaning that they would not otherwise have. Zizioulas does, however, reiterate that in the Eucharist we offer creation 'as our own personal gift,

---

[44] John D. Zizioulas, *Communion and Otherness. Further Studies in Personhood and the Church* (London: T. & T. Clark, 2006), 92.

[45] John Zizioulas, 'Relational Ontology: Insights from Patristic Thought', in John Polkinghorne (ed.), *The Trinity and an Entangled World: Relativity in Physics and Theology* (Grand Rapids/Cambridge: Eerdmans, 2010), 146–56.

[46] Ibid., 155.

[47] Zizioulas, *Communion and Otherness*, 10–11, 94.

as our own creation. Thus the eucharistic way of being involves an act of dedication or "setting apart," a sacralization of creation; ... not because of some sacred quality inherent in created nature but because of the sacrality of communion ....'[48] One might wonder whether this is reconcilable with Schmemann's assertion that consecration does *not* create a separate class of sacred objects; and if not, who is right.

'Liturgy' and 'Offering' in St Maximos

We have referred already to the reliance of the 'priest of creation' metaphor on Maximos the Confessor. Indeed, it is often now asserted, by a form of shorthand, that Maximos describes man as 'priest of creation'[49] or creation as a 'cosmic liturgy';[50] but strictly speaking, he does neither. 'Priest of creation' seems to have been extrapolated from the imagery of man as a 'natural bond' mediating between the 'divisions' in creation and thus able to bring them into unity. 'Cosmic liturgy' is a term coined by H. U. von Balthasar to characterize both Maximos's theological approach[51] and his understanding of the Divine Liturgy itself, as 'a way of drawing the entire world into the hypostatic union, *because both world and liturgy share a Christological foundation*'[52] (my emphasis). The key text here is Maximos's *Mystagogy*, in which we see the Church, the church building, and the Liturgy celebrated within it as encapsulating the event of communion in which God becomes

---

48 Ibid., 93.
49 e.g. Radu Bordeianu, 'Maximos and Ecology: The Relevance of Maximos the Confessor's Theology of Creation for the Present Ecological Crisis', *Downside Review*, 127 (2009), 117–19.
50 John Chryssavgis (ed.), *Cosmic Grace, Humble Prayer: The Ecological Vision of the Green Patriarch Bartholomew I* (Grand Rapids, MI: Wm. B. Eerdmans, 2009), Introduction, 49.
51 Hans Urs von Balthasar, *Cosmic Liturgy: The Universe according to Maximos the Confessor* (San Francisco: Ignatius Press, 2003), 85.
52 Ibid., 322.

one with us, and we are united with and in Him. 'Cosmic liturgy' represents what Metropolitan John calls the movement of creation 'to its blessed *peras*, its final goal which is unity in Christ without confusion'.[53] Man was intended to be the catalyst for this process; but since he failed in this, the task was accomplished by God made man.[54] It is easy to see how the pervasive eucharistic paradigm in Maximos has encouraged the equation of 'natural bond' with 'priest of creation', though we might also wonder why Maximos himself does not take this step.

Maximos shows remarkably little inclination to fit his cosmological thinking into a single eucharistic metaphor. Rather, one has the sense that the Divine Liturgy itself images an all-pervasive underlying pattern of God's working in His creation.

This is very true of the opening chapters of the *Mystagogy*, where we find liturgical imagery aplenty – but not in as tidy a form as the modern interpreter might wish.[55] Maximos begins with an extended discussion of the symbolism of the church building, which for him is a highly comprehensive image. It images: God (because all are brought together into unity); the world visible and invisible; the sensible world of heaven and earth; man, with his tripartite constitution of soul, spiritual intellect, and body; and the soul with its various faculties brought into unity.

The focal point of the church is the 'mystery upon the altar': the mystery of union with God, divinization. The focus is all on God's work, which effects this union. The mystical union is only really discussed *à propos* of man and the soul, but its relevance to the entire creation becomes clear at the end of this discussion: man and the world are both destined for resurrection, for a spiritual transformation. But instead of giving us one single image for the process leading up to this union, Maximos points to recurring patterns found throughout creation (and revelation). And the patterns are to some extent superimposed, because they exist on different levels. Thus man and the sensible world share the same destiny because they mirror

---

53 Zizioulas, 'Relational Ontology', 151.
54 See *Ambiguum* 41, *PG* 91: 1304D–1312B.
55 Chapters 1–7, *PG* 91: 664D–688B. For an excellent concise summary and interpretation, see Andrew Louth, *Maximos the Confessor* (London: Routledge, 1996), 74–7.

Priest of Creation or Cosmic Liturgy? 203

each other: man is a world and vice versa. Certainly, in Maximos's thought the total cosmic movement is towards unity in God, and man is the catalyst, the 'natural bond' through which this is achieved; it is not that there are several parallel courses. Yet this movement is worked out on multiple levels in the natures and characteristic activities of various creatures, all of them bearing the same pattern. The signature of the Word in the world has a holographic quality.

In contrast to most modern eucharistic imagery, we cannot fail to notice how little interest the *Mystagogy* shows in the human work of offering (and less still in the priestly role, which seems to come within Maximos's purview chiefly when he is writing to a hierarch).[56] True, it is explained that man is a 'mystical church' because, *inter alia*, he offers to God the principles of sensible things through natural contemplation in the 'sanctuary' of his soul. But the overwhelming focus is on union with God. At one point Maximos speaks of this in nuptial imagery, as 'the most holy embrace in which God becomes one flesh and one spirit with the Church and the soul'.[57] This is interesting, because where I have found nuptial imagery in the context of 'priest of creation', it is taken in quite another direction: 'Priesthood... is the very essence of manhood, man's creative relation to the "womanhood" of the created world.'[58] Now, the inherent flexibility of imagery means that these metaphors do not have to be mutually exclusive. But we might wish to ponder the rather different implications of seeing ourselves as the bride of Christ, or the bridegroom of the rest of creation.

The lack of prominence given to 'offering' in the *Mystagogy* does not mean that Maximos ignores this theme. Indeed, one of his most detailed discussions of humans' relationship with visible nature frames it in the rather broader context of giving and receiving gifts.[59] As with so many of Maximos's writings, the imagery is determined by the text he is explicating

---

56 See discussion in von Balthasar, *Cosmic Liturgy*, 324.
57 *Mystagogy* 5, *PG* 91: 860D–861A.
58 Schmemann, *For the Life of the World*, 92–3; cf. Clément, *On Human Being*, 109.
59 *To Thalassius*, *PG* 90: 476C–482D. See further discussion in Nikolaos Loudovikos, *A Eucharistic Ontology: Maximus the Confessor's Exchatological Ontology of Being as Dialogical Reciprocity* (Brookline, MA: Holy Cross Orthodox Press, 2010), 36–42.

– in this case, 2 Chron. 32: 23, which speaks of 'gifts' (*dora*) to God and 'presents' (*domata*) to the king. Again, there is no simple linear process, but a whole nexus of offerings. Creation brings its offering *through* us; creation brings gifts *from* God *to* us; we offer to God the gifts derived from creation though natural contemplation. The verbs Maximos uses are *proskomizo* and *prosphero*, and the eucharistic echoes are obvious. And in order to be in a position to receive and convey creation's offering, the mind must become, lest we wonder, a king – by attaining to the state of dispassion in which all creation is subject to man. If we are looking for a sustained and comprehensive eucharistic metaphor, we shall be disappointed. But Maximos leaves us in no doubt that the eucharistic pattern is woven into the texture of the universe.

'Priest of Creation' and Its Problems

Our brief overview so far has shown a considerable evolution in ideas, a shift from 'priesthood' as human quality to 'priest of creation' as a role, and a veritable explosion in the amount of conceptual space 'priesthood' occupies in Orthodox cosmological and ecological thinking. It also suggests that the developed idea of 'priest of creation' is not as close to Maximos's 'cosmic liturgy' as is usually suggested. And it raises the question of whether there is a pattern in the use of priestly imagery, with the most developed and assertive versions being favoured by (some) members of the ministerial priesthood, while lay writers incline more to ideas of offering and receiving, within a strongly delineated framework of 'cosmic liturgy'.

Turning now to some of the problems generated by 'priest of creation' language, we find some unresolved questions, and also some persistent misunderstandings. The imagery of priesthood and liturgy seems able to create lasting impressions that may be quite at odds with the detail of what is being said.

First of all, does 'priest of creation' imagery manage to avoid cosmic clericalism? A recurring suspicion is reflected in the comment that it 'deflects attention from our evolutionary kinship with animals' and our dependency on all other creatures.[60] The second is an entirely fair criticism of the way 'priest of creation' imagery is typically used. The first charge seems at first somewhat obtuse: is it not repeatedly pointed out that a priest has to belong to the community that he represents? But then the kinship between priest and community is relevant only if all creation is seen *as* the community, the 'laity' in the cosmic liturgy (as well as being the gifts and the temple); whereas proponents of 'priest of creation' typically elide the 'community' completely and speak as if there were only two parties involved, the priest and the gifts. It is not that a communal and conciliar understanding of the Church or a sense of cosmic concelebration is by any means lacking in modern Orthodox thinking; the latter indeed is quite pronounced, especially in some monastic writers.[61] But typically, writers who take this view of all creation use 'priesthood' language little if at all. In practice, 'cosmic concelebration' and 'priest of creation' do not mix.[62] And that is a pity, because concelebration does not mean congregationalism; 'cosmic concelebration' offers a promising framework for speaking of human 'membership' in creation, while recognizing a unique human ministry.

Closely related to the perception of 'cosmic clericalism' is the criticism of 'priest of creation' language as 'anthropocentric'.[63] Since 'anthropocentrism'

---

60   Christopher Southgate, *The Groaning of Creation. God, Evolution and the Problem of Evil* (Louisville, KY/London: Westminster John Knox Press, 2008), 106.
61   See further Elizabeth Theokritoff, 'Liturgy, Cosmic Worship and Christian Cosmology', in John Chryssavgis and Bruce V. Foltz (eds), *Towards an Ecology of Transfiguration: Orthodox Christian Perspectives on Environment, Nature and Creation* (New York: Fordham University Press, 2013), 295–306.
62   One honourable exception, which rather proves the rule, is John Chryssavgis's delicate description of man as 'the liturgical celebrant of [the] innate joy of the world', in *Beyond the Shattered Image* (Minneapolis, MN: Light and Life Publishing, 1999), 5.
63   e.g. Richard Bauckham, 'Joining Creation's Praise of God', *Ecotheology*, 7: 1 (2002), 45–59; Christina M. Gschwandtner, 'Creativity as Call to Care for Creation? Between John Zizioulas and Jean-Louis Chretien', in Bruce Benson, Norman Wirzba, and Brian Treanor (eds), *Being-in-Creation: Essays for an Endangered World* (New York: Fordham University Press, forthcoming). I am grateful to Dr Gschwandtner for the opportunity to read this paper before its publication.

is still something of an obsession in ecological theology, one must always consider how the term is being used and whether the characteristic in question is necessarily a defect in the given case. Certainly, the Orthodox understanding of cosmic salvation is formally 'anthropocentric' in a way that requires no apology, in that man is the focus for the convergence of all things for the sake of unity with God.[64] But there is also a reasonable concern that 'priest of creation' is 'anthropocentric' in the same way that a manual for celebrants is hieratic. It by no means ignores the interest of all creation in the process. But it does 'zoom in' on the human role in such a way that the rest of the 'cosmic liturgy' is blurred. When 'priest of creation' is used to the exclusion of other images, it becomes hard to see the bigger picture of God's work in the world.

Something more than a matter of focus seems to be at stake when we look at the role ascribed to human creativity.[65] Many people find the emphasis on creativity disturbing, not least because mankind's creative efforts have had a somewhat chequered history. And what are we to make of the suggestion that the world needs to be 'humanized' in order to be brought to its fulfilment? This sounds as if the intrinsic value and integrity of other creatures is being denied, although several writers strongly stress the 'isness' (Metropolitan Kallistos) or 'otherness' (Metropolitan John) of each creature, grounded in its own *logos*.

There is no doubt that humans are creative, but the association of this characteristic with priesthood seems less obvious. In the Eucharist, the priest offers up the gifts worked and offered by the community. In the Divine Liturgy, celebrated by the human community, this offering is indeed a distinctively human product. But the moral of this is not self-evident. It is usually now taken to mean that we should make analogous, 'creative' use of creation in general in order to offer it up. But it could suggest, more modestly, that whenever we do 'take creation in our hands' in any sense, we should make it an offering to God. It could also remind us that after all our skill and labour and ingenuity, we still have nothing to offer that is not totally 'God's own' already. The first interpretation suggests that human

---

64 See Bordeianu, 'Maximos and Ecology', 103, 111.
65 See further Gschwandtner, 'Creativity'.

creativity is *required for* cosmic liturgy; the second and third suggest that it is to be *conditioned by* it.

The first interpretation introduces a difficulty that the Fathers did not face: how do we take creation into our hands and 'humanize' it? Turning everything into a human product seems undesirable on a planetary scale and ridiculous on a cosmic scale. The image of *microcosm* suggests a simpler solution, however: we *are* the cosmos humanized, 'the hypostasis of the whole cosmos which participates in [our] nature'.[66] As Olivier Clément elaborates, more poetically: 'What is our body but the form that our "living soul" impresses on the universal "dust" which constantly penetrates and passes through us?'[67] Our freedom determines whether creation-in-us is brought into unity with God or alienated from Him, but the fact that we carry creation with us depends entirely on our nature.

Subsuming human creativity – or development – into priestly imagery seems to invite confusion between human and divine transformations. Celebration of the Eucharist requires bread, a human product; but the point of the Eucharist is not that matter becomes bread, but that matter – the bread, our body – becomes Christ. The priest as president of the offering community is the *instrument* of this divine 'development' (as well as undergoing it himself), but he is by no means the author or craftsman of it.

There seems to be renewed interest recently in the less invasive notion of creativity as the work of the poet, which we met earlier in Sherrard. Fr Romilo Knežević identifies the priestly role with the poetic in the sense that man 'gives to the Lord the intellectual meanings of things'.[68] This is Maximos's terminology, but he also draws on modern writers such as Paul Claudel (a probable influence on Schmemann)[69] and Jean-Louis Chrétien.[70]

---

66 Vladimir Lossky, *Orthodox Theology: An Introduction* (Crestwood, NY: St Vladimir's Seminary Press, 1989), 71.
67 Olivier Clément, 'L'homme dans le monde', *Verbum Caro*, 12: 45 (1958), 11–12.
68 Romilo Knežević, <http://www.academia.edu/1392983/Man_-_Priest_or_a_Poet_of_Creation_sermon> (accessed 14 September 2015).
69 I am grateful to Fr Alexis Vinogradov, friend and translator of Schmemann, for confirmation that Claudel receives several mentions in the diaries.
70 Romilo Knežević, <http://www.academia.edu/3515945/Homo_Theurgos_-_Priest_or_Poet_On_the_Sacramental_Nature_of_Poetry> (accessed 14 September 2015).

Their vision of a poetic 'creativity' conditioned by what creation itself has to say has also caught the attention of some other Orthodox writers,[71] though they do not comment on the extraordinary similarities to Maximos.

The role of human agency is central to one of the most contentious issues thrown up by 'priest of creation': does all creation praise God only through man? And does this mean that man controls all the channels of communication between God and His world – that creation could offer no praise before the appearance of man?[72]

It is hard to believe that the latter proposition, at least, is intended by any Orthodox theologian who speaks of man as 'priest of creation'. But one can see how this impression is created by the language of 'relating creation to God' and 'bestowing grace on the world'. Few are as unequivocal as Olivier Clément, who says quite explicitly that 'there is not only an anthropocosmic connection, there is a theocosmic connection: the world is bathed in the omnipresent glory of God, the fire of His energy; there is in each thing a divine idea, a *logos*, a word addressed to us.'[73] Yet even here, so much depends on the weight given to 'addressed to us'.

At one end of the spectrum is Leontios's statement, quoted above, that 'creation does not venerate the Maker directly and by itself'. The context for his claim is not cosmology, however, but the fight against iconoclasm, which filled the churches with decorative depictions of nature while denying that matter can be a vehicle for *human* prayer and worship. Despite Leontios's choice of words, it seems unlikely that he intended to brush aside centuries of (mainly liturgical) tradition that sees all creation as precisely praising its Maker.[74] So much depends on how literally 'praise' is being used. If we think in terms of the *logoi*, the 'words' in things, then surely creatures will have echoed the Creator word from their inception.

---

71 Gschwandtner, 'Creativity as Call to Care for Creation'; Michael Donley, 'Paul Claudel (1868–1955) – Poet of the Sacred Cosmos', *Temenos Academy Review*, 8 (2005), 34–57.
72 See Bauckham, 'Joining Creation's Praise', and Gschwandtner, 'Creativity'.
73 Clément, 'L'homme dans le monde', 12.
74 See further Theokritoff, 'Liturgy, Cosmic Worship and Christian Cosmology'.

Confusion arises because the imagery of worship evoked by 'priest of creation' readily gives the impression that man's primary role is to offer praise on behalf of creation. There is indeed such a tradition, and Schmemann's *homo adorans* comes close to it. But the very strong language of man's unique calling to 'relate creation to God' comes out of a rather different understanding of cosmic 'priesthood'. Its frame of reference is not a 'cosmic Lauds' but specifically a cosmic *Eucharist*. And the eucharistic Liturgy, to quote Schmemann again, is a procession – 'the journey of the Church into the dimension of the Kingdom'.[75] The Godward movement of all creation, which *is* its ontological praise and its very structure, can only depend directly on its Creator. But the movement is intended to culminate in the mystery of union on the altar, and for this man is the appointed instrument.

In Conclusion: Broadening the Perspective

We have seen that emphasis on the human 'priest' can lead to suspicions that the integrity of non-human creatures is being ignored. An emphasis on cosmic liturgy can lead to an apparently different concern, which however also comes down to failure to take the rest of creation seriously: the criticism that we are ignoring the ambiguity of creation, its 'fallenness'.[76] Related to this is another question raised in the ecological context: how does it help transfigure any part of creation if we 'offer it up'?

To respond to either of these questions, we have to broaden our horizons. We have to insist on the dynamic quality of 'cosmic liturgy' and its eschatological reference, but we must also recognize the complexity of

---

75 Schmemann, *For the Life of the World*, 26.
76 Christopher Southgate's criticism in these terms seems to result from his identification of 'cosmic liturgy' with 'a mere static hymn of praise', *contrasted with* the redemption/transfiguration of the cosmos: *Groaning of Creation*, 112–13.

the work of offering that it involves, which cannot readily be described in 'priestly' or even liturgical images.

The concern about the ambiguity of creation is ironic, because this is the subject of untold volumes of Orthodox literature – it is called the ascetic tradition. Asceticism is regularly, and rightly, emphasized as essential to the exercise of our 'priestly' vocation. What is not usually explained, but is very clear in Maximos, is that the very vision of 'cosmic liturgy' depends on the purification that comes from ascetic discipline. It requires perceiving things according to their *logoi*, rather than in the disordered condition in which we ordinarily experience them. At this point, it is hard to avoid reintroducing another traditional and familiar image: before we can participate in the cosmic liturgy we have to exercise our *kingship* of creation, ruling our senses and the things they apprehend. 'Ruling' things here means *not being ruled by them* – or, more precisely, by our possessiveness of them and the impassioned responses that they provoke.

Asceticism is also the most obvious way in which spiritual life practically affects the way we live in the world. If this seems an inadequate answer to the query about the practical effects of human 'priestly' offering, it may be because that is the wrong question. When we hear 'priest of creation' in an ecological context, it creates the expectation of a sort of 'stewardship' or 'creation care' – with a sacramental quality, certainly, but still an image for how man acts in the world. 'Cosmic liturgy', however, is an image of how God acts in His creation; in this context, man as 'link' or 'priest' is an instance of how God appoints all things to work together with Him. It indicates a unique responsibility, but one that is in a way indirect. 'Creation seeks but one thing', says Archimandrite Vasileios: 'for us to be truly human … returning to our life according to our God-given nature.'[77]

It is in order to become truly human, then, that we offer back to God whatever we touch with our hands, our senses, or our minds. It is in order to become truly human that we do not simply consume the world in the same way as every other living organism – we consume it in the awareness that we are feeding on God's sacrificial love. It is in order to become truly

---

77 Archimandrite Vasileios of Iviron, *Ecology and Monasticism* (Montreal: Alexander Press, 1996), 19.

human that we 'till and keep' whatever aspects of the world are entrusted to us, while simultaneously cultivating the 'words' of matter in which God speaks to us.

This helps to restore, I believe, the balance between our dignity and our creaturehood which 'priesthood of creation' sometimes seems to skew. We act in the world, but in the awareness of a crucial gap between what we can possibly offer and what God does in return. We offer that which becomes part of our own life – not because it cannot otherwise be united with God, but because only thus can we take our place in the Liturgy whose celebrant is the Word. It is the way we follow the pattern of Christ, who has taken up His creation and declared it to be His body.

Bibliography

Donley, Michael, 'Paul Claudel (1868–1955) – Poet of the Sacred Cosmos', *Temenos Academy Review*, 8 (2005), 34–57.
Gschwandtner, Christina M., 'Creativity as Call to Care for Creation? Between John Zizioulas and Jean-Louis Chretien', in Brian Treanor, Bruce Ellis Benson and Norman Wirzba (eds), *Being-in-Creation: Human Responsibility in an Endangered World* (New York: Fordham University Press, 2015), 100–112.
Theokritoff, Elizabeth, 'Liturgy, Cosmic Worship and Christian Cosmology', in John Chryssavgis and Bruce V. Foltz (eds), *Towards an Ecology of Transfiguration: Orthodox Christian Perspectives on Environment, Nature and Creation* (New York: Fordham University Press, 2013), 295–306.
Wirzba, Norman, 'A Priestly Approach to Environmental Theology: Learning to Receive and Give Again the Gifts of Creation', *Dialog: A Journal of Theology*, 50: 4 (Winter 2011, December), 356–64.
Zizioulas, Metropolitan John, 'Man the Priest of Creation', in A. Walker and C. Carras (eds), *Living Orthodoxy in the Modern World* (London: SPCK, 1996), 178–88.
——, 'Proprietors or Priests of Creation?' (Keynote address, Baltic Symposium, June 2003) <http://www.orthodoxytoday.org/articles2/MetJohnCreation.php> (accessed 15 September 2015).

DIMITRI CONOMOS

17 C. S. Lewis and Church Music[1]

> You have hundreds of feelings that can't be put into words. And that is why I think that in a sense music is the highest of the arts, because it really begins where the others leave off.
>
> C. S. Lewis, *Surprised by Joy: The Shape of My Early Life*
> (London: Geoffrey Bles, 1955)

Secular Music

In the writings of C. S. Lewis, typical references to musical compositions, whether secular or sacred, are remarks in some learned works on completely different subjects or opinions pronounced in correspondence. But there are two exceptions: first, a few paragraphs containing random thoughts on the qualities of music both vocal and instrumental in the chapter entitled 'How the Few and the Many use Pictures and Music' from *An Experiment in Criticism*;[2] and secondly the more important essay, 'On Church Music'.[3] Together, these sources expose the dichotomy that existed in Lewis's understanding of secular and sacred music. He openly admitted that, on matters

---

1   I wish to express my gratitude to Walter Hooper, the last private secretary of C. S. Lewis, whom I interviewed at his home in Oxford on 4 March 2015. Mr Hooper provided me with valuable information and anecdotes about Lewis and his musical tastes, details of which appear in this paper.
2   In C. S. Lewis, *An Experiment in Criticism* (Cambridge: Cambridge University Press, 1961), 22–6.
3   In *English Church Music*, vol. 19 (April 1949); reprinted in W. Hooper (ed.), *C. S. Lewis: Christian Reflections* (London: HarperCollins, 1967; 2nd edn, 1980), 120–6.

musical, he was a layman who possessed no musical knowledge, yet he knew what he liked to hear and what he didn't – indeed, he did not hold back from airing his views.

In his correspondence with friends he expressed his love for the works of nineteenth-century European composers. In particular, he was greatly moved by the symphonies of Beethoven, the virtuoso piano preludes of Chopin, and Wagner's *Der Ring des Nibelungen*. Lewis was struck by the manner in which Wagner had created the great epic story of the *Ring* by fusing elements of diverse German and Scandinavian myths and folk tales, but especially features from the twelfth-century German poem, the *Nibelungenlied*, which was the original inspiration for the *Ring*. In fact, during the 1930s, he and his close friend, J. R. R. Tolkien, apparently began working on a translation of the *Ring*. With this in mind, one might recall that in *The Magician's Nephew* two magic rings, which convey people to the 'Wood between the Worlds' – a connecting chamber between parallel universes – are central to the story: a yellow ring, when touched, sends one to the wood, while a green ring is used to conduct people into a world of their choosing. These rings were created by the magician 'Andrew' who made use of magical dust from Atlantis.

Among twentieth-century British composers, Lewis enjoyed the works of Edward Elgar and Gustav Holst, especially the latter's *The Planets*. In a letter to Sister Penelope[4] he confessed:

> I heard Mars and Jupiter long ago and greatly admired them ... but his characters are rather different from mine I think ... On Jupiter I am closer to him; but I think he is more 'jovial' in the modern sense of the word. The folk tune on which he bases it is not regal enough for my conception.[5]

---

4   Sister Penelope was a nun at the Community of St Mary the Virgin in Wantage, Oxfordshire. She had an engaging personality and Lewis corresponded with her throughout his life. They discussed a wide range of topics, beginning with her letter of praise for *Out of the Silent Planet*. She sent him a postcard of the Shroud of Turin that he kept for the rest of his life, and he sent her the manuscript of *The Screwtape Letters* for safekeeping and eventually allowed her to sell it to raise money for charity.
5   Letter to Sister Penelope: 31 January 1946 in W. H. Lewis (ed.), *Letters of C. S. Lewis*, revised and enlarged edition by W. Hooper (London: Collins, 1988), 381.

In March 1933 Lewis's brother, Warnie, purchased a superb gramophone together with a complete set of Beethoven's nine symphonies as well as other compositions chiefly from the European Romantic repertory. Every Sunday evening Joy and the brothers would greatly enjoy listening to the latest recordings of orchestral masterpieces. All the same, Lewis was not a devotee of merry 'noises'. He insisted that 'music means not the noises it is nice to make, but the noises it is nice to hear'.[6] The difficulty here is to fathom Lewis's understanding of the operative 'noise'. His musical diet was weighted heavily in favour of nineteenth-century opera and symphonic masterpieces with scant acknowledgement of the baroque masters (Bach and Handel) or of the accomplishments of the first Viennese school (Haydn and Mozart). Indeed, on one occasion he remonstrated 'how operatic the whole building up of the climax is in *Perelandra*'.[7]

Yet, only very occasionally is direct homage paid to music in his writings – simply because he knew so little about its evolution from monophonic chant to contemporary abstract genres. For example, in his discussion of the impacts, both positive and negative, of music in his aforementioned 'How the Few and the Many use Pictures and Music', Lewis confines himself exclusively to compositions that operate within the realm of fundamental tonal melodies and tonic/dominant functional harmonies. No mention is made of the plethora of styles that characterize twentieth-century music whether on the Continent or in Britain: impressionists, expressionists, the jazz-influenced movement, atonality, dodecaphony, and above all the flowering of new, experimental types of choral evensong compositions. Most British nationalists are equally ignored: Benjamin Britten, Ralph Vaughan Williams, and Michael Tippett.

But in spite of this narrow perspective, Lewis speaks bluntly of the music that is within his sphere of experience. And he has his prejudices, especially in vocal works where he insists that word must override melody.

---

6   *A Preface to 'Paradise Lost'* (London: Oxford University Press, 1942), 21.
7   Letter to Charles A. Brady, 29 October 1944, in W. Hooper (ed.), *C. S. Lewis: Collected Letters II* (London: HarperCollins, 2004), 629.

As for instrumental compositions, he does not deny the magn
'tunes': how at first we are inclined to imitate, whistle, and h
in so doing, he adds, we tend to ignore the composer's orch
structuring of the piece as a whole, and the manner of its ren
players. Secondly, there is the emotional response. A tune 'se
us to become convivial or pensive or animated. Here lie the re
his use of the cautionary 'seems', since some musicologists (in
author) feel that the appropriateness of melodies or themes
emotions is an illusion. Indeed, the association of tone and en
recedes with every progression in genuine musical perception.
conjectured that, on occasion, 'emotional responses are dicta
much by the fanciful verbal titles which have been attached to certain
compositions as by the music itself.'[8] Perhaps he had in mind sobriquets
such as *Götterdämmerung* and *Eroica*.

Finally, Lewis confesses that he has experienced some 'simple airs, quite
apart from what is done with them and quite apart from the execution,
[which] are intrinsically vile and ugly. Certain popular songs and hymns
come to mind.'[9] The sole example given by Lewis is, in his words, 'the
odious' 'Home, Sweet Home',[10] a telling indication of his confidence in his
own subjectivity. He would unequivocally condemn what he considered
to be repugnant or crude music. But at the same time he would concede
that, in the hands of a master musician, even elements of 'Home, Sweet
Home' might well contribute to the creation of a good symphony.[11] On
this point, it is interesting to note that this particular song, composed by
an Englishman, Sir Henry Bishop[12] (lyrics by the American John Howard

8   'How the Few and the Many use Pictures and Music', 23.
9   Ibid., 25.
10   Ibid. No hymn is mentioned.
11   Ibid.
12   1786–1855.

Payne),[13] for his 1823 opera, *Clari, or the Maid of Milan*, has remained well known and loved by many for nearly two hundred years.[14]

Sacred Music

Turning now to Lewis's opinions on church music, one might do well to begin with a cogent passage from Screwtape's eleventh letter to his nephew, the novice Wormwood.[15] Retreating atypically from his insistence on the sovereignty of word over tone, Lewis has the senior demon comparing the laughter of joy as something analogous to 'that detestable art which the humans call Music, and something like it occurs in Heaven – a meaningless acceleration in the rhythm of celestial experience, quite opaque to us. Laughter of this kind does us no good and should always be

---

13 Mid pleasures and palaces though we may roam,
    Be it ever so humble, there's no place like home;
    A charm from the skies seems to hallow us there,
    Which seek thro' the world, is ne'er met elsewhere.
    Home! Home!
    Sweet, sweet home!
    There's no place like home
    There's no place like home!

14 As early as 1827 the song was quoted by Swedish composer, Franz Berwald, in his *Konzertstück for Bassoon and Orchestra* and Gaetano Donizetti used the theme in his opera, *Anna Bolena* (1830). It is also used in Sir Henry Wood's *Fantasia on British Sea Songs* and in Alexandre Guilmant's *Fantasy for Organ* op. 43 (the *Fantaisie sur deux mélodies anglaises*). In 1857 composer/pianist Sigismond Thalberg wrote a series of variations for piano (op. 72) on the theme of 'Home, Sweet Home'. In 1909 it was featured in the silent film, *The House of Cards*. The song was reputedly banned from being played in Union Army camps during the American Civil War for being too redolent of hearth and home and so likely to incite desertion. The song is also famous in Japan as *Hanyū no Yado* ('My Humble Cottage').

15 See the passage quoted below, p. 220, and C. S. Lewis, *The Screwtape Letters* (London: Fontana, 1956).

discouraged.'[16] In an article on Lewis, Metropolitan Kallistos (Ware) has shown that, whereas the writings of the Church Fathers seem to play very little part in his intellectual formation, Lewis's thinking and theological orientation 'is profoundly in harmony with the patristic and Orthodox standpoint'.[17] The description of heavenly music is a case in point: it demonstrates Lewis's intuitive affinity with at least two medieval Neoplatonists. In his *The Celestial Hierarchy*, Dionysios the Areopagite (*c*.500) makes reference to the ranks of angels who in heaven are united in song. Each choir sings hymns, the music of which is passed from the highest and nearest to the throne of God down the ranks of the angelic choirs to the lowest, before finally being transmitted to the praying congregations of the Church militant.[18] In the medieval West an apposite point of view was expressed by Remigius of Auxerre (*c*.841–*c*.908): 'True music is always in the heavens ...'[19] Accordingly, Screwtape's 'detestable art' is in fact the human imitation of divine song, whose music is comparable to 'the laughter of joy'.

Lewis is frequently accused of loathing the Victorian hymn settings that prevailed in Oxford's Anglican churches, especially those accompanied by the organ (an instrument that he abhorred and which he described as 'one long roar').[20] Indeed, at church on Sundays and at college through the week, he frequently chose to attend only 'said' services, because, for Lewis, these hymns were the 'dead wood' of a worship liturgy.[21] On occasion he exaggerated his feelings, as in remarks such as 'those fifth-rate poems set to

16 Ibid., 50.
17 Kallistos Ware, 'C. S. Lewis: An "Anonymous Orthodox"?', *Sobornost*, 17: 2 (1995), 14–15.
18 A. Louth, 'The Reception of Dionysius in the Byzantine World: Maximus to Palamas', in S. Coakley and C. M. Stang (eds), *Dionysius the Areopagite* (Oxford: Blackwell, 2009), 64–6.
19 C. E. Lutz, *Remigii Autissiodorensis Commentum in Martianum Capellam*, vol. 2 (Leiden: Brill, 1962), 304f.: 'Musica enim vera semper in caelo est.'
20 R. Green and W. Hooper, *C. S. Lewis: A Biography* (New York: Harcourt, Brace, Jovanovich, 1974), 104.
21 Letter to Eric Routley, 16 July 1946, in W. Hooper (ed.), *C. S. Lewis, Collected Letters II*, 720.

sixth-rate music',[22] something that we shall see in more detail later. Lewis despised hymns, on the one hand, because the lyrics were not good poetry – they were frequently bathetic and paltry with 'confused or erroneous sentiment'[23] – and on the other, because he found the melodies, like those of certain popular songs, repulsive and distasteful.

As with secular music, so with sacred, Lewis was the unwitting victim of the constraints of conventional, or standard, repertories. In the former, the choice was his own, according to his tastes, and there he admitted he was musically illiterate. In the latter, choice was monopolized by clerics and church musicians whose preoccupations were to decide on what constituted acceptable hymnody. Lewis was right: their choices were often ponderous, sentimental, and far from inspiring. It would take more or less the passage of a decade following his death for Anglican churches to expand their musical repertoires not only with boiler-plate hymns both 'ancient and modern' (all of which were frequently arranged in the mediocre, lumbering, nineteenth-century style), but also with authentic plainchant, Renaissance polyphony, and innovative contemporary compositions with fresh texts. Lewis may have welcomed these developments, but he would still have had to endure the organ. Prejudices notwithstanding, Lewis was far from proscribing hymn singing in worship. What he wanted was first-class verses set to first-class music. At the same time, neither verse nor tone, singly or collectively, must be considered as ends in themselves. They are pathways, not destinations; any opposing viewpoint would be tantamount to idolatry:

> The books or the music in which we thought the beauty was located will betray us if we trust to them; it was in them, it only came through them, and what came through them was longing. These things the beauty, the memory of our own past – are good images of what we really desire; but if they are mistaken for the thing itself they turn into dumb idols, breaking the hearts of their worshippers. For they are not the thing

---

22 C. S. Lewis, 'Answers to Questions on Christianity' (1944), originally a pamphlet; later included in W. Hooper (ed.), *God in the Dock* (Grand Rapids, MI: Eerdmans, 1970), 62.
23 'Christianity and Culture', in W. Hooper (ed.), *C. S. Lewis: Christian Reflections*, 3.

itself; they are only the scent of a flower we have not found, the echo of a tune we have not heard, news from a country we have never yet visited.[24]

His artistic palate, in due course, was mitigated by ethical and religious constraints to the degree that his point of view soon took an about-face. In *The Screwtape Letters*, for example, written in 1942, he remarked: 'Provided that any of those neighbours sing out of tune, or have boots that squeak, or double chins, or odd clothes, the patient will quite easily believe that their religion must therefore be somehow ridiculous.'[25] Such remarks may be compared with the following, written two years later:

> I disliked very much their hymns, which I considered to be fifth-rate poems set to sixth-rate music. But as I went on I saw the great merit of it. I came up against different people of quite different outlooks and different education, and then gradually my conceit just began peeling off. I realized that the hymns (which were just sixth-rate music) were, nevertheless, being sung with devotion and benefit by an old saint in elastic-side boots in the opposite pew, and then you realize that you aren't fit to clean those boots. It gets you out of your solitary conceit.[26]

Music in Letters

On 13 July 1946 Erik Routley (1917–82), an English Congregational minister, composer, and musicologist (educated at Lancing College and at Magdalen and Mansfield Colleges in Oxford), wrote a letter of request to C. S. Lewis. The Hymn Society of Great Britain and Ireland was opening a file of new hymns to which modern hymn writers were to be asked to contribute. Would Lewis be willing to be a member of the panel to which

---

24   This sermon, delivered at Oxford University's church of St Mary the Virgin on 8 June 1941, is included in W. Hooper (ed.), *The Weight of Glory and Other Addresses by C. S. Lewis* (New York: HarperCollins, 1980), 25–46.
25   *Screwtape Letters*, 16.
26   'Christianity and Culture', in W. Hooper (ed.), *C. S. Lewis: Christian Reflections*, 61–2.

new hymns may be submitted in order that their merit may be assessed? Such a request rightly suggests that Lewis would be expected to evaluate the hymn *texts*. But Lewis's curt reply, written just three days later from Magdalen College, addresses both the poems and their musical settings:

> The truth is that I'm not in sufficient sympathy with the project to help you. I know that many of the congregation like singing hymns: but am not yet convinced that their enjoyment is of a spiritual kind. It may be: I don't know. To the minority, of whom I am one, the hymns are mostly the dead wood of the service. Recently in a party of six people I found that all without exception would like fewer hymns. Naturally, one holding this view can't help you.[27]

There are echoes here of earlier statements ('fewer hymns', 'music as an end in itself', etc.) and they will be repeated in later correspondence. In a letter to Mrs R. E. Halvorson, dated March 1956,[28] Lewis brings up the issue of the *effect* of music on the churchgoer by dividing the worshippers into two categories: (a) the musically illiterate who merely receive a single, emotional effect; and (b) musical scholars who receive both emotional and intellectual satisfaction. In terms of religious experience, for both (a) and (b), music can be either a preparation or a medium for encountering God or a distraction, an impediment. All things that are both natural and sinless, he continues, have the capability to be of service in the spiritual life, but this is not automatic. When the 'thing' does not serve, it becomes merely trifling – as music is to millions of people – or a dangerous idol. Lewis argues that, at times, the emotional effect of music might not only be a distraction but also a deception. Certain emotions felt in church may easily be mistaken for religious emotions when they may be wholly natural.

> That means that even genially religious emotion is only a servant. No soul is saved by having it or damned for lacking it. The love we are commanded to have for God and our neighbour is a state of the will, not of the affections (though if they ever also play their part so much the better). So that the test of music or religion or even

---

27 Letter to Eric Routley, 16 July 1946, in W. Hooper (ed.), *C. S. Lewis, Collected Letters II*, 720.
28 W. Hooper (ed.), *C. S. Lewis, Collected Letters III* (London: HarperCollins, 2006), 731–2.

visions if one has them is always the same – do they make one more obedient, more God-centred, and neighbour-centred and less self-centred? 'Though I speak with the tongues of Bach and Palestrina and have not charity etc.!'[29]

Routley was so disappointed by Lewis's response that on 18 September 1946 he produced a very long letter which, together with Lewis's correspondence, was later printed in the periodical *The Presbyter* under the heading, 'Correspondence with an Anglican who dislikes hymns'.[30] Routley begins by pointing out that: 'It is a matter of plain fact that you have as much influence on religious thought among ordinary Christians in this country at the present time as any other one person; if you had less influence it wouldn't matter so much that you take the view you do about hymns.' Routley then, in a very loquacious and convoluted manner, insists that Lewis's understanding of term 'hymn' may be flawed. Hymns, he insists, were never meant to be a garnishment to the service – never a medium for community singing, or for aesthetic, non-spiritual indulgence – but a vital part of the liturgy itself (precisely as *troparia* function in celebrations of the Byzantine rite). As such, Routley maintains that congregational responses are what epitomize the authentic hymn: when the faithful participate in the action of the ritual by responding to the gestures or actions of the celebrant. The Eucharist, he insists, is constructed skilfully and satisfyingly along these lines.

The discussion ends with a reply from Lewis to Routley on 21 September 1946.[31] He begins with an apology in case of a misunderstanding. Lewis declares it was never his intention to give the impression that active participation by the people or that hymns were bad in principle. This is followed by a rather extraordinary remark:

> In modern England, however, we can't sing as well as the Welsh and Germans can. Also (a great pity, but a fact) the art of poetry has developed for two centuries in a private and subjective direction. That is why I find hymns 'dead wood'. But I spoke only for myself and a few others.

---

29 Ibid. A rewriting of 1 Corinthians 13: 1.
30 *The Presbyter: A Journal of Reformed Churchmanship*, 6: 2 (1948), 15–20.
31 Ibid., 20.

This oversimplification may be judged by some as bordering on the facetious, but more likely it is tongue-in-cheek. After all, which and in what way are the 'Welsh and Germans' superior singers to the English? Is the 'private and subjective direction' of poetry from the mid-eighteenth century meant to refer to all poetry, or only hymnody? Are the 'few others' mentioned here the same as the aforementioned 'party of six people'? Elsewhere, one notes that these *few* become '*many* laymen' whose 'chiefly desire are fewer, better, and shorter hymns; especially *fewer*'. It was noted above, moreover, that in 1944 Lewis 'went on [to see] the great merit' of hymn singing (in spite of the low-brow words and music) when he observed others with 'quite different outlooks and different education' sing with devotion and benefit from it. He concludes by conceding that, if an improved hymnody (or even the present repertory) edifies other people, it would of course be 'an elementary duty of charity and humility for me to submit'. Indeed Lewis insisted to intellectual converts to Christianity that sacrifice of personal tastes and a self-effacing acquiescence in anything that may edify their uneducated parishioners (no matter how appalling it seems to the educated 'natural man') are the first lessons they must learn. 'The door is *low* and one must stoop to enter.'[32]

That Lewis did not disdain all hymns is made evident by an event recorded in the eleventh volume of the Lewis Papers. Very early on 1 May 1930 (Mayday) Lewis and his brother, Warren, ascended to the top of Magdalen College's tower. There at dawn they heard the Magdalen College School boys' choir sing 'a Latin hymn which was very effective and a beautiful tune: why on earth don't they sing these hymns in church?'[33] Perhaps if unaccompanied Latin plainchants were sung in Anglican churches in

[32] *The Presbyter*, 20.
[33] Lewis Papers, vol. 11. 11. The Lewis Papers consist of deposited manuscripts, including literary manuscripts, correspondence, photographs, essays, notebooks, letters, papers, and microfilms. The papers in this collection were acquired by the Bodleian Library from various sources between 1968 and 1989. The originals of the majority of the photocopies in the collection are held by the Marion E. Wade Center, Wheaton College, Illinois, USA. In 1982 selections from Warren Lewis's diary were published under the title *Brothers and Friends*.

place of Victorian hymns, Lewis might have had more inspiring remarks to make about hymn texts and their settings.

Polemics For and Against Church Music

By 1949 Lewis had solidified his views on sacred song in the form of a short but telling article originally submitted in April of that year to the journal *English Church Music*, edited at that time by the musician Leonard Blake (1907–89). Blake himself was a composer of organ-accompanied Anglican hymns whose musical settings and choice of religious poetry could scarcely have enthused Lewis. Nevertheless, Blake was a friend and he especially invited Lewis to contribute a paper. The result, entitled 'On Church Music', has been reprinted in *C. S. Lewis: Christian Reflections* and is the only piece of writing by Lewis to deal solely with the nature, materials, forms, and forces of church music according to his personal proclivities. In this manifesto Lewis begins by describing himself as a 'layman ... who can boast no musical education', lacking the experience of a lifelong churchgoer and, as such, far from being qualified to teach on the subject. But having agreed to express his opinions, he is prepared to stick his neck out and speak. Unfortunately, many have read into this essay much more than he had actually expressed.

Lewis's opening assumptions are that:

1. 'nothing should be done or sung or said in church which does not aim directly or indirectly at glorifying God or edifying the people or both';[34]
2. church services may have a cultural value but this is not what they exist for.

---

34 *Christian Reflections*, 120.

Both here and above (in Lewis's second letter to Erik Routley) we encounter the word 'edify'. Here he praises church music so long as it edifies the faithful, whereas in the letter he discredits church music if it failed to do so.[35] What is new in this article, however, is the reference to 'glorification' and its connection with 'edification'. Briefly put, Lewis's premise takes the following trajectory: whenever we edify people (through gesture, song, or spoken word) we glorify (God), but in glorifying (God) we do not always edify (people). He considers that to edify others is an act of charity and obedience 'and therefore in itself a glorification of God'. But it is also possible for someone to glorify God in ways that do not edify his neighbour. The two examples he offers as acts of glorification that obfuscate fellow worshippers are those who speak in tongues (untranslated) and the singing of hymns set to tasteless (to some – but not to others) music. After a meandering discussion, he dismisses both erstwhile paradigms as inapposite to edification and glorification precisely because the one has to do with uttered words and the other with wordless utterances.

Lewis then proffers somewhat unconvincing remarks about 'the idea behind Church Music' which, he maintains,

> [...] *glorifies God by being excellent in its own kind*;[36] almost as the birds and flowers and the heavens themselves glorify Him. In the composition and highly trained execution of sacred music we offer our natural gifts at their highest to God, as we do also in ecclesiastical architecture, in vestments, in glass and gold and silver, in well-kept parish accounts, or the careful organization of a Social.

The difficulty here is that Lewis confines himself in this article solely to the sonic aspect of church music. But, aside from organ *obbligati*, church music is exclusively song and, as such, any judgement on church song that makes no reference to both word and tone, melody and prosody, considerably weakens one's assumptions. The ultimate question is: what makes sacred music sacred? The words, the music, or both? From medieval times

---

35 See above, p. 223. In both instances it is not absolutely clear if Lewis is referring to the poetry, the tune, or both.
36 *Christian Reflections*, 121. Author's italics.

examples exist in the East as well as in the West of profane parahymnography[37] set as *contrafacta*[38] to liturgical music. Does the liturgical melody here independently retain its sanctity, its capability to edify and glorify? When it comes to modern church music – what Lewis refers to as 'popular hymns' – his opinions are vehemently negative: 'I do not yet seem to have found any evidence that the physical and emotional exhilaration which it produces is necessarily, or often, of any religious relevance.'[39] Hence the deduction, cited also in his letter to Mrs R. E. Halvorson, that 'What I, like many other laymen, chiefly desire in church are fewer, better, and shorter hymns, especially fewer.'[40] Such aesthetic, non-spiritual exhilaration was experienced by Lewis in 1922 (before his conversion). Together with Arthur and Maureen Moore, he attended choral evensong as if in an auditorium at New College chapel. Having listened to some choral psalmody and Charles Villiers Stanford's *Magnificat*, among some other pieces, he admitted to enjoying the performance immensely: 'I wondered why I had never troubled to go before', he added.[41]

In order to place Lewis's ruminations into some kind of perspective it is important to find the answer to the question: can there be a true church music style? By definition, *church* music is music composed, adapted, or deemed suitable for church use, or for Christian worship, ritual, thanksgiving, or commemoration. Two fundamental issues of church music define its style: (a) what is the correct manner of performance? and (b) what are the range and depth of the hymnography's sentiments that the music may seek to express? Musicological debate on the historical evolution of church music has provoked as many difficulties as it has solved. Yet all of these 'difficulties' deal with or rise out of what are perceived as fundamental

---

37   See K. Mitsakis, 'Byzantine and Modern Greek Parahymnography', in D. Conomos (ed.), *Studies in Eastern Chant*, vol. 5 (Crestwood, NY: St Vladimir's Seminary Press, Crestwood, 1990), 7–9.
38   New texts substituted for the original one without substantial change to the music.
39   *Christian Reflections*, 122.
40   Ibid., 122–3.
41   W. Hooper (ed.), *All My Road before Me: The Diary of C. S. Lewis, 1922–1927* (London: HarperCollins, 1991), 71.

categories of church music: an appropriate textual and melodic repertory and an appropriate compositional and performing style. The nature of that appropriateness and the authority to determine it are the primary issues that the historical evolution has sought to address.

The evidence of history provides no answers to the question of what the characteristics and features of true church music are. But academic discourse over the centuries has raised this question unremittingly and certain recognizable patterns have sporadically emerged, though none has prevailed. The criterion of verbal intelligibility affected all of the music of the Reformation and Counter-Reformation, but this matter arose initially as an impassioned concomitant doctrinal issue at the Council of Trent (1545–63)[42] that subsequently sought to realize itself in musical terms. As early as the fourth century, St Niketas of Remesiana (*c.* 335–414) had insisted that singing in church should be executed 'without distraction to the meaning of the words being sung'.[43] Lewis was not directly absorbed by these verbal matters. His arguments centred on taste (that is, *his* taste) and intention: the quality of the melody, its execution, its prosody, and how these edify and/or glorify. By limiting his range of focus to Victorian hymn compositions, his conclusions eschew such genres as psalmody, biblical tropes, antiphonal and responsorial compositions, liturgical responses, choral motets, plainchant, and many more.

Towards the end of the nineteenth century, a genus known as *a cappella* singing came to the fore. It attempted to set the standard by which English church music could be identified, irrespective of sonant lucidity or even lingual origin. Ideally this was a form that shunned musical instruments and employed identifiable triadic functional harmony. For Lewis, who, as stated earlier, disdained the organ, this feature was a source of satisfaction,

---

42 This Roman Catholic council was convened by Pope Paul III. Among many other topics, it dealt with the reform of liturgical music. A principal aim of the reforms and of the music composed with them in view was the intelligibility of the liturgical texts.

43 Niketas of Remesiana, 'On the Benefit of Psalmody', in O. Strunk (ed.), *Source Readings in Music History: The Early Christian Period and the Latin Middle Ages*, trans. J. McKinnon (New York: Norton, 1978), 21.

but even the *a cappella* repertory, despite its moderate popularity, did not satisfy congregations in general. Indeed, no qualifications about hymns' texts, musical style, or melodic structures have ever produced acceptable answers or provided by themselves a high-quality style of church music.

More directly relevant to Lewis's arguments in 'On Church Music' are two more fundamental issues. The first derives from the nature of music itself, while the second is related to the nature of music as an invocation of the divine. Lewis realized that, first, church music tends quickly to occupy a dominant position from which it orders and controls, and even comes to interpret, content. Secondly, if left to their own devices, composers and performers may tend to forget church music's *raison d'être* and instead take delight only in their own activities. As a result, Lewis, together with some of his colleagues, criticizes church music – that is to say, the (limited) kind of church music that he had experienced – as being not so much an enhancement of sacred services as an obstruction:

> The first and most solid conclusion which (for me) is that both parties, the High Brows and the Low, assume far too easily the spiritual value of the music they want. Neither the greatest excellence of a trained performance from the choir, nor the heartiest and most enthusiastic bellowing from the pews, must be taken to signify that any specifically religious activity is going on. It may be so, or it may not.[44]

In particular, Lewis disputed the spiritual value of (Anglican) church music: did it glorify God, or was it merely an aesthetic emotion rather than a profound spiritual feature of worship? He was also troubled by the way in which both 'intellectual' (what he calls 'highbrow') and boorish church songs isolated and separated the faithful. As such, the presence of music could counterbalance its potential advantages.[45] Having made the distinction, Lewis neither offers examples of either type nor states his criteria for classification. On the other hand, he observed that such differences in taste can be an opportunity for engaging in humility and self-effacement.

---

44 *Christian Reflections*, 123.
45 Ibid., 123–4.

It can teach us humility and charity towards simple lowbrow people who may be better Christians than ourselves. I naturally loathe nearly all hymns: the face and life of the charwoman in the next pew who revels in them teach me that good taste in poetry or music are not necessary for salvation.[46]

There is one instance, however, when Lewis himself chose a popular Victorian hymn by Henry Alford[47] when King Frank (also known as the 'Cabby') urged the entire party, newly landed in Narnia, to remain calm, and suggested that the best thing they could do to 'pass the time' would be to sing a "ymn".[48] This the Cabby proceeded to do. He struck up at once a harvest thanksgiving hymn: all about crops being 'safely gathered in'. Would this be a sample of 'highbrow/non-boorish'? Ultimately, Lewis declares, God has no need of human offerings, whether martyrdom or music, since at one level they are superfluous: 'like the intrinsically worthless present of a child, which a father values indeed, but values only for the intention'.[49]

Music as Metaphor

Lewis well understood the power of music: how it is able to affect attitudes; how it can have a decisive influence on human behaviour; and, both metaphorically and metaphysically, how it can represent the divine harmony and symmetry of the spheres and of the material world. Whereas the Genesis account of the creation *ex nihilo* gives us an act of creation through the Word (εἶπεν ὁ Θεός), which in a Christian context is read as creation through the second person of the Trinity, the creation story of Narnia has the Christ-like Aslan performing the same action, but this time through the medium of

---

46 *Collected Letters*, 7 December 1950.
47 'Come, ye thankful people, come', a thanksgiving poem by Henry Alford (1810–71), set to music by George Elvey (1816–93).
48 C. S. Lewis, *The Magician's Nephew* (London: Bodley Head, 1955), ch. 8.
49 *Christian Reflections*, 126.

pitched, wordless, unmeasured vocal intonation.[50] In both cases the 'Voice' is the originator and architect; sound and song (respectively) are inexorably foundational in the two creation stories. A further consequence of these mystagogic enactments is the manifestation of *joy*. The union of joy with song is a theme expounded in the prophecy of Sophonias (= Zephaniah): '*Sing*, O daughter of Zion; shout, O Israel; be glad and *rejoice* with all the heart, O daughter of Jerusalem' (Zeph. 3: 14) and 'The Lord thy God ... will save, he will *rejoice* over thee with joy; he will rest in his love, he will joy over thee with *singing*' (Zeph. 3: 17). Singing here represents the joy of God who saw that everything was 'good'. The Hebrew phrase 'he will rejoice over you with singing' can also be translated literally as 'he rejoices over you with a shout of joy'.

Thus at the emergence of Narnia there was song: the mellifluous voice of a Lion; a voice that intoned everything into existence. Out of the primordial darkness, a distant Voice began to sing. This song, wordless, tuneless, now close, now far, ever multidirectional, was a 'noise' so beautiful that it almost became unbearable. Lewis then extends this metaphor of a life-creating music by introducing a second, antiphonal choir of 'more voices than you can possibly count' which sang in harmony with the solo Voice but at a higher *tessitura*: 'cold, tingling, and silvery'. Instantly, and at the very moment the populous choir emerged singing, the black, cloudless firmament became ablaze with stars: myriads of shining points of light leaping into existence; 'single stars, constellations, and planets, brighter and bigger than any in our world'. Surely it was the stars themselves, fashioned by music of the deep First Voice, which were singing.

Without a pause, the Voice continued with added vigour its song of creation. In their turn, hills began to form close to the distant horizon and, as the Voice rose and rose in pitch and volume, it 'swelled to the mightiest and most glorious sound it had yet produced', the sun rose in all its glory shooting beams across the land. With the rising of the sun, the singer himself, a magnificent, bushy, immensely pleased Lion appeared on earth. He stood facing the risen sun with mouth wide open in song.

50 *The Magician's Nephew*, ch. 9.

But now the song changed; it was a 'new song',[51] a melismatic jubilus intoned by the Lion as he strode through the sprawling, barren terrain. In contrast with the previous incantation which had summoned up the heavenly lights, this euphony resounded *pianissimo* and yet also *rapsodico* as it echoed in every gully and hill, above the high peaks, the ridges, and crevices of the newly formed landscape. Then suddenly, as the Lion moved, singing, over the face of the land, the ground responded by sending up shoots of grass, followed by bushes, and finally elegant trees whose branches were raised high in a gesture of praise and thanksgiving. Polly Plummer, one of the witnesses of the creation of Narnia,[52] realized that there was a connection between the music and the phenomena that were taking place. For example, when a row of firs appeared out of nowhere on a ridge near to her, she sensed that this was the material equivalent of the immaterial musical phrases – a sequence of deep, sustained pitches – which had been sung by the Lion moments before.

> And when he burst into a rapid series of lighter notes she [Polly] was not surprised to see primroses suddenly appearing in every direction. Thus, with an unspeakable thrill, she felt quite certain that all the things were coming (as she said) 'out of the Lion's head'. When you listened to his song you heard the things he was making up: when you looked round you, you saw them …

In other words, creation was music transfigured: for 'the deepest, wildest voice they had ever heard was saying: "Narnia, Narnia, Narnia, awake. Love. Think. Speak. Be walking trees. Be talking beasts. Be divine waters."'

---

51   Psalm 98: 1.
52   *The Magician's Nephew*, ch. 9.

Conclusion

In spite of his negative statements about the state of Anglican church music and poetry in the mid-twentieth century, C. S. Lewis believed that sacred music could be a source of assistance to Christian congregations. He did not go so far as to say that one could derive spiritual benefits from music, but at the same time he made deft references to vocal and instrumental music, both of which inform and permeate his writings and speeches. It would be difficult to overemphasize the importance of music in Lewis's life, thought, and works. It gave him great pleasure, informed his writing in a variety of ways, and as a source of longing helped lead him to the Christian faith.

Reading through the pages of his formal and informal writings, one observes that Lewis's approach to liturgical song was sometimes cautious, decidedly candid, occasionally compliant, recurrently calumnious, and markedly contradictory. His statements percuss with unanswered questions, not unexpected for a wide-ranging thinker who draws conclusions only after considerable deliberation. Lewis lived at a time when choirs and their masters, especially in cathedral ceremonies, usurped the functions of the clergy. The conductor 'became' the celebrant; the soloists the acolytes. Houses of worship were transformed into auditoriums and in them the High Mass assumed the demeanour of a concert for the modern bourgeoisie. The eminent music critic, Eric Blom (1888–1959), affirmed that attendance at a concert performance should be counted as equivalent to attendance at a divine service. Indeed, at Guildford Cathedral it was known that the sermon was at times replaced by a motet. Few agreed with Dean Inge (1860–1954) who allegedly remarked that 'there is little to justify the notion that God enjoys nothing better that a serenade.' Lewis would certainly have concurred. Furthermore Karl Barth's (1886–1968) adage, which would have had considerable backing, claimed that 'when the angels go about their task praising God, they perform only Bach. I am sure, however, that when they are together *en famille*, they sing Mozart.'

Now Barth's apophthegm suggests that many – but probably not C. S. Lewis – consider there to be a viable link between music and religion, and in this link the former shares (or perhaps overtakes) the space of the latter. The eminent journalist Bernard Levin (1928–2004), whose background was non-religious, admitted that listening to first-class music suffices to make one acquire faith. On the other hand, for the conductor Colin Davis (1927–2013), music was undeniably a religious and mystical experience. To these two positions Lewis responds:

> I must insist that no degree of excellence in the music, simply as music, can assure us that ...[a]... paradisal state has been achieved. The excellence proves 'keenness'; but men can be 'keen' for natural, even wicked, motives. The absence of keenness would prove that they lacked the right spirit; its presence does not prove that they have it. We must beware of the naïve idea that our music can 'please' God as it would please a cultivated human hearer.[53]

Is music, then, a source of revelation in its own right? It is curious that, of all the sacred arts, music was the last to develop fully. For many centuries music stood in an equivocal and ambiguous affinity to Christianity, but eventually it surfaced for some as a dominant fountainhead of revealed truth. At the heart of Lewis's questioning was the popular conception of music as epiphany. It is a fact that, today, in their frequenting of concert halls or listening to CDs, people have discovered a substitute sacrament. Lewis would place this action into the realm of an illusory euphoria that eschews any authority to objective doctrine. He would also ask whether church hymns constitute a truly spiritual or only an ecstatic aspect of public prayer. Instead of genuine worship, there is the danger of an 'aesthetic religion of "flowers and music"', which for Lewis is far from the calling of God to active obedience.[54]

---

53   *Christian Reflections*, 126.
54   *God in the Dock*, 328–9.

Bibliography

Green, R., and W. Hooper, *C. S. Lewis: A Biography* (New York: Harcourt, Brace, Jovanovich, 1974).
Hooper, W. (ed.), *C. S. Lewis: Christian Reflections* (London: HarperCollins, 1967; 2nd edn, 1980).
—— (ed.), *God in the Dock* (Grand Rapids, MI: Eerdmans, 1970).
—— (ed.), *All My Road before Me: The Diary of C. S. Lewis, 1922–1927* (London: HarperCollins, 1991).
—— (ed.), *C. S. Lewis, Collected Letters II: Books, Broadcasts and War 1931–1949* (London: HarperCollins, 2004).
Lewis, C. S., *A Preface to 'Paradise Lost'* (London: Oxford University Press, 1942).
——, 'Answers to Questions on Christianity' (1944), originally a pamphlet; later included in W. Hooper (ed.), *God in the Dock*.
——, 'On Church Music', originally published in *English Church Music*, vol. 19 (April 1949); reprinted in W. Hooper (ed.), *C. S. Lewis: Christian Reflections*, 120–6.
——, *The Screwtape Letters* (London: Fontana, 1956).
——, *An Experiment in Criticism* (Cambridge: Cambridge University Press, 1961).
——, 'Christianity and Culture', in W. Hooper (ed.), *C. S. Lewis: Christian Reflections*.
——, *The Weight of Glory and Other Addresses by C. S. Lewis* (New York: HarperCollins, 1980).
Lewis, W. H. (ed.), *Letters of C. S. Lewis*, revised and enlarged edition by W. Hooper (London: Collins, 1988).
Louth, A., 'The Reception of Dionysius in the Byzantine World: Maximus to Palamas', in S. Coakley and C. M. Stang (eds), *Dionysius the Areopagite* (Oxford: Blackwell, 2009).
Lutz, C. E., *Remigii Autissiodorensis Commentum in Martianum Capellam*, vol. 2 (Leiden: Brill, 1962).
Mitsakis, K., 'Byzantine and Modern Greek Parahymnography', in D. Conomos (ed.), *Studies in Eastern Chant*, vol. 5 (Crestwood, NY: St Vladimir's Seminary Press, 1990).
Ware, K., 'C. S. Lewis: An "Anonymous Orthodox"?', *Sobornost*, 17: 2 (1995), 9–27.

Epilogue

KALLISTOS WARE

18 Fifty-Four Years as an Athonite Pilgrim

'A High Mountain Apart'

Among all the sacred places on this earth, the Holy Mountain of Athos is the one that I personally find most immediately attractive.[1] Since my first visit in 1961, I have been drawn back to the 'mountain of monks' more frequently than I can now remember: perhaps some fifteen times, possibly more often. With good reason Athos has been styled 'the monastic magnet',[2] and certainly its magnetic force is something I have felt continually since my initial pilgrimage fifty-four years ago, and indeed for a number of years before that.

During those fifty-four years, what have I come to understand about the inner meaning and the spiritual message of the Holy Mountain? What changes have I seen? What have I come to regard as its contribution to the wider community of the outside world, throughout the Church as a whole and, indeed, beyond its boundaries? 'We know that when any one of us falls, he falls alone', states Aleksei Khomiakov, 'but no one is saved alone.'[3] How, then, do the monks of Athos contribute to the salvation of others?

---

1   In this paper I have incorporated material from two earlier articles: 'Mount Athos Today', *Christian*, 3: 4 (1976), 322–33; 'The Holy Mountain: Universality and Uniqueness', in G. Speake and K. Ware (eds), *Mount Athos: Microcosm of the Christian East* (Oxford: Peter Lang, 2012), 175–203.
2   Compare the title of the book edited by R. Gothóni and G. Speake, *The Monastic Magnet: Roads to and from Mount Athos* (Oxford: Peter Lang, 2008).
3   'The Church is One', section 9, in W. J. Birkbeck (ed.), *Russia and the English Church during the Last Fifty Years*, vol. 1 (London: Rivington, Percival & Co., 1895), 216.

Let me begin with what has been for me the single most memorable experience on the Holy Mountain, when I ascended alone during the night to the summit of Athos in summer 1971.[4] My intention was to reach the peak at sunrise. I was about to set out from St Anne's around 10 pm, when there was a sudden and violent fall of rain; and I wondered if it might be prudent to postpone my journey. 'Go', said Fr Elias, the monk with whom I was staying, 'you may not ever again have another such opportunity. And if you go, you will never forget your experience.' I am glad that I took his advice. In fact there was no more rain that night.

It was a lengthy climb. My starting point at St Anne's was about 300 metres above sea level, but to reach the summit I had to mount upwards for another 1,700 metres or more. I had chosen a night when there was a full moon, but in practice the moon was less helpful than I had expected; for I had forgotten that much of the walk was through thick woods where the moonlight could not penetrate. My immediate objective was the little chapel of the Panagia, about 500 metres below the summit, where I intended to rest before embarking on the final stages of the ascent. I came out from the woods into a rocky wilderness where the chapel ought to have been, but I could not see it anywhere. To make matters worse, I lost the path. Moonlight has the effect of flattening the landscape and making everything appear different. Blundering about in confusion for many minutes, eventually I sat down defeated. Then I looked up and saw to my surprise the chapel no more than 200 metres away. How strange that I had not noticed it before!

After a short sleep on the chapel floor and a drink of cool water from the nearby cistern, I set out in the pale morning light for the peak of the Holy Mountain. The path is good, and there is no danger at all as long as one does not wander from it. But I kept in mind that, not long before, three Germans had left the proper route and fallen to their deaths. I arrived at the summit just as I had hoped, at the exact moment when the sun emerged in the east from the low clouds across the sea.

---

4 I had previously ascended to the summit during the day in 1966, in the company of Gerald Palmer.

I was confronted by an astonishing spectacle. After gazing for some time at the rising sun in the east, I turned and looked northward, and saw the whole Athonite peninsula, thousands of metres below me, stretching away towards the mainland. It was like a relief map, with rocks and paths standing out with an amazing clarity. I could distinguish all the paths that I had been following for the past ten days, and even the exact points where I had missed the right turning (for in those days there were few effective signposts).[5] Then, with my back to the rising sun, I looked westward, once more over the sea. The sight that met me was something I had never expected, and it will always remain etched in my memory. I saw the shadow of the Holy Mountain as a great pyramid of darkness, extending many miles over the sea and shrinking perceptibly as the sun behind my back rose higher. Surely there are few places in the world where such a phenomenon can be seen.

As I stood in this way, alone at sunrise in the piercing cold on the top of Mount Athos, beside the (then) ruined chapel of the Transfiguration, I was given a dim inkling of the significance of the Mountain as a holy sanctuary, as a point in sacred space, a 'thin place' where the wall of partition between earth and heaven, between the present age and the Age to come, becomes so attenuated as to be virtually transparent.[6]

Wolves, Snakes, and Frogs

I have begun these recollections of my visits to Athos over fifty-four years by speaking of the Mountain itself, and this I have done for an important reason. Athos is indeed a mountain full of *holy persons*, of dedicated monks; and of this I shall speak in a moment. It is also a mountain full

---

[5] The working parties organized each summer in recent years by the Friends of Mount Athos have helped to remedy this.

[6] On the phrase 'a thin place', see Evelyn Underhill, *Collected Papers*, ed. Lucy Menzies (London: Longmans, Green & Co., 1946), 196.

of *holy objects*, of churches and chapels, icons, relics, chalices, crosses, and illuminated Gospel books. But, beside all this, it is more fundamentally in itself a *holy mountain*. While admiring the saints and ascetics who have dwelt and still dwell there, and while rejoicing in the spiritual beauty of the many works of art that it contains, we need also to appreciate the physical reality of the Mountain as such, the intrinsic sacredness of the material environment in which these persons and objects are to be found. In the words of Fr Nikon (1875–1963), the hermit of Karoulia who inspired the English translation of the *Philokalia*, 'Here every stone breathes prayers.'[7] In common with other holy places – such as Jerusalem and Patmos, Iona and Walsingham – the Holy Mountain of Athos acts as a sacrament of God's presence, as a burning glass concentrating the rays of the spiritual Sun with an especial intensity, manifesting the immediacy of the Eternal.

To appreciate this physical reality, this intrinsic sacredness, the best way for the pilgrim is to travel on foot – not to be driven in a minibus or Land Rover but to *walk*, if possible alone. This will frequently prove exhausting. The ancient mule paths are often steep, sometimes neglected, full of loose, sharp stones and overgrown with brambles.[8] In summer the pilgrim will inevitably suffer from heat and thirst. But only so will he come face to face with the basic reality of Athos as a centre of stillness, a shrine of the Divine Presence.

Along with the holiness of the Mountain, the pilgrim who travels on foot will also be struck by its outstanding natural beauty. Because of the presence of streams on every side and the absence of marauding goats, Athos – especially in springtime – is a veritable paradise. There are meadows bright with wild flowers, and trees covered with blossom; and everywhere there is the surrounding sea, with waves breaking over the rocks. Prince

---

7   On Fr Nikon, see K. Ware, 'Gerald Palmer, the *Philokalia*, and the Holy Mountain', in *Friends of Mount Athos: Annual Report 1994*, ed. Graham Speake (published in 1995), 23–8.
8   On the neglect of the ancient paths of Athos, see P. Sherrard, *Athos the Holy Mountain* (London: Sidgwick & Jackson, 1982), 43–8. This incorporates material from P. Sherrard, 'The Paths of Athos', *Eastern Churches Review*, 9: 1–2 (1979), 100–7.

Fifty-Four Years as an Athonite Pilgrim

Mishkin's words come to mind, in Dostoevsky's novel *The Idiot*: 'Beauty will save the world.'

This Athonite beauty is not vacant and static, but it is full of sounds and movement; for the Mountain is a refuge for many living creatures, non-human as well as human. On my earlier visits, as I set off to walk alone through the more remote uplands, the monks warned me to beware of the wolves. I never saw any, but doubtless they saw me as they looked watchfully from the thick undergrowth beside the paths. I am told that there are now no more wolves on Athos, because they have all been shot. This is in some respects a pity, for wolves in their own way are hesychasts, seeking solitude and avoiding contact with humans; and so their continuing presence was an assurance that the Mountain has not ceased to be a place of seclusion.

While I have never seen any wolves on my Athonite wanderings, I have twice met wild boar. The first occasion was just outside the skete of the Prophet Elijah. The second was in the deserted region above the Serbian monastery of Hilandar, on the path leading to Chromitsa, close to the border with Ouranoupolis. Here I encountered a whole family, father, mother, and two youngsters. Not more than 50 metres away, all four of them stopped in their tracks and stared at me, with curiosity but without apparent hostility. After I greeted them, they continued peacefully on their way, disappearing among the bushes.

The solitary walker will also come across snakes, both great and small, which abound on the Holy Mountain. When I was staying for several weeks at Hilandar, working on the English translation of the *Philokalia* with my friends Gerald Palmer and Philip Sherrard – both frequent visitors to Athos – I used to go alone for a walk each afternoon in the surrounding woods. Every day, in exactly the same place on the path, I met a snake some 3 metres long, basking in the sunshine. On the first day I banged on the ground with my staff, but he showed no inclination to move, until I had addressed him politely, asking him to let me through. Then he slid into a gap in the adjoining wall; but as soon as I had passed I heard a swishing sound immediately behind me, as he slid out once more to resume his place in the sun. On the second day I had no need to bang on the ground, for as soon as I asked him he moved out of the way. On the third day I did not even have to ask, much less to bang on the ground, for of his own accord he moved aside as soon as he saw me approaching. Such is the rapport with the realm of nature that even a town-dweller such as myself can quickly establish during visits to the Mountain. The monks who live there permanently, especially the hermits, frequently build up a relationship that is far closer. The many stories in monastic sources about beasts and saints are not mere legends.[9]

Not all my encounters with Athonite snakes have been as benign as my acquaintance with the snake of Hilandar. Once, in one of the more solitary regions of the Mountain, I heard nearby a strange sound, and I turned aside from the path to discover the cause. A rabbit had come down to a pool to drink and a large water snake had seized hold of its head and was gradually swallowing it whole, as the rabbit screamed aloud. I took note that it would be sensible not to bathe in isolated pools on the Mountain. The monks may not eat meat, but there are other residents on Athos who do so.

I wondered at the time whether I should intervene to try and save the rabbit, but I decided that it was not my business to meddle in the affairs of Athonite wild life. I bore in mind the experience of a friend of mine who was making his way through the woods on the Mountain in the company of a monk. My friend has the ability to imitate bird song; and since the Athonite woods are full of birds he practised this gift as the two of them walked together. He called out to the birds and the birds duly replied. In tones of disapproval, the monk said to him: 'Would you mind not doing that?' 'Why, what's wrong?' asked my friend. And the monk replied severely, 'You are disturbing the natural order.'

Along with the snakes and birds, Athos is home to innumerable frogs. I know few sounds in nature as attractive as the singing of frogs, and Athos is one of the best places in which to enjoy batrachian harmony. Once I was staying, around the season of Pentecost, at the skete (or monastic village) of St Anne's. Here each of the scattered dwellings has a garden, with its own cistern and its own contingent of melodious frogs. As I sat on a balcony

---

9   See the classic anthology by H. Waddell, *Beasts and Saints* (London: Constable, 1934); and compare the two books by J. Stefanatos, *Animals and Man: A State of Blessedness* (Minneapolis, MN: Light and Life, 1992), and *Animals Sanctified: A Spiritual Journey* (Minneapolis, MN: Light and Life, 2001).

around sunset, first I could hear the frogs many metres below me on the steep hillside, and then came an answering group many metres above. Others joined in from various cisterns on either side, and before long the whole evening was alive with frog-sourced music. I wished that it would never end.

There is an Athonite anecdote, typical of the monastic sense of humour, about a group of monks who were celebrating the morning service. The frogs in the cistern outside were making an astonishing noise. So the superior went out of the chapel and said: 'Frogs! We've just ended the Midnight Office and are about to begin Matins. Would you mind keeping quiet until we've finished?' Whereupon the frogs replied: 'We've just ended Matins and we are about to begin the First Hour. Would *you* mind keeping quiet until *we've* finished!'

Decline and Renewal: Threats and Hopes

Having reflected on the natural environment, both inanimate and animate, of the Holy Mountain of Athos, let us turn our attention to the monks themselves. I am grateful that, on my first visit in 1961, I was in time to see Athos in what may be termed its 'pre-industrial era'. There were at that time virtually no roads suitable for vehicles, and indeed no actual vehicles to use such roads. The pilgrim, arriving at the port of Daphni, did not find a bus to take him up to the monastic capital of Karyes; he had to walk. But coming events cast their shadow before: on my second visit, in 1962, I found that a vehicle road from port to capital was under construction, in preparation for the celebrations of the Athonite millennium in 1963. In 1961 the only vehicle road was from the Russian monastery of St Panteleimonos, leading up far above to the woods that belonged to the monastery. The community had a lorry to bring down timber to the harbour. Through the modest sale of this timber the Russian monks hoped to raise a little money, for their economic position at that time was altogether dire. This road, however, did not connect St Panteleimonos with any of the other monasteries. With this one exception, I do not think that in 1961 any monastery possessed a lorry, Jeep, or Land Rover. I was told that the Serbian monastery had a tractor donated by Tito, but I never saw it.

Alas! Today the situation has changed out of all recognition. A network of vehicular roads – many of them ugly gashes across the hillside – now joins all the twenty 'ruling' monasteries to one another, with the sole exceptions (as far as I know) of Grigoriou and Dionysiou, which have in any case outlets immediately on to the sea. Vehicles are to be found everywhere. The monks are surprised that I deliberately choose, whenever possible, to walk from one monastery to another, not out of voluntary asceticism, but because of the delight which such walks afford. They consider that this behaviour is unsuitable for a bishop.

Other aspects of the 'pre-industrial era' on Athos remain clearly in my memory. There was no electricity, and lighting was provided by oil lamps or candles. An electric system had been installed in Vatopedi in the 1920s or 1930s, but when I visited in 1961 it no longer worked. There was no running hot water in the monasteries; it had to be heated on a cauldron balanced on a primus stove. The monasteries were not connected directly to the outside world by telephone, although there was a primitive and inefficient telephone system joining the monasteries to each other. I believe that this was set up during the German occupation in World War II. It is easy to look back with nostalgia to the days of Athonite oil lamps, but more modern devices certainly have advantages from a practical point of view. There is, after all, nothing intrinsically numinous about primus stoves and oil lamps.

Coming to Athos in 1961, all around me I saw evidence of decline. The monks constituted a shrinking and ageing population. Everywhere I was surrounded by grey beards, while the few beards that were black stood out as a marked exception. The fall in numbers was by no means new, but had started before World War I. In 1903 there were 7,432 monks, more than half of them non-Greeks. By 1913 the number had dropped to 6,345: this was due mainly to the expulsion of some 800 Russian monks in the course of the dispute concerning 'Glorifiers of the Name' (*Imyaslavtsy*). Following the 1917 revolution, no more recruits came from Russia, and few Greeks chose to join the Athonite monasteries; in consequence, by 1943 there were only 2,878 monks, and by 1959 the number had fallen to 1,641. A low point was reached in 1971, by which time there were only 1,145. Most of these were over sixty years of age, and so there was every prospect that the decrease would continue.

Surprisingly this did not happen. In 1972, for the first time since 1914, the number of monks actually increased, rising by a figure of one from 1,145 to 1,146. This upward movement has steadily continued since then, and today there are perhaps 2,000 monks on the Mountain. More importantly, these are not predominantly elderly, but are distributed more or less evenly among the different age groups. Indeed, there are monasteries where it is difficult to discover a grey beard among the serried ranks of black whiskers. Recently the overall numbers have ceased to grow noticeably; there has, however, been no significant diminution.

This growth in numbers has been accompanied by a major alteration of spiritual atmosphere in the different communities. In almost all the monasteries that I visited during my visits in the 1960s, on a practical level there was a lack of hope among the monks, an absence of any expectation that the demographic situation would improve. Those with whom I spoke did not doubt that the Mountain enjoyed the special blessing of Christ and His Mother; but they viewed the future with quiet resignation rather than with any sense of confidence. I remember, for example, a conversation I had in 1968 with Fr Evdokimos, the senior *epitropos* in the monastery of Philotheou (it was at that time idiorrhythmic). 'We are seventeen monks here', he said, 'but we are mostly old men, and so all the work has to be done by about three or four. I am afraid that Athos will soon become like the monasteries of Egypt – just ruins.' (In fact since then there has been a notable revival of monasticism in the Coptic Church of Egypt, but that is another story.)

I do not hear any of the Athonite monks speaking today in the way that Fr Evdokimos did fifty years ago. Today, combined with the quest for inner stillness, there is among the monks a sense of practical purpose, of dynamic energy. Sometimes one hears the phrase 'springtime in the garden of the Panagia', and this aptly describes the prevailing mood. Everywhere buildings are being restored – sometimes, I fear, unwisely: there was a disastrous example some time ago at Dionysiou when a substantial part of the attractive external balconies was destroyed. But at any rate there are no longer the signs of structural decay that were all too apparent in the

1960s. There is better sanitation in the quarters both of the monks and of the visitors; there are proper washing facilities, with hot water, and there is electric light. In most monasteries there is a welcome improvement in the cooking: no longer do lukewarm beans form the main staple of the diet, but eggs, green salads, and fresh fruit are usually provided.

As for the monks themselves, there has been an evident change in educational level. In 1961, throughout the whole of Athos, I doubt whether more than a dozen monks had received a university education. Today in virtually every community there are members with university degrees – not exclusively in theology but often in subjects such as medicine, law, or politics – and there are a number who have studied outside Greece in western centres of learning. Several are authors of substantial doctrinal texts. Some of us, recalling the humble simplicity and the purity of the vision found so notably among the monks of an earlier era, may feel that there has been a certain loss. Needless to say, university education does not necessarily produce good monks. Yet so long as Athos contained virtually no monks who had pursued higher studies, it was difficult for the Mountain to provide the articulate inspiration and leadership that are so greatly needed by the Church at large.

One of the most encouraging changes has been in the liturgical worship on Athos. In the 1960s, despite the lack of younger monks, the daily round of services was conscientiously performed in full; but often this was done in a hurried and perfunctory manner. A non-Orthodox visitor said to me in 1961, 'They perform their worship as a duty, but without joy.' I thought this unduly harsh, but I saw his point. Now, however, in almost every monastic house the outward prayer life is markedly different. The standard of singing is greatly improved; the reading of the Psalms is more intelligible; the ceremonial actions are carried out with greater reverence; there is less talking in church.

Most important of all, there has been a decisive revival of frequent communion. When I first visited the Mountain in 1961, it was the practice almost everywhere for the monks to receive the sacrament no more than once every forty days, that is to say, ten times a year, even though the Liturgy was celebrated daily, except in Lent.[10] It was also the custom for them to observe before communion a strict fast of two or three days, without any use of oil in cooking. Since oil is allowed on all Saturdays throughout the year, with the sole exception of Holy Saturday (the Saturday immediately before Easter), this meant that, apart from Easter day, the monks never received communion on Sunday, but as a rule on Saturday. This was surely a strange anomaly.

On my first visit to Athos, I attended the feast of the Nativity of the Mother of God (8/21 September) at the Great Lavra. If I recall rightly, the feast fell on a Sunday. There was an all-night vigil, with the participation of some eight priests and four deacons. But, when we came to the Liturgy, this was served by a single priest, without a deacon. At the moment of Holy Communion, out of a congregation of about 150, monks and lay pilgrims, to my astonishment not a single person came forward to receive the sacrament. I had a sad feeling of anticlimax. Today it is unthinkable that this should happen at a great feast in any of the main Athonite houses. At Simonopetra, for example, it is the norm for lay monks to receive Holy Communion two or three times a week. Throughout the Mountain there has been a true Eucharistic renaissance.[11]

What has been the main reason for this increase in the number of monks on the Holy Mountain, and for the renewal of the spiritual and liturgical life? Among the various possible answers, the most significant reason in my view has been the presence on Athos, over the past fifty years, of charismatic elders (*gerontes*), endowed with the gifts of discernment and pastoral guidance. The ministry of the *abba* (or 'father in God') has

---

10   Among the twenty ruling monasteries at that time, the only exception to the forty-day practice was at Dionysiou, where, under the guidance of great Abbot Gabriel, the monks received communion once every two weeks. There may also have been more frequent communion in a few of the hermitages.

11   On reception of the Eucharist on Athos, see Hieromonk Patapios and Archbishop Chrysostomos, *Manna from Athos. The Issue of Frequent Communion on the Holy Mountain in the Late Eighteenth and Early Nineteenth Centuries* (Oxford: Peter Lang, 2006). St Nikodimos of the Holy Mountain (1748–1809), along with other Athonite members of the Kollyvades movement, was a firm advocate of frequent communion, and indeed even of daily communion.

been a constant feature of Eastern monasticism from the time of the first monks such as St Antony and St Makarios of Egypt in the fourth century up to the present day; but there have been periods of decline followed by periods of revival. On Athos the second half of the twentieth century has definitely been a period of revival. Prominent examples of such charismatic elders, from the 1960s onwards, are Fr Vasileios at Stavronikita and Iviron, Fr Aimilianos at Simonopetra, Fr George at Grigoriou, and Fr Ephraim at Philotheou (he has more recently established some sixteen monasteries in North America). It is a striking fact that, when Athonite monasteries have revived, this has been particularly in houses where the abbot is endowed with the gift of eldership. Today young people drawn to the monastic life are attracted not so much by the abbey as by the *abba*. They are looking, not primarily for a famous house with a distinguished history, but for a personal guide.

Spiritual fathers on the Holy Mountain are of course to be found not only in the main monasteries but in the sketes such as Great and Little St Anne's and Kafsokalyvia. One such *geronta*, in the middle of the twentieth century, was Fr Joseph of New Skete (1898–1959). He gathered round himself a group of disciples who practised the Jesus Prayer with special devotion. Setting out from New Skete, his followers have played an important role throughout the Mountain and elsewhere. More recently, a greatly revered elder was the hermit Paisios (1924–94), who was glorified as a saint in 2015. I shall never forget the two hours that I spent with him in 1971, when we spoke at length about St Isaac the Syrian. I was greatly struck by his lightness of heart and his spirit of joy.

Guarding the Walls

What, finally, has been the contribution of the Holy Mountain to the outside world? Although, as already noted, there are now well-educated monks on Athos who are authors of serious spiritual works, the Holy Mountain is by no means a centre of scholarship, in any way comparable to the Benedictine Maurist congregation in eighteenth-century France. What is said by Fr Theoklitos of Dionysiou, a leading Athonite spokesman in the mid-twentieth century, is basically true, although somewhat overstated:

> In the Eastern Church, the existence of the 'scholar' monk is quite unknown...The monk finds no justification, under the ascetic and mystical theology that has been developed by the Fathers, except as a worker of virtue, as a contemplative soul called by God, giving to his brethren in Christ, because of his love for them, out of the abundance of his experience of the divine...Hence, the cell of the monk is not a room for scholarly research and writing, but a place for prayer, work, meditation and the tempering of the soul for special spiritual struggles, in an unworldly, solitary, quiet region.[12]

Much more important than scholarship and literary work is the provision of hospitality by the Athonite monasteries. From the earliest beginnings of monasticism this has been seen, in both East and West, as an integral part of the monastic vocation. As St Benedict of Nursia insists in his *Rule*, 'Let all guests be received as Christ Himself, for He says "I was a stranger, and you welcomed me" (Matt. 25: 35).'[13] Such also is the tradition of the Mountain. Abbot Gabriel of Dionysiou once said to me, 'We divide all the money received by the monastery into three equal parts: one third for upkeep of the buildings, one third for the monks, one third for hospitality to visitors and pilgrims.'

Yet here there is today a major difficulty. In the past the majority of the visitors were genuine pilgrims and, because travel was difficult, their number was relatively restricted. When I stayed for a week at Great Lavra during October 1962, for the whole of that time I was the only visitor. Today, especially throughout the summer, the main monasteries are all but overwhelmed by a constant influx of visitors. Despite a strict quota system, the numbers are disturbingly large: perhaps nearly a hundred each night at the more accessible houses. What is more, most of these visitors are tourists rather than pilgrims; they come to Athos out of curiosity

---

12   Quoted in C. Cavarnos, *Anchored in God. An Inside Account of Life, Art, and Thought on the Holy Mountain of Athos* (Athens: Astir/Papademetriou, 1959), 210–12.
13   Benedict, *Regula Monachorum*, 53.

rather than religious devotion. The monks do their best to cope with this incursion, but the inevitable result is that one no longer finds on Athos the stillness and silence that was such an impressive feature on my visits to the Mountain fifty years ago.

It is only to be expected that those who come to the Holy Mountain as genuine pilgrims are in many cases not content simply to attend the church services and to venerate the icons and relics, but they also hope to find monks to whom they can open their hearts, and from whose words they can receive healing. This brings us to a second way, alongside hospitality, in which Athonite monasticism serves the Christian community at large. From the very beginning of its history the Mountain has nurtured elders, charismatic guides who can offer spiritual direction. We have already spoken of the crucial role played by these elders in the revival of monastic life on Athos during the past half-century. Not only do these elders provide assistance to the monks permanently resident on the Mountain, but they also minister to the many pilgrims who seek them out. But the visitor should not expect that he will easily and casually discover such elders. Often they are hidden.

It is of course true that the ministry of eldership is not limited to monks. Spiritual guides are to be found among the married clergy and in monasteries for women as well as men, and likewise among the laity, both men and women. There are many *ammas* as well as *abbas*. But it can justly be claimed that the Mountain, while enjoying no monopoly, is yet to a preeminent degree a centre where such Spirit-filled counsellors are to be found.

What is it that enables someone to act as a spiritual father or mother? It is above all their entry into the deep mystery of inner prayer. The true *geronta* is not merely someone who *says* prayers from time to time, but someone who *is* prayer all the time, a living flame of prayer, without interruption day and night, whether in solitude or in the company of others. And so we come to a third way in which Athos serves the world. Today, as in the past, the Holy Mountain continues to be an oasis of living prayer. I am not thinking only of intercessory prayer, although this does indeed play a prominent role in the prayer life of the Athonite monk. Yet beyond this all prayer – not only prayer of intercession and petition but prayer that is exclusively contemplative – supports and strengthens the Christian community as a whole. Every place where genuine prayer is offered, and *par excellence* each of the monasteries and hermitages of the Mountain, acts as a focal point, a powerhouse of noetic electricity, that renders the desert of the secular world less arid and forlorn.

This, in the last resort, is the only way in which a monastic centre such as Athos can find its justification and *raison d'être*. For those who do not believe in the value of prayer, monastic life on the Holy Mountain will appear futile and pointless, a perverse waste of human talent. But for those who believe that the world is upheld by the prayers of the saints, the Mountain is indeed providing a service to the world that is creative and indispensable.

The value of the Holy Mountain, and equally of every monastic house of prayer, is well illustrated in a story from fourth-century Egypt. When the young Palladios was suffering from discouragement, he went to see his spiritual father Makarios of Alexandria and said to him, 'Father, what shall I do? For my thoughts afflict me, saying: "You are making no progress, go away from here."' Makarios replied, 'Tell your thoughts: "For Christ's sake I am guarding the walls."'[14]

I am guarding the walls: the Church is like a city; the monks are sentinels on the walls, keeping watch so that the other inhabitants of the city can pursue their occupations in safety and security. *Against whom* are the monks guarding the walls? The monks of Athos have a clear and specific answer: against the demons, who are the common enemies of humankind. The warfare waged by monks against the forces of evil is thus a battle fought on behalf of every one of us alike. *With what weapons* do the monks fight? With the weapon of prayer, and beyond that with the totality of their ascetic dedication and their personal sanctification. Such in essence is the way in which the Athonite monk assists the world: not so much by what he *does* as by what he *is*; not actively but existentially; not primarily by preaching, teaching, writing, or by external works of mercy, but by his very existence, by his continual prayer of the heart.

---

14   Palladios of Helenopolis, *The Lausiac History* 18, section 29.

Because there are persons of living prayer on the slopes of Mount Athos, our lives wherever we may be – in North Oxford, in Chelsea, or Camden Town – are rendered more stable, more fruitful, more joyful. We are never alone. Let us bless God for our Athonite companions, for the mystical support of our monastic partners and fellow workers.

Bibliography

Bryer, A., and M. Cunningham (eds), *Mount Athos and Byzantine Monasticism*. Papers from the Twenty-eighth Spring Symposium of Byzantine Studies, Birmingham, March 1994 (Aldershot: Variorum, 1996).

Dawkins, R. M., *The Monks of Athos* (London: George Allen & Unwin, 1936).

Dora, V. della, *Imagining Mount Athos: Visions of a Holy Place from Homer to World War II* (Charlottesville and London: University of Virginia Press, 2011).

Golitzin, A., *The Living Witness of the Holy Mountain: Contemporary Voices from Mount Athos* (South Canaan, PA: St Tikhon's Seminary Press, 1996).

Gothóni, R., and G. Speake (eds), *The Monastic Magnet: Roads to and from Mount Athos* (Oxford: Peter Lang, 2008).

Sherrard, P., *Athos: The Holy Mountain* (London: Sidgwick & Jackson, 1982).

Speake, G., *Mount Athos: Renewal in Paradise*, 2nd edn (Limni: Denise Harvey, 2014).

Speake, G., and K. Ware (eds), *Mount Athos: Microcosm of the Christian East* (Oxford: Peter Lang, 2012).

Notes on Contributors

HILARION ALFEYEV is a hierarch of the Russian Orthodox Church, a theologian, a church historian, and a composer. At present he is the Metropolitan of Volokolamsk, chairman of the Department of External Church Relations, and a permanent member of the Holy Synod of the Patriarchate of Moscow. Under the guidance of Metropolitan Kallistos he completed his DPhil at the University of Oxford in 1995. He is also author of several volumes on dogmatic theology, Patristics, and church history, numerous articles in various languages, and musical compositions for choir and orchestra.

ANDREAS ANDREOPOULOS was raised in Greece and studied psychology, sociology, and theology in Greece, Canada, the UK, and the USA. He is now Reader in Orthodox Christianity at the University of Winchester. His publications include *Gazing on God: Trinity, Church and Salvation in Orthodox Thought and Iconography* (2013), *This is my Beloved Son: The Transfiguration of Christ* (2012), *The Sign of the Cross: The Gesture, the Mystery, the History* (2006), *Art as Theology: From the Postmodern to the Medieval* (2006), and *Metamorphosis: The Transfiguration in Byzantine Theology and Iconography* (2005).

JOHN BEHR is the Dean of St Vladimir's Orthodox Theological Seminary in New York. His most recent publications are an edition and translation of the fragments of Diodore of Tarsus and Theodore of Mopsuestia, a monograph on Irenaeus, and a more poetic and meditative work entitled *Becoming Human: Theological Anthropology in Word and Image* (2013). He is currently working on a new edition and translation of Origen's *On First Principles* and a study of the Gospel of St John.

SEBASTIAN BROCK is Emeritus Reader in Syriac Studies at the University of Oxford and Emeritus Fellow of Wolfson College. Among his publications are *The Luminous Eye: The Spiritual World Vision of St Ephrem* (1992),

The Hidden Pearl: The Syrian Orthodox Church and its Ancient Aramaic Heritage, 3 vols (2001), and *Fire from Heaven: Studies in Syriac Theology and Liturgy* (2006).

JOHN CHRYSSAVGIS, Archdeacon of the Ecumenical Patriarchate, was born in Australia, completed a theology degree in Athens, and pursued doctoral studies in Oxford. A member of the Office of Ecumenical and Inter-Faith Affairs of the Greek Orthodox Archdiocese of America, he currently serves as theological adviser to the Ecumenical Patriarch on environmental issues. His recent publications include *Light through Darkness: The Orthodox Tradition* (2004), *Beyond the Shattered Image: Insights into an Orthodox Christian Ecological Worldview* (1999), and *In the Heart of the Desert: The Spirituality of the Desert Fathers and Mothers* (2009).

DIMITRI CONOMOS is primarily a musicologist with interests in the medieval Christian chant traditions of the Greek, Slavonic, and Latin Churches. He has written many books and articles in these fields and continues to lecture in universities and theological institutions throughout Europe and Australia. Lately he has also turned to studies in Byzantine hymnography. His non-musicological endeavours include publications on Orthodoxy and ecology and the mythology of Africa and Russia.

MAXIMOS CONSTAS is Senior Research Scholar at Holy Cross Greek Orthodox School of Theology in Brookline, Massachusetts. He holds a PhD in Patristics and Historical Theology from the Catholic University of America in Washington, DC. For many years he was professor of theology at Harvard Divinity School, after which he became a monk at the monastery of Simonopetra on Mount Athos. He is author of *The Art of Seeing: Paradox and Perception in Orthodox Iconography* (2014), an edition and translation of *Maximos the Confessor, On Difficulties in the Church Fathers: The Ambigua to Thomas and the Ambigua to John*, 2 vols (2014), *Proclus of Constantinople and the Cult of the Virgin in Late Antiquity* (2003), as well as numerous scholarly articles and translations, including three volumes of the works of the contemporary Athonite Elder Aimilianos of Simonopetra.

He is currently working on a translation of St Maximos the Confessor, *The Questions to Thalassios*.

NIKOLAOS HATZINIKOLAOU studied physics at the Aristotelian University of Thessaloniki, astrophysics at Harvard University, and mechanical engineering at MIT. He holds a doctorate in Biomedical Engineering and Applied Mathematics from Harvard. He also studied theology at Holy Cross Greek Orthodox School of Theology, and holds a PhD from the University of Thessaloniki on Orthodox Christian Ethics and Bioethics. In 1989 he was tonsured a monk on Mount Athos and then was ordained a deacon and a priest. He served for a number of years at the Metochion of Holy Ascension, a dependency of Simonopetra monastery in Athens. In 2004 he was elected Metropolitan of Mesogaia and Lavreotiki in Greece and, among his other activities, he founded the first hospice in Greece under the auspices of the Church.

ELIZABETH JEFFREYS is Bywater and Sotheby Professor of Byzantine and Modern Greek Language and Literature Emerita at the University of Oxford and Emeritus Fellow of Exeter College. She has published widely on topics in Byzantine literature.

FRANCES JENNINGS converted from Anglicanism to Orthodoxy in 2009 under the spiritual guidance of Bishop Kallistos. She is a partner in a firm of chartered accountants and serves on the board of trustees of her parish of St Nicholas the Wonderworker in Oxford. She joined the Executive Committee of the Friends of Mount Athos in 2015.

EPHREM LASH was born in India into a military family. After studying classics at Oxford University, he served for some years as a schoolmaster. Ordained priest in 1985, he was tonsured a monk at the monastery of Dochiariou on Mount Athos. On his return to the UK he became chaplain to the monastery of the Assumption at Whitby, and from 2006 served the community of St Anthony the Great and St John the Baptist in Islington, London. He was best known for his translations of church services and patristic texts from Greek, Aramaic, and Syriac. He died on 15 March 2016.

ANDREW LOUTH is Professor Emeritus of Patristic and Byzantine Studies at the University of Durham and Honorary Fellow in the Faculty of Theology at the Free University of Amsterdam. He is an archpriest of the Diocese of Sourozh, Moscow Patriarchate, and serves the Orthodox parish in Durham. He is author of several books and many articles, most recently *Modern Orthodox Thinkers: From the 'Philokalia' to the Present* (2015).

STEPHEN PLATT is Rector of the Russian Orthodox Church of St Nicholas the Wonderworker, Oxford. He is also General Secretary of the Fellowship of St Alban and St Sergius.

MARCUS PLESTED is Associate Professor of Greek Patristic and Byzantine Theology at Marquette University, Wisconsin. He wrote his doctorate under the supervision of Metropolitan Kallistos at the University of Oxford. He was received into the Orthodox Church on the Holy Mountain in 1992. From 2000 to 2013 he worked at the Institute for Orthodox Christian Studies in Cambridge, latterly as its Vice-Principal and Academic Director. He has been a member of the Center of Theological Inquiry and the Institute for Advanced Study in Princeton, New Jersey, and has taught, lectured, and published widely in patristic, Byzantine, and modern Orthodox theology. He is author of two books to date: *The Macarian Legacy: The Place of Macarius-Symeon in the Eastern Christian Tradition* (2004) and *Orthodox Readings of Aquinas* (2012).

NIKOLAI SAKHAROV studied music before being tonsured a monk at the monastery of St John the Baptist at Tolleshunt Knights, Essex. He completed a doctorate at Oxford University on the theology of Elder Sophrony (his great uncle) under the supervision of Metropolitan Kallistos. He is author of *I Love Therefore I Am: The Theological Legacy of Archimandrite Sophrony* (2002).

GRAHAM SPEAKE is founder and Chairman of the Friends of Mount Athos. Having studied classics at Trinity College, Cambridge, he holds a doctorate in Greek from the University of Oxford and is a Fellow of the Society of

Antiquaries of London. He is author of *Mount Athos: Renewal in Paradise* (2nd edn, 2014), for which he was awarded the Criticos Prize.

ELIZABETH THEOKRITOFF completed a doctorate in Liturgical Theology at the University of Oxford under Metropolitan Kallistos. She is an independent scholar and theological translator. Her publications include *Living in God's Creation: Orthodox Perspectives on Ecology* (2005).

KALLISTOS WARE holds a doctorate from the University of Oxford where from 1966 to 2001 he was Spalding Lecturer in Eastern Orthodox Studies. Since 1970 he has also been Fellow of Pembroke College. He is a monk of the monastery of St John the Theologian, Patmos, and an assistant bishop in the Greek Orthodox Archdiocese of Thyateira and Great Britain. In 2007 he was raised to the rank of metropolitan.

ROWAN WILLIAMS is Master of Magdalene College, Cambridge, having formerly been Archbishop of Canterbury from 2002 to 2012. He is author of several theological works, most recently *The Edge of Words: God and the Habits of Language* (2014) and *On Augustine* (2016).

Index

Agathon 87
Aimilianos, Fr, of Simonopetra 248
akedia 126–8
Alfeyev, Hilarion, Metropolitan of
 Volokolamsk 2, 15
Alford, Henry 229
Alypios the Stylite, St 137
animals 241–3
Annunciation 2, 105–10
Ansgar, St 21
Antony, St 116, 248
Apophthegmata Patrum 86
Arianism 44
Athenagoras, Archbishop 13–14
Athos, Mount 28, 36, 40, 57, 134, 137, 138,
 143–4, 237–52
Augustine, St 153

Bach, Johann Sebastian 215, 232
Balthasar, Hans Urs von 165, 201
baptism 50, 52–4, 81, 182
Barsanouphios, Abba 136
Barsanouphios and John, Sts 89, 134
Barth, Karl 232
Basil the Great, St 83, 134
Bath 27
Beethoven, Ludwig van 214, 215
Behr, Fr John 2
Benedict of Nursia, St 249
Bishop, Sir Henry 216
Blake, Leonard 224
Blake, William 40
Blom, Eric 232
Blowers, Paul 42
Britten, Benjamin 215

Brock, Sebastian 2
Bryson, Bill 15
Buddhism 185
Bulgakov, Sergei 2, 20, 152, 154, 155–6,
 159, 178

Carlyle, Thomas 45
Carras, Costa 30
Chopin, Frédéric 214
Chrétien, Jean-Louis 207
Chryssavgis, Deacon John 2
Clark, Elizabeth 160–2
Claudel, Paul 207
Clément, Olivier 196, 207–8
Cleopa, Fr 134
confession 9–10, 81, 83, 91–3
Conomos, Dimitri 3
Constantine Manasses 106
Constas, Fr Maximos 2
Copts 147, 245
Corinthians, St Paul's first epistle to 71, 99
Counter-Reformation 227
Cyril and Methodios, Sts 4

Daley, Brian 42
David of Thessaloniki, St 137
Davidman, Joy 215
Davis, Colin 233
Dawkins, Richard 121
deification 3, 38–9, 60, 97, 100–1, 114,
 119, 128, 171–87, 191, 202
Deir al-Surian monastery 51
Derrida, Jacques 161
Diadochos of Photike, St 58, 78
Dionysios the Areopagite 51, 173, 218

Dionysiou monastery 113, 244, 245
Divine Liturgy 2, 34, 49, 115, 192, 201–2, 206, 246–7
Dochiariou monastery 27
Dorotheos, Abba 82–3, 134
Dositheos 82–3
Dostoevsky, Fyodor 45, 241

Ecumenical Councils 60
ecumenism 31, 34, 44
Eirene, *Sevastokratorissa* 107
Elchaninov, Fr Alexander 35
Elgar, Edward 214
Ephraim of Arizona, Elder, formerly of Philotheou 139, 248
Ephraim the Syrian, St 134
eschatology 115–18
Eustratios, St 79
Evagrios of Pontos 2, 59–72, 77, 80, 87, 117, 119, 122, 127–8, 149
Evdokimos, Fr, of Philotheou 245
Evdokimov, Paul 193

Farley, Edward 156
fasting 88–9, 144
Fellowship of St Alban and St Sergius 20
Florovsky, Fr Georges 2, 42, 43, 152–4, 156
Fraser, Canon Giles 30
Friends of Mount Athos 1

Gabriel, Abbot of Dionysiou 249
Géhin, Paul 62
George, bishop of the Arab Tribes 49, 50
George, Fr, of Grigoriou 248
Gillet, Fr Lev 192
'Glorifiers of the Name' 244
Gorodetzky, Nadejda 191–2
Great Lavra monastery 247, 249
Gregory Nazianzen, the Theologian, St 69, 81, 99, 100, 191, 194

Gregory of Nyssa, St 68–9, 195
Gregory of Sinai, St 58, 122
Gregory Palamas, St 24, 42, 45, 60, 128, 137, 154
Grigoriou monastery 244

Halvorson, Mrs R. E. 221, 226
Handel, George Frideric 215
Hanson, Richard 158–9
Harnack, Adolf von 157
Hatzinikolaou, Nikolaos, Metropolitan of Mesogaia and Lavreotiki 2
Haydn, Joseph 215
Heidegger, Martin 167
Hellenism 153–4
Henry, Michael 166, 168–9
hesychasm 31, 36–7, 42
hesychasts 57, 60, 114, 241
Hilandar monastery 241, 244
Holst, Gustav 214
Husserl, Edmund 166–7
hypostasis 3

icons 44, 109–10, 151, 166–9
Inge, Dean William 232
Iona 240
Irenaeus 164–5
Isaac the Syrian, St 77, 86, 118, 128, 134, 135–6, 147, 248
Isaiah of Scetis, Abba 121, 124, 134
Ischyrion, Abba 149

James, M. R. 45
Jameson, Fredric 161
Jeffreys, Elizabeth 2
Jennings, Simon 7–9
Jerusalem 240
Jesus Prayer 7, 31, 37, 58, 114, 191–2, 248
John, St, Gospel of 71
John the Baptist, St 133
John Cassian 113, 116

Index

John Chrysostom, St 45, 51
John of the Cross, St 178
John Klimakos, St 35, 77, 78, 80, 81, 82,
    85–6, 87, 90, 100, 117, 118, 134, 137
John Paul II, Pope 45
John Tzetzes 106
Jones, Tamsin 166, 168
Joseph the Hesychast, Elder, of New
    Skete 134, 248
Jung, Carl Gustav 39
Justin the New, St 134

Kadloubovsky, E. 58
Kafsokalyvia, skete of 248
Kallistos and Ignatios, Sts 118, 123
Kannengiesser, Charles 42
Kant, Immanuel 166
Karoulia, skete of 113, 143
Karyes 243
Katounakia, skete of 143
Kelly, J. N. D. 157
kenosis 174–8, 180–3
Khomiakov, Aleksei 237
Khrapovitsky, Antonii 178
Kiev Caves, monastery of the 134, 138,
    143–4, 149
King, John 29, 31
Knežević, Fr Romilo 207

Lappa-Zizika, Eurydice 62
Leontios of Cyprus, St 197, 208
Levin, Bernard 233
Lewis, C. S. 3, 213–31
Lewis, Warren 215, 223
Lossky, Vladimir 3, 42, 179, 180, 184
Louth, Fr Andrew 7, 42
Luke, St, Gospel of 169
Luther, Martin 27
Lyotard, Jean-François 161
Maitland Moir, Fr John 28
Makarian Homilies 81

Makarios of Corinth, St 57
Makarios of Egypt, St 89, 134, 248, 251
Makris, Fr Amphilochios 14, 16, 40, 134
Manganeios Prodromos 105–10
Manuel Komnenos, Emperor 107
Marion, Jean-Luc 166–9
Mark the Monk, St 34, 58, 134
Mary of Egypt, St 9, 137
Maximos the Confessor, St 2, 59–72,
    100, 114, 115, 128, 191, 194–6, 198,
    200–4, 207–8, 210
Montgomery, Bernard Law 28
Moore, Arthur and Maureen 226
Moshe bar Kepha 50–1
Mozart, Wolfgang Amadeus 215, 232
music 3, 213–31

Neilos of Sinai, St 80, 125–6
New Skete 113
Nibelungenlied 214
Nicholas Kallikles 106
Nicolas of Cusa 173
Niketas of Remesiana, St 227
Nikitas Stithatos 119–20, 148
Nikodimos of the Holy Mountain, St 38,
    57, 114, 132, 136
Nikon of Karoulia, Fr 36, 240

Optina monastery 134
Origen 69, 72, 81
Ottomans 43

Pachomios, St 87–8, 89, 90
Paisios of Athos, St 134, 139, 147, 150, 248
Paisy Velichkovsky, St 134
Palladios of Helenopolis 251
Palmer, Gerald 35, 36, 40, 58, 241
Papadiamantis, Alexandros 45
Patmos 13–14, 131, 240
Paulos mar Gregorios, Metropolitan of
    Delhi 195–6

Payne, John Howard 216–17
Penelope, Sister, of Wantage 214
Philaret, Metropolitan of Moscow 178, 193
Philokalia 2, 10, 30–1, 35–9, 57–60, 113–28, 131, 134, 148, 240, 241
Philotheou monastery 139, 245
Plato 23
Poimin 88–9
Porphyrios of Athos, St 134
Potter, Beatrix 24
praxis 17, 149
Prophet Elijah, skete of 241
Psalms 36, 78, 79, 135
psychology 39

Rahmani, Ignatius Ephrem II, Syrian Catholic Patriarch 50–2
Reformation 227
Remigius of Auxerre, St 218
Romans, St Paul's epistle to 65–6, 173
Routley, Erik 220–1, 225
Russian Revolution 244

St Anne, skete of 238, 242–3, 248
St Catherine's monastery, Sinai 49–50, 109
St John the Baptist, monastery of, Essex 139
St Mamas, monastery of 81
St Panteleimonos, monastery of 243
Sakharov, Fr Nicholas 176, 178–9, 181
Sakharov, Fr Sophrony 3, 134, 171, 175–87
Sara, St 136
Schelling, F. W. J. von 155
Schmemann, Fr Alexander 193–4, 196–8, 201, 207, 209
Seraphim of Sarov, St 134, 138
Sherrard, Philip 33, 35, 196–7, 207, 241
Silouan, St 134
Simon the Myrrhbearer, St 137

Simonos Petra monastery 137, 139, 247
Sinkiewicz, Robert 42
Society of St Francis 13
Sophonias, prophecy of 230
Sophronios of Jerusalem, St 137
Sophrony, Fr *see* Sakharov, Fr Sophrony
Speake, Graham 131
Stanford, Charles Villiers 226
Staniloae, Fr Dumitru 194–5
Stoudion monastery 134
Symeon the New Theologian, St 2, 75–6, 91–102, 114, 123, 148
Symeon the Studite, St 2, 75–102
Syriac 2, 49–52

Talmud 155
Teilhard de Chardin, Pierre 192
Theodore of Edessa, St 78
Theodore of Mopsuestia 51
Theodore Prodromos 106
Theodore the Studite, St 100
Theognostos, St 124
Theoklitos, Fr, of Dionysiou 249
Theokritoff, Elizabeth 3
Theophan the Recluse, St 35, 131, 134, 138
theoria 16, 66, 128
Theotokos 2, 105–10, 133
Thomas Aquinas, St 24, 127
Tigger 31
Tippett, Michael 215
Tito, Josip Broz 244
Tolkien, J. R. R. 214
Trent, Council of 227
Trisagion 30, 78
Turner, H. J. M. 96
Tyndale, William 27

Underhill, Evelyn 45
Valamo monastery 134
Vasileios, Archimandrite, of Iviron 210, 248

Index

Vatopedi monastery 244
Vaughan Williams, Ralph 215
Vianney, John 45

Wagner, Richard 214
Walsingham 240
Ware, Everald 19, 28
Ware, Kallistos, Metropolitan of Diok-
    leia 1–4, 7–45, 49, 58–9, 75, 115,
    116, 121, 131, 151, 196–7, 206, 218
  Eustratios Argenti 34
  The Festal Menaion 29, 35
  The Lenten Triodion 29, 35
  The Orthodox Church 27–8, 34–5, 37
  The Orthodox Way 28–9, 34–5
Williams, Rowan 2–3, 43, 163
women priests 31
World Council of Churches 44

xeniteia 87, 93, 95

Yannaras, Christos 42

Zernov, Militza 20
Zernov, Nicolas 34
Zizioulas, John, Metropolitan of Perga-
    mum 42, 165, 190, 196, 198–202,
    206